Possession, Relative Title, and Ownership in English Law

Possession, Relative Title, and Ownership in English Law

LUKE ROSTILL

OXFORD

UNIVERSITY PRESS

OXFORD
UNIVERSITY PRESS

Great Clarendon Street, Oxford, OX2 6DP,
United Kingdom

Oxford University Press is a department of the University of Oxford.
It furthers the University's objective of excellence in research, scholarship,
and education by publishing worldwide. Oxford is a registered trade mark of
Oxford University Press in the UK and in certain other countries

First Edition published in 2021

Impression: 1

Published in the United States of America by Oxford University Press
198 Madison Avenue, New York, NY 10016, United States of America

British Library Cataloguing in Publication Data

Data available

Library of Congress Control Number: 2020948226

ISBN 978–0–19–884310–8

DOI: 10.1093/oso/9780198843108.001.0001

Printed and bound by
CPI Group (UK) Ltd, Croydon, CR0 4YY

Preface

This book has a relatively long history. It is based on my DPhil thesis, which I completed at Oxford in 2016. For the most part, the claims that are advanced and defended in this book are the same as those that I argued for in the thesis.

The thesis that I submitted is not the thesis I originally intended to write. Initially, the aim was to individuate the various types of proprietary interest that English law recognises in respect of chattels. It soon became clear, however, that there are competing conceptions of 'possessory title', and that adopting one conception rather than another has important implications for the status of ownership in English law and the limits of relativity of title. It was obvious that one could not adequately engage with these matters in a single chapter. So, the aim of individuating various kinds of proprietary interest was replaced with the aim of understanding the nature of the 'title' that is acquired through possession. This is the central objective of this book.

Shortly before this book was completed, Dr Michael Crawford's important contribution, *An Expressive Theory of Possession*,[1] was published. It has not been possible to incorporate a detailed discussion of Dr Crawford's views into the text of this book (though I have been able to include a number of references to them in the notes). I hope it may assist the reader if I briefly set out my understanding of the relationship between the two books.

Dr Crawford's answer to the question with which this book is primarily concerned is that the fact of possession generates an 'ownership interest'.[2] But this question is not the main focus of his book. Rather, Dr Crawford's central aim is to answer two related questions:[3] what, for the purposes of the rule, is the nature of possession? And why does possession, as opposed to some other mechanism, fulfil the function of creating property rights in tangible things? Dr Crawford's thought-provoking answer to the first question differs, in some important respects, from the answer provided and defended in Chapter 2 of this book.

---

[1] Michael JR Crawford, *An Expressive Theory of Possession* (Hart 2020).
[2] ibid 10, 54–58.
[3] ibid 7.

As for the second question, Dr Crawford denies that the 'origin' of the possession rule 'can be traced to some elusive rationale'.[4] Rather, 'the possession convention was so pervasive in life that it was, consciously or otherwise, incorporated into the law's formal system of rights and duties'.[5] This book aims to provide a sound account of the current rules and the main considerations upon which they are based. It does not aim to provide a full explanation of how and why the rules emerged and evolved. It is argued, in Chapter 4, that the modern rules that confer fees simple on possessors of land were established by the courts in order to fulfil, or to aid the fulfilment of, objectives that Parliament adopted by enacting the Real Property Limitation Act 1833; objectives which Parliament reaffirmed its commitment to on more than one occasion in the 20th century. Is this compatible with Dr Crawford's thesis? I think the answer depends on what is meant by the 'origin' of the rules. For while, according to the account in Chapter 4 of this book, the modern rules regarding land were instituted by the courts in the 19th century in order to achieve certain goals, legal rules providing protection in trespass to possessors of land, and rules conferring proprietary interests on those who were seised of land, emerged much earlier. It would be consistent with the views defended in this book to claim that Dr Crawford's theory explains why these rules, as well as the rules that confer property rights on possessors of chattels, emerged. But since I do not aim in this book to provide a complete genealogy of the rules, and since I cannot do justice to Dr Crawford's arguments here, I will not comment on whether this claim should be accepted.

I owe many debts of gratitude. One of the oldest is owed to the Warden and Fellows of Wadham College, Oxford. Wadham was my academic home for nearly a decade. This was a mighty privilege from which I benefited in countless ways. I particularly benefited from the instruction, guidance, mentorship, and support of the college's law tutors: Jeffrey Hackney, Laura Hoyano, Wanjiru Njoya and, later, Simon Douglas, Rachel Taylor, Hannah Glover, Tarun Khaitan, Eveline Ramaekers, and Sandy Steel. Jeffrey and Laura supported and assisted me at every stage of my journey from law fresher to law lecturer and I wish to express my profound gratitude to them.

While writing my DPhil thesis, I shared a house with three other Wadham postgraduate research students: Diana Greenwald, Katia Mandaltsi, and Marie Tidball. They were the best housemates I could have wished for and I will always treasure our time together.

---

[4] ibid 87.
[5] ibid 113.

I would not have been able to embark on postgraduate study, or to write the thesis, without the financial support that I received from various quarters. My sincere thanks to 3 Verulam Buildings, Sir Roy Goode, the Oxford Law Faculty, Wadham College, and the Arts and Humanities Research Council.

The final stage of my DPhil was completed while I was a Supernumerary Teaching Fellow in Law at St John's College, Oxford. St John's was a wonderful place to teach and study and I would like to thank the President and Fellows of the college for giving me such a valuable opportunity. I am particularly grateful to my former colleagues in law: Paul Craig, Richard Ekins, and Simon Whittaker; and my predecessor, Jeremias Adams-Prassl.

Since 2016 I have been a Fellow of Trinity College, Oxford. I am conscious of how lucky I was to join such an impressive, vibrant, and friendly academic community. I would like to record my thanks to the Senior Tutor, Valerie Worth, and to the Senior Law Fellow, Nick Barber, who helped me to find time to research and write.

One of the benefits of writing this book, and the thesis on which it is based, at Oxford is that I was able to meet and learn from many outstanding private lawyers. I am especially grateful to Susan Bright, Simon Douglas, Joshua Getzler, and Bill Swadling for discussing the subject matter of this book, and a host of related issues, with me on many occasions over the last decade. I learned a great deal from them as a student and continue to learn from them as a colleague. Simon also agreed to examine the thesis, in conjunction with Robert Chambers. Their feedback was invaluable and I wish to express my gratitude to them.

One of my greatest debts is to Ben McFarlane, who supervised my DPhil. He was a model supervisor and went beyond the call of duty on many occasions—he even generously agreed to continue supervising the project after he had moved to UCL. As the pages of this book demonstrate, my thinking on possession, relativity of title, and ownership has been greatly influenced by his own. I am extraordinarily grateful to him.

I also benefited from discussing the ideas in this book with students on the Oxford undergraduate personal property course and the BCL/MJur advanced property and trusts course. I was also able to present my work at various conferences and workshops, including the Young Property Lawyers Forum in Stellenbosch in 2012; the Modern Studies in Property Law Postgraduate Conference in Liverpool in 2014; a workshop on property and trusts at UCL in 2015; meetings of the Oxford Property Law Discussion Group; an Oxford Law Faculty research seminar; and a colloquium on intersections in private law at the University of Sydney in 2019. I would like to thank all those who provided comments or questions on these or other occasions, particularly: Bram Akkermans, John Armour, Elise Bant, Anna Berlee, Alexandra Braun, Adrian Briggs, John Cartwright, Matthew Conaglen, Michael Crawford, Paul S Davies, Sjef van Erp, Jamie Glister, Roy Goode, James Goudkamp, Sarah Green, Louise Gullifer, Birke Häcker, Robin Hickey, Björn Hoops, Emma Lees, Mike Macnair, Charles Mitchell, Aleksi Ollikainen-Read, Kenneth Reid, Jill Robbie, Joseph W Singer, Roger Smith, Robert Stevens, Andreas Televantos, Nicholas Tiverios, André van der Walt, Charlie Webb, and Sarah Worthington.

In the final stages, I received excellent research assistance, and many insightful comments, from Hin Liu, to whom I am grateful. I would also like to thank Jamie Berezin, Iona Jacob, Paulina dos Santos Major, and the rest of the team at OUP.

This book would not have been written were it not for the unconditional support, at every stage, of my parents Mark and Jackie, my sister Holly, and my grandparents Joan, Les, Doreen, and Clifford. When I arrived at Wadham in 2007, academia and the legal world were as new to them as they were to me. They did all they could to enable me to explore and, eventually, inhabit these worlds.

Finally, my ardent thanks to Sarah, for more than I can say, and to whom this book is dedicated.

Luke Rostill
Oxford, August 2020

Contents

List of Abbreviations   xiii
Table of Cases   xvii
Table of Legislation   xxv

1. Introduction   1

2. Possession   7
  2.1 The Aims and Scope of the Enquiry   7
  2.2 Scepticism of Possession   8
    2.2.1 Ambiguity   9
    2.2.2 Vagueness   10
    2.2.3 Variation   11
    2.2.4 Implications   13
  2.3 The Nature of Possession   14
    2.3.1 The General Possession Rule   16
      2.3.1.1 Exclusive physical control   16
      2.3.1.2 The intention to possess   19
      2.3.1.3 Possession through another   21
      2.3.1.4 Joint possession   22
    2.3.2 Special Possession Rules   22
  2.4 Possession of Estates and Interests   23

3. Possession and Title: Three Views   25
  3.1 Introduction   25
  3.2 Three Views of Title by Possession   27
    3.2.1 The Possessory Right View   27
    3.2.2 The Strong Proprietary Interest View   31
    3.2.3 The Presumed Property View   34
    3.2.4 Combining the Three Views   36
  3.3 The Importance of Distinguishing the Three Views   36
    3.3.1 Distinguishing Rules of Acquisition from Rules of Presumption   37
    3.3.2 Is the Distinction Important?   41
  3.4 Conceptual Objections to Presumptions of Property   42
    3.4.1 The First Argument   43
      3.4.1.1 Presumptions and rules of presumption   43
      3.4.1.2 Presumptions, facts, and the law of proof   46
    3.4.2 The Second Argument   50
  3.5 Conclusion   51

4. Possession and Title to Land   53
   4.1 Introduction   53
   4.2 The Incidents of a Possessor's Interest   55
       4.2.1 Possession and Rights   56
       4.2.2 Possession-dependence and Alienability   61
             4.2.2.1 Possession and ejectment   62
             4.2.2.2 The emergence of a new rule   67
                     4.2.2.2.1 *Davison v Gent*   68
                     4.2.2.2.2 *Asher v Whitlock*   72
             4.2.2.3 Alienability and possession-dependence: the modern law   77
       4.2.3 The Incidents of a Possessor's Interest: Conclusions   80
   4.3 Objections to the Strong Proprietary Interest View   81
       4.3.1 The Illegitimate Judicial Innovation Objection   81
             4.3.1.1 The Limitation Acts   82
             4.3.1.2 The source of a squatter's title   84
       4.3.2 The Objection based on the Doctrine of Tenure   88
       4.3.3 The Objection based on the Law of Property Act 1925   90
       4.3.4 The Abandonment Objection   90
   4.4 The Scope of the Acquisition Rule   94
       4.4.1 Adverse and Non-adverse Possession   94
       4.4.2 Title by Possession and the Land Registration Act 2002   96
   4.5 Conclusion   98

5. Possession and Title to Chattels   99
   5.1 Introduction   99
   5.2 The Incidents of a Possessor's Interest   99
       5.2.1 Possession and the Right to Exclusive Possession   100
       5.2.2 Possession-dependence   104
       5.2.3 Alienability   109
       5.2.4 The Incidents of a Possessor's Interest: Conclusions   112
   5.3 Objections to the Strong Proprietary Interest View   113
       5.3.1 The First Objection: Possession and the Presumption
             of Ownership   114
       5.3.2 The Strong Proprietary Interest View and the *Jus Tertii*   117
             5.3.2.1 The *jus tertii* and the common law   119
             5.3.2.2 The *jus tertii* and the Torts (Interference with Goods)
                     Act 1977   124
   5.4 Conclusion   125

6. The Grounds of Relative Title   127
   6.1 Introduction   127
   6.2 Obligation-based Arguments   130
       6.2.1 Finders, Wrongful Possessors, and Obligation-based Reasons   131
       6.2.2 Obligation-based Reasons in the Law   143

6.3 The Security and Certainty of Title   144
    6.3.1 The Security and Certainty of Title to Unregistered Land   145
    6.3.2 Registered Land and Title by Possession   149
    6.3.3 The Security and Certainty of Title to Chattels   151

7. Ownership and Relativity of Title   155
  7.1 Ownership in General   155
  7.2 Ownership of Land and Chattels in English Law   164
    7.2.1 Landownership and Tenure   166
    7.2.2 The Doctrine of Estates and Relativity of Title   168
    7.2.3 The Difficulty of Identifying the Best Title   169
    7.2.4 The Protection of Proprietary Interests   169
  7.3 Ownership and Relative Title   170
  7.4 Conclusion   174

Index   175

List of Abbreviations

Ad & El	Adolphus & Ellis' Queen's Bench Reports
Ad & El (NS)	Adolphus & Ellis' Queen's Bench Reports (New Series)
Adelaide L Rev	Adelaide Law Review
Am J Comp L	American Journal of Comparative Law
APQ	American Philosophical Quarterly
B & Ad	Barnewall & Adolphus' King's Bench Reports
B & Ald	Barnewall & Alderson's King's Bench Reports
B & C	Barnewall & Cresswell's King's Bench Reports
B & S	Best & Smith's Queen's Bench Reports
Bing	Bingham's Common Pleas Reports
Bing NC	Bingham's New Cases, Common Pleas
Bl Comm	Blackstone, *Commentaries on the Laws of England*
Bligh	Bligh's House of Lords Reports
Bulst	Bulstrode's King's Bench Reports
Burr	Burrow's King's Bench Reports
Car & M	Carrington & Marshman's Reports
Car & P	Carrington & Payne's Reports
CB	Common Bench Reports
CB (NS)	Common Bench Reports, New Series
CLR	Commonwealth Law Reports
CLWR	Common Law World Review
Cmd	Command papers (1919-56)
Cmnd	Command papers (1957-86)
Co Litt	Coke, *Commentary upon Littleton*
Com	Comyn's King's Bench Reports
Co Rep	Coke's King's Bench Reports
Cox CC	Cox's Criminal Cases
CPR	Civil Procedure Rules
CRA 2015	Consumer Rights Act 2015
CUP	Cambridge University Press
Cro Eliz	Croke's King's Bench Reports
CTLC	Consumer and Trading Law Cases
DLR (3d)	Dominion Law Reports (Third Series)
Dyer	Dyer's King's Bench Reports
East	East's King's Bench Reports
Edinburgh LR	Edinburgh Law Review
Edinburgh UP	Edinburgh University Press

EGLR	Estates Gazette Law Reports
El & Bl	Ellis & Blackburn's Queen's Bench Reports
Eur Rev Private L	European Review of Private Law
Exch	Welsby, Hurlestone & Gordon's Exchequer Reports
FCR	Federal Court Reports (Australia)
Harv L Rev	Harvard Law Review
H & C	Hurlstone & Coltman's Exchequer Reports
H & N	Hurlstone & Norman's Exchequer Reports
HC Deb	House of Commons Debates (Hansard)
HL Deb	House of Lords Debates (Hansard)
HLC	House of Lords Cases
HUP	Harvard University Press
IJNS	Irish Jurist (New Series)
ILT	Irish Law Times
Ir J Rep	Irish Jurist Reports
Ir LR	Irish Law Reports
J Eur Tort L	Journal of European Tort Law
J of Equity	Journal of Equity
JLS	Journal of Legal Studies
J of Philosophy	Journal of Philosophy
J Political Philosophy	Journal of Political Philosophy
Jac & W	Jacob & Walker's Chancery Reports
Jerusalem Rev LS	Jerusalem Review of Legal Studies
Johnson	Johnson's Chancery Reports
Jur	Jurist Reports
Jur (NS)	Jurist Reports (New Series)
KCLJ	King's College Law Journal
LA 1939	Limitation Act 1939
LA 1980	Limitation Act 1980
Law & History Rev	Law and History Review
Law Com CP No	Law Commission Consultation Paper Number
Law Com No	Law Commission Report Number
Ld Raym	Lord Raymond's King's Bench and Common Pleas Reports
LEG	Legal Theory
Legge	Legge's Supreme Court Cases (New South Wales)
Leon	Leonard's Reports
LJ Ex	Law Journal Reports, Exchequer New Series
LJKB	Law Journal Reports, King's Bench New Series
LJQB	Law Journal Reports, Queen's Bench New Series
Ll L Rep	Lloyd's List Law Reports
LRA 2002	Land Registration Act 2002
LR Ex	Law Reports, Exchequer Reports
LR Ex D	Law Reports, Exchequer Division

LR HL	Law Reports, House of Lords
LR KB	Law Reports, King's Bench
LR QB	Law Reports, Queen's Bench (Second Series)
LS	Legal Studies
LT	Law Times Reports
LTOS	Law Times Reports, Old Series
Macq	Macqueen's Scotch Appeal Cases
Melbourne U L Rev	Melbourne University Law Review
Mich LR	Michigan Law Review
Minnesota LR	Minnesota Law Review
M & G	Manning and Granger's Common Pleas Reports
M & Rob	Moody & Robinson's Nisi Prius Reports
Mood & M	Moody & Malkin's Nisi Prius Reports
M & W	Meeson & Welsby's Exchequer Reports
Neb L Rev	Nebraska Law Review
NILQ	Northern Ireland Legal Quarterly
NW	North Western Reporter (US)
NZLR	New Zealand Law Reports
OUP	Oxford University Press
Saund	Saunders' King's Bench Reports
SGA 1979	Sale of Goods Act 1979
SR (NSW)	State Reports (New South Wales)
Strange	Strange's King's Bench Reports
Style	Style's King's Bench Reports
Syd LR	Sydney Law Review
Taunt	Taunton's Common Pleas Reports
Term Reports	Durnford & East's Term Reports, King's Bench
TIL	Theoretical Inquiries in Law
TLR	Times Law Reports
Tort L Rev	Tort Law Review
Tulane L Rev	Tulane Law Review
Tulsa Law Rev	Tulsa Law Review
U of Queensland LJ	University of Queensland Law Journal
UCLA L Rev	University of California at Los Angeles Law Review
UTLJ	University of Toronto Law Journal
Ves Jr	Vesey Junior's Chancery Reports
Virginia LR	Virginia Law Review
Washington ULQ	Washington University Law Quarterly
Yale LJ	Yale Law Journal

Table of Cases

Adams v Naylor [1944] KB 750 (CA) 58
Agency Co Ltd v Short (1888) 13 App Cas 793 (PC) 83
Alan Wibberley Building Ltd v Insley [1999] 1 WLR 894 (HL) 2, 25, 59, 72
Alfred McAlpine Construction Ltd v Panatown Ltd (No 1) [2001] 1 AC 518 (HL) 116
Aliakmon, The. See Leigh & Sullivan Ltd v Aliakmon Shipping Co Ltd
Allan v Liverpool Overseers (1874) LR 9 QB 180 (QB) 16, 58, 70–71
Allen v Rivington (1670) 2 Saund 111; 85 ER 813 68–69
Allen v Roughley (1955) 94 CLR 98 (HCA) 32–33, 65–66, 77
Anchor Brewhouse Developments Ltd v Berkley House
    (Docklands Development) Ltd [1987] 2 EGLR 173 (Ch) 165–66
Anderson v Gouldberg (1892) 53 NW 636 29–30
Anon (1652) Style 368; 82 ER 784 62–63
Armory v Delamirie (1722) 1 Strange 505; 93 ER 664 105
Ashby v Tolhurst [1937] 2 KB 242 (CA) 132
Asher v Whitlock (1865) LR 1 QB 1; (1865) 35 LJQB 17;
    (1865) 11 Jur (NS) 925 ....67–68, 70–71, 72–77, 78, 79, 82
Astor's Settlement Trusts, Re [1952] Ch 534 (Ch) 127
Atkinson and Horsell's Contract, Re [1912] 2 Ch 1 (CA) 3–4, 37, 81, 85
Atlantic Computer Systems Plc, Re [1992] Ch 505 (CA) 11–12
Attenborough v London and St Katharine's Dock Co (1878) 3 CPD 450 (CA) 123–24
Attorney-General (Ontario) v Mercer (1883) 8 App Cas 767 (PC) 88, 89
Attorney-General v Brown (1847) 1 Legge 312 (NSWSC) 90

Back v Daniels [1925] 1 KB 526 (CA) 165–66
Bannerman Town v Eleuthera Properties Ltd [2018] UKPC 27 .... 21, 22, 94–95
Barker v Furlong [1891] 2 Ch 172 (Ch) 122–23
Basset v Maynard (1600) Cro Eliz 819; 78 ER 1046 102
Baxter v Taylor (1832) 4 B & Ad 72; 110 ER 382 55
Beckham v Drake (1849) 2 HLC 579; 9 ER 1213 67
Berrington d Dormer v Parkhurst (1811) 13 East 489; 104 ER 460 64
Betts v Metropolitan Police District Receiver [1932] 2 KB 595 (KB) 108
Biddle v Bond (1865) 6 B & S 225; 122 ER 1179 (QB) 119–20
BMW Financial Services (GB) Ltd v Bhagwanani [2007] EWCA Civ 1230;
    [2007] CTLC 280 101–2
Bocardo SA v Star Energy UK Onshore Ltd [2010] UKSC 35;
    [2011] 1 AC 380 .... 16, 165–66
Boosey v Davis (1987) 55 P & CR 83 (CA) 18
Borwick Development Solutions Ltd v Clear Water Fisheries Ltd [2020]
    EWCA Civ 578 27–28
Bourne v Fosbrooke (1865) 18 CB (NS) 515; 144 ER 545 (CP) 101
Brest v Lever (1841) 7 M & W 593; 151 ER 904 57
Bridges v Hawkesworth (1851) 15 Jur 1079 .... 103, 105, 121–22
Bristow v Cormican (1878) 3 App Cas 641 (HL) 58, 59
Brown, Re [1954] Ch 39 (Ch) 165–66

Bruton v London & Quadrant Housing Trust [2000] 1 AC 406 (HL) 95–96
Buckinghamshire County Council v Moran [1990] Ch 623 (CA) 16, 18, 19–20, 21
Buckley v Gross (1863) 3 B & S 566; 122 ER 213; (1863) 32 LJQB 129;
    (1863) 9 Jur (NS) 986 .... 102, 107–8
Burton v Hughes (1824) 2 Bing 173; 130 ER 272 143–44
Buttle v Saunders [1950] 2 All ER 193 (Ch) 161–62

Carter v Johnson (1839) 2 M & Rob 263; 174 ER 283 .... 101, 120
Cary v Holt (1745) 2 Strange 1238; 93 ER 1154 57
Central London Commercial Estates Ltd v Kato Kagaku Co Ltd [1998]
    4 All ER 948 (Ch) 80–81
Chabbra Corp Pte Ltd v Jag Shakti (Owners) (The Jag Shakti) [1986]
    AC 337 (PC) 116–17
Chambers v Donaldson (1809) 11 East 65; 103 ER 929 58
Chambers v Havering London Borough Council [2011] EWCA Civ 1576;
    [2012] 1 P & CR 17 17
Chinery v Viall (1860) 5 H & N 288; 157 ER 1192 141
Cholmondeley v Clinton (1820) 2 Jac & W 1; 37 ER 527 147
Cholmondeley v Clinton (1821) 4 Bligh 1; 4 ER 721 67
Chung Ping Kwan v Lamb Island Developments Co Ltd [1997] AC 38 (PC) 85
City of London Corp v Appleyard [1963] 1 WLR 982 (QB) 21–22
Clarke v Clarke (1868) IR 2 CL 395 (QB) 77
Clowes Developments (UK) Ltd v Walters [2005] EWHC 669 (Ch); [2006]
    1 P & CR 1 20
Club Cruise Entertainment & Travelling Services Europe BV v
    Department for Transport (The Van Gogh) [2008] EWHC 2794 (Comm) 101
Cochrane v Moore (1890) 25 QBD 57 (CA) 151–52
Coggs v Bernard (1703) 2 Ld Raym 909; 92 ER 107 53–54
Coldman v Hill [1919] 1 KB 443 (CA) 132, 134
Colley v Overseas Exporters [1921] 3 KB 302 (KB) 109
Conway v George Wimpey & Co Ltd [1951] 2 KB 266 (CA) 56
Cosslett (Contractors) Ltd, Re [1998] Ch 495 (CA) 35
Costello v Chief Constable of Derbyshire Constabulary [2001]
    EWCA Civ 381; [2001] 1 WLR 1437 .... 2, 103, 105, 106–9, 112,
                                                          121–22, 124, 151–52
Cowan v Scargill [1985] Ch 270 (Ch) 161–62
Crinion v Minister for Justice [1959] Ir J Rep 15 21–22

Dalton v Angus & Co (1881) 6 App Cas 740 (HL) 60–61
Dalton v Fitzgerald [1897] 2 Ch 86 (CA) 77, 85
Danford v McAnulty (1883) 8 App Cas 456 (HL) 59, 64
Davison v Gent (1857) 1 H & N 744; 156 ER 1400; (1857) 3 Jur (NS) 342;
    (1857) 26 LJ Ex 122; (1857) 28 LTOS 291 .... 67–72, 74–75
de Franco v Commissioner of Police of the Metropolis, The Times,
    8 May 1987 (CA) 124
Delaney v TP Smith Ltd [1946] KB 393 (CA) 58
Doe d Carter v Barnard (1849) 13 Ad & El (NS) 945; 116 ER 1524 .... 67, 70–71
Doe d Hall v Penfold (1838) 8 Car & P 536, 537; 173 ER 607 .... 64–65, 66
Doe d Harding v Cooke (1831) 7 Bing 346; 131 ER 134 65–66
Doe d Hughes v Dyeball (1829) Mood & M 346; 173 ER 1184,
    sub nom Doe d Hughes v Dyball (1829) (1829) 3 Car & P 610;
    172 ER 567 .... 68–69, 74

Doe d Humphrey v Martin (1841) Car & M 32; 174 ER 395 64–66
Doe d Jukes v Sumner (1845) 14 M & W 39; 153 ER 380 85
Doe d Smith and Payne v Webber (1834) 1 Ad & El 119; 110 ER 1152 64–66
Donald v Suckling (1866) LR 1 QB 585 (QB) 99–100
Douglas Valley Finance Co Ltd v S Hughes (Hirers) Ltd [1969] 1 QB 738 138

East West Corp v DKBS AF 1912 [2003] EWCA Civ 83; [2003] QB 1509 135–36
Eastern Construction Co Ltd v National Trust Co Ltd [1914] AC 197 (PC) 116
Elwes v Brigg Gas Co (1886) 33 Ch D 562 (Ch) 22
Esso Petroleum Co Ltd v Southport Corp [1953] 3 WLR 773 (Assizes);
    [1954] 2 QB 182 (CA); [1956] AC 218 (HL) 56
Ezekiel v Fraser [2002] EWHC 2066 (Ch) 70–71, 79–80, 81

Fairweather v St Marylebone Property Co Ltd [1963] AC 510 (HL) 80–81, 85
Flack v National Crime Authority (1997) 80 FCR 137 (FCA) 12–13
Foster v Warblington Urban DC [1906] 1 KB 648 (CA) 59–60
Fouldes v Willoughby (1841) 8 M & W 540; 151 ER 1153 .... 101, 172
Franklin v Neate (1844) 13 M & W 480; 153 ER 200 .... 99–100, 116–17

Garlick v W & H Rycroft Ltd (CA, 30 June 1982) 132, 134
Gerrarde v Worseley (1580) Dyer 374a; 73 ER 839 62–63
Gilchrist Watt & Sanderson Pty Ltd v York Products Pty Ltd [1970]
    1 WLR 1262 (PC) 133–34, 135–36
Giles v Glover (1832) 9 Bing 128; 131 ER 563 101
Gledhill v Hunter (1880) 14 Ch D 492 (Ch) 63
Gough v Chief Constable of the West Midlands Police [2004] EWCA Civ 206 .... 103, 105
Government of Iran v The Barakat Galleries Ltd [2007] EWCA Civ 1374; [2009] QB 22   102
Graham v Peat (1801) 1 East 244; 102 ER 95 .... 57, 58
Greenmanor Ltd v Pilford [2012] EWCA Civ 756 .... 16, 18–19

Hamps v Darby [1948] 2 KB 311 (CA) 101
Hannah v Peel [1945] KB 509 (KB) 22, 105–6, 121–22, 151–52
Harker v Birkbeck (1764) 3 Burr 1556; 97 ER 978 57
Harper v Charlesworth (1825) 4 B & C 574; 107 ER 1174 .... 58, 59, 66–67
Hartley v Moxham (1842) 3 Ad & El (NS) 701; 114 ER 675 101
Hawdon v Khan (1920) 20 SR (NSW) 703 (NSWSC) 32–33, 77, 79, 81
Heaney v Kirkby [2015] UKUT 0178 (TCC) 96–97
Heydon and Smith's Case (1610) 13 Co Rep 67; 77 ER 1476 143–44
Hollins v Fowler (1875) LR 7 HL 757 (HL) 20–21, 133–34, 172
Houghland v RR Low (Luxury Coaches) Ltd [1962] 1 QB 694 (CA) 132, 134
Hunt v Peake (1860) Johnson 705; 70 ER 603 60–61
Hunter v Canary Wharf [1997] AC 655 (HL) 59–60, 61, 72

Isaack v Clark (1614) 2 Bulst 306; 80 ER 1143 .... 20–21, 133–34
Ironmonger v Bernard International (Estate Division) (CA, 9 February 1996) 92–93
Irving v National Provincial Bank Ltd [1962] 2 QB 73 (CA) 108

J A Pye (Oxford) Ltd v Graham [2000] Ch 676 (Ch) 145–46, 149–50
J A Pye (Oxford) Ltd v Graham [2001] EWCA Civ 117; [2001] Ch 804 .... 145–46, 147–48
J A Pye (Oxford) Ltd v Graham [2002] UKHL 30; [2003]
    1 AC 419 .... 15, 16–17, 18, 19–20, 21, 22, 87,
                                                 94–95, 145, 146–47, 149–50

J A Pye (Oxford) Ltd v United Kingdom (2006) 43 EHRR 3; (2008) 46 EHRR 45 . . . 145–46
J Alston & Sons Ltd v BOCM Pauls Ltd [2008] EWHC 3310 (Ch); [2009]
    1 EGLR 93 . . . . 20, 94–95
Jag Shakti, The. *See* Chabbra Corp Pte Ltd v Jag Shakti (Owners).
Jan De Nul (UK) Ltd v Axa Royale Belge SA [2002] EWCA Civ 209; [2002]
    1 Lloyd's Rep 583 58–59
Jayne v Price (1814) 5 Taunt 326, 128 ER 715 65–66
Jeffries v Great Western Railway Co (1856) 5 El & Bl 802;
    119 ER 680 . . . . 49, 67, 99, 101, 102, 120, 144
Johnson v Diprose [1893] 1 QB 512 (CA) 101
Jolliffe v Willmett & Co [1971] 1 All ER 478 (QB) 56
Jones v Chapman (1849) 2 Exch 803, 154 ER 717; 18 LJ Ex 456 . . . . 58, 59, 70–71
Joslin v Hipgrave [2015] UKFTT 0497 (PC) 96–97
Jupiter (No 3), The [1927] P 122 (PDA) 119–20

Kay v Lambeth LBC [2006] UHKL 10; [2006] 2 AC 465 95–96
Kenny v Preen [1963] 1 QB 499 (CA) 23
Kirk v Gregory (1876) LR 1 Ex D 55 101
Kowal v Ellis (1977) 76 DLR (3d) 546 (Manitoba Court of Appeal) 133–34
Kulkarni v Manor Credit (Davenham) Ltd [2010] EWCA Civ 69 110–11
Kuwait Airways Corp v Iraqi Airways Co (Nos 4 & 5) [2002] UKHL 19;
    [2002] 2 AC 883 . . . . 101–2, 137–38, 140–41, 172

Lambeth London Borough Council v Blackburn [2001] EWCA Civ 912;
    (2001) 82 P & CR 494 19–20
Lancashire & Yorkshire Railway Co v MacNicoll (1918) 88 LJKB 601 (KB) 172
Lawrence v Fen Tigers Ltd [2014] UKSC 46; [2015] AC 106 165–66
Leach v Jay (1878) 9 Ch D 42 (CA) 53, 85
Leake v Loveday (1842) 4 M & G 972; 134 ER 399 120–21
Leigh & Sullivan Ltd v Aliakmon Shipping Co Ltd (The Aliakmon) [1986]
    AC 785 (HL) 58–59, 102–3, 112
Letang v Cooper [1965] 1 QB 232 (CA) 56, 101
Lord Advocate v Young (1887) 12 App Cas 544 (HL) 17
Lowe's Will's Trust, Re [1973] 1 WLR 882 (CA) 88
Lynn Lewis Ltd v The Environment Agency [2007] EWLandRA REF/2005/1068 . . . 96–97

M'Donnell v M'Kinty (1847) 10 Ir LR 514 83
M'Dowell v Ulster Bank (1899) 33 ILT 225 21–22
McPhail v Doulton [1971] AC 424 (HL) 127
McPhail v Persons, Names Unknown [1973] Ch 447 (CA) 63
Mabo v Queensland (No 2) (1992) 175 CLR 1 (HCA) 88, 90
Marcq v Christie Manson & Woods Ltd [2003] EWCA Civ 731; [2004] QB 286 135–36
Mainline Private Hire Ltd v Nolan [2011] EWCA Civ 189; [2011] CTLC 145 . . . . 16–17, 19
Makepiece v Fletcher (1734) 2 Com 457; 92 ER 1158 64
Malik v Malik [2019] EWHC 1843 (Ch) 20, 21
Marsden v Miller (1992) 64 P & CR 239 (CA) 15, 16, 18–19, 21
Mayfair Property Co v Johnston [1894] 1 Ch 508 (Ch) 55
Mayor of London v Hall [2010] EWCA Civ 817; [2011] 1 WLR 504 . . . . 53–54, 81
Metters v Brown (1863) 1 H & C 686; 158 ER 1060; (1863) 32 LJ Ex 138 . . . . 49, 65–66
Mexfield Housing Co-operative Ltd v Berrisford [2011] UKSC 52; [2012] 1 AC 955 . 94–96
Michael v Chief Constable of South Wales Police [2015] UKSC 2; [2015] AC 1732 132
Mills v Brooker [1919] 1 KB 555 (DC) 165–66

Mitchell v Ealing London Borough Council [1979] QB 1 (QB) 132, 134
Mitchell v Glasgow City Council [2009] 1 AC 874 (HL) 132
Moon v Raphael (1835) 2 Bing NC 310; 132 ER 122 141
Morice v Bishop of Durham (1804) 9 Ves Jr 399; (1805) 10 Ves Jr 522 127
Morris v CW Martin & Sons Ltd [1966] 1 QB 716 (CA) 132
Morrison Steamship Co Ltd v Greystoke Castle [1947] AC 265 (HL) 116
Morritt, Re (1886) 18 QBD 222 (CA) 99–100
Moses v Lovegrove [1952] 2 QB 533 (CA) 83
Mount Carmel Investments Ltd v Peter Thurlow Ltd [1988] 1 WLR 1078 (CA) .. 77, 90–93

National Coal Board v J E Evans & Co (Cardiff) Ltd [1951] 2 KB 861 (CA) 56, 101
National Crime Authority v Flack (1998) 86 FCR 16 (FCAFC) 12–13, 106
National Employers' Mutual General Insurance Association Ltd v Jones [1990]
    1 AC 24 (HL) 110–11
National Provincial Bank Ltd v Ainsworth [1965] AC 1175 (HL) 58
Nelson v Cherrill (1832) 8 Bing 316; 131 ER 415 120
Nepean v Doe d Knight (1837) 2 M & W 894; 150 ER 1021 87
Network Rail Infrastructure Ltd v Conarken Group Ltd [2010]
    EWHC 1852 (QB); [2010] BLR 601 56
Newman v Bourne & Hollingsworth (1915) 31 TLR 209 (DC) 133–34
Nicholls v Ely Beet Sugar Factory [1931] 2 Ch 84 (Ch) 70–71

O'Sullivan v Williams [1992] 3 All ER 385 (CA) 116
Ocean Estates Ltd v Pinder [1969] 2 AC 19 (PC) 2, 19–20
Odessa, The [1916] 1 AC 145 (PC) 99–100, 116–17
Ofulue v Bossert [2008] EWCA Civ 7; [2009] Ch 1 145–46
Oxford Meat Co Pty v McDonald [1963] 63 SR (NSW) 423 70–71

Parker v British Airways Board [1982] QB 1004 (CA) 2, 12–13, 16, 19,
                                                    21–22, 28–29, 103, 121–22
Parker v Godin (1728) 2 Strange 813; 93 ER 866 172
Patel v Mirza [2016] UKSC 42; [2017] AC 467 106
Peaceable d Uncle v Watson (1811) 4 Taunt 16; 128 ER 232 64–65
Pemberton v Southwark LBC [2000] 1 WLR 1672 (CA) 59–60
Perry v Clissold [1907] AC 73 (PC) 70–71, 72, 77
Phillips v Vaughan [2016] UKFTT 0320 (PC) 96–97
Phipps v Pears [1965] 1 QB 76 (CA) 165–66
Pioneer Container, The [1994] 2 AC 324 (PC) 135–36
Port of London v Ashmore [2009] EWHC 954 (Ch) 18
Port of London Authority v Mendoza [2017] UKUT 146 (TCC) 21
Powell v McFarlane (1977) 38 P & CR 452 (Ch) 15, 16–17, 19–20, 21, 94
Prangnell-O'Neill v Lady Skiffington 1984 SLT 282 (IH) 151–52

R v Allpress [2009] EWCA Crim 8; [2009] 2 Cr App R (S) 58 114–16
R v D'Eyncourt and Ryan (1888) 21 QBD 109 (DC) 103
R v Lambert [2001] UKHL 37; [2002] 2 AC 545 11–12
R v McNamara (1988) 87 Cr App R 246 (CA) 11–12
R v May [2008] UKHL 28; [2008] 1 AC 1028 114–15
R v Ngan [2008] 2 NZLR 48 (Supreme Court of New Zealand) 133–34
R v Thomas Smith (1855) 6 Cox CC 554 4
R (Best) v Chief Land Registrar [2015] EWCA Civ 17; [2016] QB 23 146
Red House Farms (Thorndon) Ltd v Catchpole [1977] 2 EGLR 125 (CA) 18

Reynolds v Clarke (1725) 2 Ld Raym 1399 56
Rhone v Stephens [1994] 2 AC 310 (HL) 165–66
Roberts v Tayler (1845) 1 CB 117; 135 ER 481 70–71
Robinson v Chief Constable of West Yorkshire [2018] UKSC 4; [2018] AC 736 132
Roe d Haldane and Urry v Harvey (1769) 4 Burr 2484; 98 ER 302 . . . . 59, 64
Rogers Sons & Co v Lambert & Co [1891] 1 QB 318 (CA) 119–20, 121–22
Rogers v Spence (1844) 13 M & W 571; 153 ER 239 67
Rooth v Wilson (1817) 1 B & Ald 59; 106 ER 22 102–3
Rosenberg v Cook (1881) 8 QBD 162 (CA) 77–79, 94–95
Rowland v Divall [1923] 2 KB 500 (CA) 110
Russell v Wilson (1923) 33 CLR 538 (HCA) 101, 106

Sandeman Coprimar SA v Transitos y Transportes Integrales SL [2003]
    EWCA Civ 113; [2003] QB 1270 135–36
Sanderson v Marsden (1922) 10 Ll L Rep 467 (CA) 137–38
Scmlla Properties Ltd v Gesso Properties (BVI) Ltd [1995] BCC 793 (Ch) 89, 167–68
Secretary of State for the Environment, Food and Rural Affairs v Meier
    [2009] UKSC 11; [2009] 1 WLR 2780 23–24
Sedleigh-Denfield v O'Callaghan [1940] AC 880 (HL) 165–66
Sevilleja v Marex Financial Ltd [2020] UKSC 31; [2020] 3 WLR 255 124–25
Sewell v Burdick (The Zoe) (1884) 10 App Cas 74 (HL) 112–13
Simpson v Fergus (1999) 79 P & CR 398 (CA) 18–19
Site Developments (Ferndown) Ltd v Cuthbury Ltd [2010] EWHC 10 (Ch);
    [2011] Ch 226 90–91
Smith v Littlewoods Organisation Ltd [1987] AC 241 (HL) 132–33
Smith v Milles (1786) 1 Term Reports 475; 99 ER 1205 101
South Staffordshire Water Co v Sharman [1896] 2 QB 44 (DC) 12–13, 14
Southcot v Bennet (1600) Cro Eliz 815; 78 ER 1041 143
St Marylebone Property Co Ltd v Fairweather [1962] 1 QB 498 (CA) 3, 72
Street v Mountford [1985] AC 809 (HL) 55, 94–95, 165–66
Sutton v Buck (1810) 2 Taunt 302; 127 ER 1094 . . . . 102, 143–44
Swire v Leach (1865) 18 CB (NS) 479; 144 ER 531 143–44
Sze To Chun Keung v Kung Kwok Wai David [1997] 1 WLR 1232 (PC) 94–95

Tapling v Jones (1865) 11 HLC 290; 11 ER 1344 165–66
Thompson v Nixon [1966] 1 QB 103 (DC) 133–34
Tichborne v Weir (1892) 67 LT 735 (CA) 85
Towers & Co v Gray [1961] 2 QB 351 (DC) 11–12
Trustees of Dundee Harbour v Dougall (1852) 1 Macq 317 (HL) 147
Tubantia, The [1924] P 78 (PDA) 16–17, 18, 19
Turner v Chief Land Registrar [2013] EWHC 1382 (Ch);
    [2013] 2 P & CR 12 . . . . 3–4, 80–81, 90
Turner v Hardcastle (1862) 11 CB (NS) 683; 142 ER 964 143–44

Umma v Appu [1939] AC 136 (PC) 18
United Australia Ltd v Barclays Bank Ltd [1941] AC 1 (HL) 137–38
USA v Dollfus Mieg et Compagnie SA [1952] AC 582 (HL) 101

Van Gogh, The. See Club Cruise Entertainment & Travelling Services Europe BV v
    Department for Transport
VFS Financial Services (UK) Ltd v Euro Auctions (UK) Ltd [2007]
    EWHC 1492 (QB) 141–42

Walgrave v Ogden (1589) 1 Leon 224; 74 ER 205 101–2
Warner v Metropolitan Police Commissioner [1969] 2 AC 256 (HL) 11–12, 13–14
Waverley Borough Council v Fletcher [1996] QB 334 (CA) 12–13, 22, 103–4
Webb v Chief Constable of Merseyside Police [2000] QB 427 (CA) 105
Webb v Fox (1797) 7 Term Reports 391; 101 ER 1037 102
Wells v Pilling Parish Council [2008] EWHC 556 (Ch); [2008] 2 EGLR 29 2
Whale v Hitchcock (1876) 34 LT 136 (DC) 64–66
Wheeler v Baldwin (1934) 52 CLR 609 (HCA) 77
White v Morris (1852) 11 CB 1015; 138 ER 778 101
White v Withers LLP [2009] EWCA Civ 1122; [2010] 1 FLR 859 101
Wilbraham v Snow (1668) 2 Saund 47; 85 ER 624, 628 99
Williams v Network Rail Infrastructure Ltd [2018] EWCA Civ 1514;
    [2019] QB 601 .... 55, 59–60
Wilson v Lombank Ltd [1963] 1 WLR 1294 123
Winder, Ex p (1877) 6 Ch D 696 (Ch) 77
Winkfield, The [1902] P 42 (CA) 49, 102–3, 116–17, 120,
                                        123–24, 128–29, 137–38, 143–44
Winter Garden Theatre (London) Ltd v Millennium Productions Ltd
    [1948] AC 173 (HL) 165–66
Wretham v Ross [2005] EWHC 1259 (Ch) 20, 21
Wuta-Ofei v Danquah [1961] 1 WLR 1238 (PC) 17

Yearworth v North Bristol NHS Trust [2009] EWCA Civ 37; [2010] QB 1 132
Young v Hichens (1844) 6 Ad & El (NS) 606; 115 ER 228 9

Zarb v Parry [2011] EWCA Civ 1306; [2012] 1 WLR 1240 .... 15, 16
Zoe, The. *See* Sewell v Burdick

Table of Legislation

UK STATUTES

Administration of Estates Act 1925
  sch 2, pt 1 167
Civil Liability (Contribution) Act 1978
  s 1(1) 141–42n.72
Common Law Procedure Act 1852 63
  s 168 63
  s 169 63
  sch A 63
Companies Act 2006
  s 859A 151–52
Consumer Rights Act 2015
  s 4(1) 110
  s 5 109
Criminal Law Act 1977
  s 6(1)–(1A) 29–30
Drugs (Prevention of Misuse)
    Act 1964 .... 12n.29
  s 1(1) 11–12
Factors Act 1889
  s 9 110–11
Human Rights Act 1998
  s 1(1)(b) 165–66
  s 4 165–66
  s 6 165–66
Insolvency Act 1986
  s 283 165–66
  s 283A 165–66
  s 306 165–66
  s 436(1) 165–66
Land Registration Act 1925
  s 75 .... 83n.207
Land Registration Act 2002   80–81, 83–84,
    96–97, 149–50
  s 4 .... 165n.64
  s 15(3) 80–81
  s 27 .... 165n.64
  s 96 .... 83–84, 149–50
  s 96(1) 149–50
  s 96(3) 149–50
  s 97 .... 83–84, 149–50
  s 98 .... 83–84, 149–50

sch 6 ..... 23–24, 83–84, 96–97, 149–50
sch 6(4) 83–84
sch 6(5)(1) 83–84
sch 6(7) 83–84
sch 6(9) 83–84
sch 6(9)(1) 80–81, 96
Law of Property Act 1922
  s 128(2) 167n.81
  s 138 .... 167n.81
  sch 12(4)–(6) 167n.81
Law of Property Act 1925 90
  s 1(1) 90
  s 1(1)(a) 55n.17
  s 51(1) 85–86n.227
  s 52 .... 165n.64
  s 95(4) 55n.17
  s 205(1)(xix) 55n.17
Limitation Act 1939 .... 83, 152–53
  s 4 83
  s 5 .... 15n.44, 83
  s 10 .... 15n.44, 83
  s 10(1) 83
  s 10(2) 83
  s 16 83
  sch 83
Limitation Act 1980 ... 15n.44, 83, 152–53
  s 2 152–53
  s 3(1) 152–53
  s 3(2) 152–53
  s 4 152–53
  s 15 .... 83, 90–91, 145, 149–50
  s 15(1) 145
  s 17 .... 83, 96–97,
               145–46, 147–50
  s 18 .... 83, 145
  s 28 145
  sch 1 83
  sch 1(1) 145
Metropolitan Police Courts Act 1839
  s 29 107–8
Misuse of Drugs Act 1971 .... 12n.29
  s 5(2) 12n.29
  s 28(3)(b)(i) 12n.29

Police and Criminal Evidence Act 1984
s 22 106
Police (Property) Act 1897
s 1 108
Presumption of Death Act 2013
ss 1–3 . . . . 44n.81
Proceeds of Crime Act 2002
s 76(4) 115
s 84(2) 115
s 84(2)(b) 115
s 84(2)(h) 115
Real Property Act 1845
s 6 53
Real Property Limitation
    Act 1833 . . . . 63, 82–83, 84–85,
                                    87, 98, 144–45
s 2 82
s 3 82
s 34 82–83
s 36 63
s 39 64
Real Property Limitation Act 1874
s 1 83
Sale of Goods Act 1979
s 2 . . . . 109, 110
s 2(1) 109
s 2(4) 109
s 2(5) 109
s 2(6) 109
s 12(1) 110
s 12(3) 110

s 24 110
s 25 110
s 25(1) 110–11
s 61(1) 109, 110
Statute of Limitations 1623
    (21 Jac 1, c 16) 64
Statute of Westminster the Third
    (Quia Emptores) 1290
    (18 Edw 1, c 1) 55–56
Supreme Court of Judicature Act 1875 . . 63
Tenures Abolition Act 1660 167
Torts (Interference with Goods)
    Act 1977 . . . . 119, 123–25
s 2(2) 101–2n.18
s 7(1) 124
s 7(2) 124
s 8(1) 116, 124–25
Wills Act 1837
s 3 . . . . 53, 55–56

UK STATUTORY INSTRUMENTS

Civil Procedure Rules 1998, SI
    1998/3132 124
r 19.5A(1) 124, 151n.125
r 19.5A(2) 124

INTERNATIONAL INSTRUMENTS

European Convention on Human Rights
Protocol 1, Art 1   165–66

1

Introduction

For centuries, jurists have reflected on the nature and significance of ownership and possession.[1] This is understandable, for the concepts of ownership and possession have played a momentous role in legal, political, and economic thought, and rules relating to ownership and possession are central components of many property systems. One issue that jurists have been particularly interested in is the relationship between ownership and possession. Indeed, Richard Posner has said that '[t]he "problem" of possession, and the source of its enduring fascination as much to the Romans, Savigny, and Holmes as to ourselves, is precisely its relation to property'.[2]

With respect to English law, a common view is that ownership and possession are fundamental concepts in the law of personal property. According to the authors of a number of practitioner and student textbooks,[3] English law recognises two kinds of legal (as opposed to equitable) proprietary interests in respect of tangible chattels:[4] legal ownership interests and possessory interests. The central questions of personal property law, on this view, include: what are legal ownership interests and possessory interests? How are these interests acquired and transferred? And how are they protected? One question that must be addressed by those who defend this view is whether, within this framework, one can make sense of the fact that English law is what Tony Honoré has called a 'multititular system', ie a system in which multiple, independent titles to certain land or a particular chattel can exist concurrently.[5]

---

[1] See David J Seipp, 'The Concept of Property in the Early Common Law' (1994) 12 Law & History Rev 29; James Gordley and Ugo Mattei, 'Protecting Possession' (1996) 44 Am J Comp Law 293; Joshua Getzler, 'Roman Ideas of Landownership' in Susan Bright and John Dewar (eds), *Land Law: Themes and Perspectives* (OUP 1998).

[2] Richard A Posner, 'Savigny, Homes, and the Law and Economics of Possession' (2000) 86 Virginia LR 535, 543.

[3] eg Sarah Worthington, *Personal Property Law: Text, Cases and Materials* (Hart 2000) 16–17, ch 2; Ewan McKendrick (ed), *Goode on Commercial Law* (5th edn, Penguin 2016) ch 2; Michael Bridge and others, *The Law of Personal Property* (2nd edn, Sweet & Maxwell 2018) chs 2, 10.

[4] Tangible chattels are sometimes called 'choses in possession'. They are corporeal, moveable things that can be the subject matter of proprietary interests (eg books, pianos, and cars). Hereinafter, tangible chattels are called simply 'chattels'.

[5] AM Honoré, 'Ownership' in AG Guest (ed), *Oxford Essays in Jurisprudence* (OUP 1961) 107, 136–39. 'Land', for present purposes, refers to corporeal hereditaments, including the surface layer of the

Possession, Relative Title, and Ownership in English Law. Luke Rostill, Oxford University Press (2021). © Luke Rostill.
DOI: 10.1093/oso/9780198843108.003.0001

In English law, this system rests on two basic principles. The first is the principle of relativity of title. This, as Lord Diplock explained in *Ocean Estates Ltd v Pinder*,[6] is the principle that '[w]here questions of title . . . arise in litigation the court is concerned only with the relative strengths of the titles proved by the rival claimants'.[7] If, for example, B brings an action to recover possession of land from C, it is not a defence that an unconnected third party, A, has a 'better title' to the land than B.[8]

The second principle is that possession is a source of 'title'. In *Alan Wibberley Building Ltd v Insley*,[9] Lord Hoffmann said: '[p]ossession is in itself a good title against anyone who cannot show a prior and therefore better right to possession'.[10] If, for example, B found A's wallet in the street and picked it up, B, by taking possession, acquired a 'title' to the wallet that is good against all the world, except those who have a better, because earlier, 'title'.[11]

It is widely recognised that these principles are foundational;[12] yet they have long been, and still are, interpreted in opposing ways by judges, practitioners, and academics. One central and divisive issue concerns the nature of the 'title' that is acquired through taking possession,[13] and how it relates to ownership. Among those who believe that English law recognises two kinds of legal proprietary interests in respect of chattels— legal ownership interests and possessory interests—some would say that B, by taking possession of the wallet, acquired a 'possessory interest'.[14] Others would say that B acquired a 'possessory title to legal ownership'.[15] Since B has a mere 'possessory title', B's interest, unlike A's, will generally determine if and when B ceases to be in possession.[16]

---

earth, an area of space above the surface, plants, buildings, and fixtures. For discussion, see Kevin Gray and Susan Francis Gray, *Elements of Land Law* (5th edn, OUP 2009) 8–55.

[6] [1969] 2 AC 19 (PC).

[7] ibid 25.

[8] See Chapter 4 (section 4.2.2.2).

[9] [1999] 1 WLR 894 (HL).

[10] ibid 898.

[11] *Parker v British Airways Board* [1982] QB 1004 (CA); *Costello v Chief Constable of Derbyshire Constabulary* [2001] EWCA Civ 381; [2001] 1 WLR 1437.

[12] See, eg *Wells v Pilling Parish Council* [2008] EWHC 556 (Ch); [2008] 2 EGLR 29 [7] (Lewison J): 'the principle of relativity of title . . . is the bedrock of English land law'.

[13] Everyone accepts that, where a person takes possession of an *unowned* chattel (res nullius), the possessor acquires an alienable proprietary interest that is capable of lasting forever and comprises a right to exclude the world at large. The debate concerns the effect of taking possession of (a) land, which is necessarily held by someone, or (b) chattels that are *not* unowned.

[14] eg Bridge and others (n 3) paras 10-004, 10-013, 10-018.

[15] eg McKendrick (n 3) paras 2.20–2.24.

[16] ibid para 2.22. It is important to recognise that the terms 'possessory title' and 'possessory interest' are multivocal. For instance, the term 'possessory interest' is sometimes used in contradistinction to 'reversionary interest'.

A contrasting view is that A and B each hold the very same kind of interest. William Swadling, for example, would say that B has the same type of right as A, namely, a 'right to exclusive possession forever'.[17] Importantly, on this view, B's right, like A's, will survive a loss of possession. The only difference is that A's right binds B, but B's right does not bind A. For Swadling, it would be a mistake to regard A or B as the owner, or to regard each of them as an owner: 'any notion of "ownership" is inconsistent with the fundamental English law principle of relativity of title'.[18] This, too, is contentious. Frederick Pollock, for instance, embraced a very different conclusion about the relationship between relativity of title and ownership in English law: possessors, he claimed, are relative owners; they are 'invested as against the world at large with all the incidents of ownership'.[19]

Lawyers also disagree over the nature of the 'title' that is acquired through taking possession of land. There are many views. A fairly common one is that the protection afforded to possessors is a consequence of rules of evidence or presumption. The possessor acquires a 'title' to the fee simple in the sense that her possession will be treated as evidence, or will give rise to a presumption, that she has the fee simple. In *Re Atkinson and Horsell's Contract*,[20] for example, Sir Herbert Cozens-Hardy MR said:

> the true view is this, that whenever you find a person in possession of property that possession is prima facie evidence of ownership in fee, and that prima facie evidence becomes absolute when . . . there is nobody who can challenge the presumption which his possession of the property gives.[21]

Cozens-Hardy MR thought that this 'explains' the protection afforded to a squatter, ie a person who is in adverse possession of land.[22] An opposing view is that by taking possession—or, more narrowly, by taking adverse possession—one actually acquires a fee simple estate in the land,

---

[17] William Swadling, 'Property: General Principles' in Andrew Burrows (ed), *English Private Law* (3rd edn, OUP 2013) paras 4.422–4.428. See also Ben McFarlane, *The Structure of Property Law* (Hart 2008) 146.

[18] William Swadling, 'Trusts and Ownership: A Common Law Perspective' (2016) 24 Eur Rev Private L 951, 959. See also WW Buckland and AD McNair, *Roman Law and Common Law: A Comparison in Outline* (FH Lawson ed, 2nd edn, CUP 1965) 68: '[English] courts deal with rights to possess where the Roman courts dealt with ownership.'

[19] Frederick Pollock, *A First Book of Jurisprudence* (5th edn, Macmillan 1923) 188.

[20] [1912] 2 Ch 1 (CA).

[21] ibid 9 (cited with approval in *St Marylebone Property Co Ltd v Fairweather* [1962] 1 QB 498 (CA) 513 (Holroyd Pearce LJ)).

[22] ibid.

comprising rights that bind every person who does not have a better right to possession.[23]

The debate over the nature of the 'title' that is acquired through possession has significant practical implications. If, for example, the 'title' that B acquired upon picking up the wallet subsists only for so long as she remains in possession of it, then, if B is dispossessed by C, and C, in turn, is dispossessed by D, B will not be able to recover possession, or a monetary remedy, from D. Furthermore, the proper limits of the principle of relativity of title depend, in part, on the nature of the possessor's 'title'. In particular, whether B has certain rights, or whether she is merely presumed to have certain rights, is relevant to: (i) the circumstances in which C, when sued by B, should be able to rely on the fact that A has a 'better title' than B; and (ii) the precise effect of allowing C to show that A has a 'better title' than B.[24]

This book seeks to illuminate the principle of relativity of title, and its relationship to possession and ownership, by addressing four main questions. First, what, for the purposes of the rules concerning the acquisition of title, is possession? It is important to address this question, for 'possession' is ambiguous and 'shifts its meaning according to the subject-matter to which it is applied'.[25] It is argued in Chapter 2 that the general rule is that one will obtain possession of certain land or a particular chattel if, and only if, one has: (a) exclusive physical control of the land or chattel; and (b) an intention, in one's own name and on one's own behalf, to exclude the world from it.[26]

Secondly, what is the nature of the 'title' that is acquired by obtaining possession? Chapters 3, 4, and 5 are concerned with this question. Chapter 3 analyses and compares three significant views of the nature of a possessor's 'title', and examines the distinction between, on the one hand, a person being presumed by a court to have a right or interest in respect of certain land or chattels and, on the other hand, a person actually acquiring a right or interest.

Chapter 4 discusses the nature of the 'title' that is acquired through taking possession of land. It argues that the traditional view, which is that 'mere possession is not a root of freehold title', is plausible only if one overlooks how the law evolved in the 19th century.[27] In the modern law, possession is a 'root of freehold title'; one can acquire a fee simple estate simply through taking

---

[23] See, eg *Turner v Chief Land Registrar* [2013] EWHC 1382(Ch); [2013] 2 P & CR 12 [13]–[16] (Roth J).

[24] See Chapter 5 (section 5.3.2).

[25] *R v Thomas Smith* (1855) 6 Cox CC 554, 556 (Erle J).

[26] See Chapter 2 (section 2.3).

[27] See Chapter 4 (section 4.2.2).

possession,[28] though the precise scope of the acquisition rule is unsettled.[29] This body of law, it is argued, can be properly understood only if one appreciates its history and, in particular, how the legal changes that were brought about by the courts—through a line of cases that includes the famous case of *Asher v Whitlock*—were necessitated by, and intended to further, purposes that Parliament embraced in the first half of the 19th century.[30] The current acquisition rule applies irrespective of whether the possessor is in possession of land in respect of which there is a registered estate, and this raises some difficult questions about the relationship between unregistered and registered land.[31] It is true, as Martin Dixon has said, that '[u]nregistered land is of diminishing importance, legally and practically';[32] but to understand the relationship between the registered land system and the (unregistered) 'title' acquired through possession, we must examine the common law rules concerning possession and relativity of title.

Chapter 5 considers the nature of the title that is acquired through taking possession of a chattel. It is argued that the possessor acquires an alienable proprietary interest that is capable of lasting forever, will survive a loss of possession, and includes a right to exclude the world at large.[33] The possessor acquires, in other words, a general property interest in possession (as opposed to in reversion). The precise scope of the rule is unclear, but it seems that the rule applies where a person who takes possession of a chattel does not take under a pre-existing right to exclusive possession, or under the grant of a new limited legal interest (eg a pledge). If all this is correct, it is a mistake to claim that the interest that is acquired through possession is 'possessory' in the sense that, once acquired, it will generally continue to exist only if the interest-holder remains in possession. It is also a mistake to claim that a possessor is protected *solely* by rules of presumption, though, as we will see,[34] a person who is in possession of a chattel will be able to take advantage of the rule that a possessor, or one who has a right to immediate possession, must be presumed to have 'absolute and complete ownership' if a person with a better right cannot be identified.

The third main question is: what are grounds of the rules that confer proprietary interests on possessors? One has an impoverished understanding of a legal rule if one is unaware of its legal basis. It is important, therefore, to ascertain

---

[28] See Chapter 4 (section 4.2).
[29] See Chapter 4 (section 4.4).
[30] See Chapter 4 (section 4.3.1).
[31] See Chapter 4 (section 4.4.2).
[32] Martin Dixon, *Modern Land Law* (11th edn, Routledge 2018) 20.
[33] See Chapter 5 (section 5.2).
[34] See Chapter 5 (section 5.3).

whether the rules have a legal rationale and, if so, what it is. It is argued in Chapter 6 that the rules are primarily based on the genuine need to provide greater certainty over title to chattels and unregistered land and to secure the position of possessors and their successors in title. But the law's reasons for applying the rule to cases involving registered land are unclear.[35]

Fourthly, what is the relationship between relativity of title and ownership? Is relativity of title incompatible with ownership? Or should we regard those who hold competing titles to a thing as independent, or relative, owners? It is argued in Chapter 7 that, despite the fact that English law is a multititular system that recognises relativity of title, land and chattels can be owned.[36] It is, however, a mistake to think that an inferior fee simple or an inferior general property interest possesses all the incidents of ownership.[37] There are significant differences between the legal positions of the person who has the best title to a thing and the person who has an inferior title. The former, it is suggested, may, depending on the circumstances, have ownership; but the latter does not. This is not a mere theoretical difference with no serious legal consequences: in some circumstances, it matters, in practice, whether one is the owner, ie the holder of the best title.

One significant implication of this book's analysis of the law concerning relativity of title and the acquisition of proprietary interests through possession is that the architecture of land law and the law of personal property are much closer than many believe. Just as there can be multiple fees simple in respect of certain land, there can be multiple general property interests in respect of a certain chattel. And, within this multititular system, there is a place for ownership: the holder of the best fee simple or the best general property interest may, depending on the circumstances, have ownership. Recognising these similarities between land law and the law of personal property is crucial if we are to relieve the latter of its status as 'underconceptualized';[38] a mere 'wallflower'.[39]

---

[35] See Chapter 6 (section 6.3).
[36] See Chapter 7 (sections 7.1 and 7.2).
[37] See Chapter 7 (section 7.3).
[38] Arianna Pretto-Sakmann, *Boundaries of Personal Property: Shares and Sub-Shares* (Hart 2005) 3.
[39] Peter Birks, 'Personal Property: Proprietary Rights and Remedies' (2000) 11 KCLJ 1, 2.

2

Possession

2.1 The Aims and Scope of the Enquiry

An examination of the law concerning the acquisition of title through possession should consider the nature of the title that one acquires and the nature of
the possession that gives rise to it. This chapter is concerned with the latter. It
aims to explain what counts as possession for the purposes of the rules concerning the acquisition of title. It does not aim to give an account of the nature
of the general concept of possession. The enquiry is, therefore, legal, not philosophical. In this respect, it can be contrasted with John Salmond's well-known
account of possession, which sought to provide 'an analysis of the conception
[of possession] itself', as opposed to 'an exposition of the manner in which it is
recognized and applied in the actual legal system'.[1]

Nor does this chapter aim to provide what might be described as a general
account of possession in English law. Consequently, it can be contrasted with
Frederick Pollock's hugely influential essay on possession.[2] In the preface,
Pollock noted that '[t]he want of any systematic account of possession in
English law-books has often been remarked upon'.[3] Pollock intended to fill the
gap; he sought to explain the 'native doctrine of possession'—as opposed to any
doctrine of Roman Law—and 'to show that a fairly consistent body of principles is contained in the English authorities'.[4] He outlined eight rules that, in his
view, 'represent, in a general way, the working method of the Common Law
with regard to Possession'.[5]

Pollock's approach gives rise to a question that he did not adequately examine in his essay: what is a general account of possession in the law actually an account of? What, in other words, is the subject matter of the account?
One might say that the subject matter is 'possession in the law'. But this answer,

---

[1] John W Salmond, *Jurisprudence* (7th edn, Sweet & Maxwell 1924) 295.
[2] Frederick Pollock and Robert Samuel Wright, *An Essay on Possession in the Common Law*
(Clarendon Press 1888). Pollock is the author of Parts I and II, Wright of Part III.
[3] ibid v.
[4] ibid vi.
[5] ibid 19.

Possession, Relative Title, and Ownership in English Law. Luke Rostill, Oxford University Press (2021). © Luke Rostill.
DOI: 10.1093/oso/9780198843108.003.0002

without elaboration, is problematic, because 'possession' is ambiguous, and its meaning depends upon the context. This might lead one to say that the subject matter is all the rules in English law that concern 'possession' in various senses of this term. But this response gives rise to other questions. What is the point of treating these laws together? And when does a law 'concern' possession? The point is not that these questions are unanswerable, but that they should be considered and discussed if one purports to provide a general account of 'possession in the law'. That, it seems, was Pollock's aim in his famous essay on possession. It is not, however, the aim of this chapter.

2.2 Scepticism of Possession

The aims and methodologies of the 19th-century writers on possession were rejected by many jurists in the 20th century. The American jurist Burke Shartel, for instance, rejected the approach of 'older writers' who had 'brought as many cases as possible together, on the basis of some feature of similarity among them, and have united them all under one conceptual head'.[6] Whereas Pollock sought to provide a general account of possession in English law, Shartel favoured an analysis that took seriously 'the particularization of problems' and which gave 'particularized form ... to our concepts and terms':[7]

> instead of attempting to develop a standard act or a standard event to cover all the cases in which proprietary relations arise, or liabilities are imposed, on the basis of dealings with things, instead of trying to define the act of taking or the act of delivery for all legally significant situations, let us try to frame standard statements more particular in type and narrower in application.[8]

Shartel acknowledged that the meaning of 'possession' depends upon the context,[9] and that there are often good reasons for the law to adopt one meaning in one context and a different meaning in another. On the basis of these considerations, Shartel and a number of other legal writers[10] maintained that the

---

[6] Burke Shartel, 'Meanings of Possession' (1932) 16 Minnesota LR 611, 612.

[7] ibid 625.

[8] ibid 624.

[9] Pollock also acknowledged that 'possession' is ambiguous and that 'careful attention must in every case be paid to the context': Pollock and Wright (n 2) 1, 28. But he nonetheless thought that it was possible and desirable to give a general account of possession in law: Pollock and Wright (n 2) 19.

[10] eg DR Harris, 'The Concept of Possession in English Law' in AG Guest (ed), *Oxford Essays in Jurisprudence* (OUP 1961) 69–72; RWM Dias, *Jurisprudence* (5th edn, Butterworths 1985) 273–89.

general accounts of possession that had been advanced by Pollock and other 'older writers' were the product of a flawed methodology. But the sceptical treatment of the older writings did not stop there; some jurists went further and concluded that possession is no more than a device of policy and convenience.[11] This conclusion should be rejected and, in order to see why, we must understand the ambiguity of 'possession', the vagueness of particular senses of 'possession', and the implications of these matters for the law, legal reasoning, and legal discourse.

2.2.1 Ambiguity

It is widely recognised that 'possession' is an ambiguous word; it has multiple meanings.[12] In legal contexts, two important clusters of meanings should be distinguished. When 'possession' is used in a way that belongs to the first cluster, it means, at least, 'physical control'. An example of 'possession' being used in this way can be found in the judgment of Lord Denman CJ in *Young v Hichens*.[13] The claimant had almost caught some fish with a net when the defendant disturbed the fish and prevented the claimant from catching them. The claimant brought trespass. Lord Denman CJ said:

> [i]t does appear almost certain that the [claimant] would have had possession of the fish but for the act of the defendant: but it is quite certain that he had not possession . . . [T]he question will be whether any custody or possession has been obtained here. I think it is impossible to say that it had, until the party had actual power over the fish.[14]

Lord Denman plainly used the term 'possession' to refer to a relationship between a person and a tangible thing whereby the person has physical control of—'actual power over'—the thing.

When 'possession' is used in a way that belongs to the second cluster, it refers to a legal interest (ie an interconnected set of rights, liberties, powers, and/ or immunities).[15] RH Kersley, for example, asserted that there are three types

---

[11] See section 2.2.4 below.
[12] See, eg Pollock and Wright (n 2) 1; Shartel (n 6) 612.
[13] (1844) 6 Ad & El (NS) 606; 115 ER 228. See also Pollock and Wright (n 2) 12, 26.
[14] (1844) 6 Ad & El (NS) 606, 611; 115 ER 228, 230.
[15] See JW Bingham, 'The Nature and Importance of Legal Possession' (1915) 13 Mich LR 535, 623, 636–40.

of legal interest that a person may have in goods: '(1) ownership, (2) bailment, (3) mere possession'.[16] More recently, Michael Bridge has said that, at common law, there are two '[p]roprietary interests in chattels': 'possession and ownership'.[17] According to these accounts of the law, it is possible to acquire possession (a kind of interest) by obtaining possession of a chattel (ie, roughly, physical control).[18]

The law might provide that X has possession even where X does not have it. Suppose that, for the purposes of a rule, 'possession' means 'physical control'. Let's refer to possession, in this sense, as 'possession (control)'. The law might provide that, in certain circumstances, a person who does not have possession (control) should be treated by the courts as though she had it. Where this is so, we can say that X has 'fictitious possession' or 'constructive possession',[19] though it should be noted that the latter term is sometimes used in other ways.[20] In such circumstances, the statement 'according to the law, X has possession (control)' is true, but 'X has possession (control)' is false. The term 'possession (control)' has the same meaning in each of these statements. Fictitious possession (control) is not a special kind of possession (control); to have fictitious possession (control) is to have possession (control) according to the law, when one does not actually have it.

2.2.2 Vagueness

Certain senses of possession are vague. A term is vague if it has borderline cases. A borderline case is one in which it is intrinsically unclear whether the term applies.[21] For instance, 'short' and 'bald' are vague: there are cases in

---

[16] RH Kersley, *Goodeve's Modern Law of Personal Property* (9th edn, Sweet & Maxwell 1949) 9.

[17] Michael Bridge, *Personal Property Law* (4th edn, OUP 2015) 30. See also Pollock and Wright (n 2) 16–20, 22–24, 119; Bingham (n 15) 636–40; Ewan McKendrick (ed), *Goode on Commercial Law* (5th edn, Penguin 2016) para 2.06; Michael Bridge and others, *The Law of Personal Property* (2nd edn, Sweet & Maxwell 2019) paras 10-004, 10-011, 10-018.

[18] If the argument advanced in Chapter 5 is correct, the interest that is acquired through obtaining possession of a chattel should not be called 'possession': see Chapter 5 (sections 5.2 and 5.4). See also Ben McFarlane, *The Structure of Property Law* (Hart 2008) 144–46; Simon Douglas, *Liability for Wrongful Interferences with Chattels* (Hart 2011) 30–33.

[19] Pollock and Wright (n 2) 25, 27; Simon Douglas, 'Is Possession Factual or Legal?' in Eric Descheemaeker (ed), *The Consequences of Possession* (Edinburgh UP 2014) 71–75.

[20] Importantly, the term is also used to refer to cases in which the possessor exercises, or is regarded as exercising, control through another: Pollock and Wright (n 2) 18, 21, 27.

[21] There has been much discussion of how to properly characterise borderline cases: see, eg Timothy AO Endicott, *Vagueness in Law* (OUP 2000) ch 3; Roy Sorensen, *Vagueness and Contradiction* (OUP 2001) ch 1.

which a person is not clearly short and not clearly non-short; and there are cases in which a person is not clearly bald and not clearly non-bald.

'Possession (control)' is vague. There are cases in which it is clear that a person has possession (control), cases in which it is clear that a person does not have it, and cases in which it is unclear. Lord Wilberforce recognised this in *Warner v Metropolitan Police Commissioner*.[22] His Lordship gave the following description of a clear case of possession:

> a possessor of a thing has complete physical control over it; he has knowledge of its existence, its situation and its qualities; he has received it from a person who intends to confer possession of it and he has himself the intention to possess it exclusively of others.[23]

Lord Wilberforce went on to distinguish such a case from 'borderline cases' in which 'one or more of [those elements] is lacking, or incompletely present'.[24]

The law cannot eliminate the indeterminacies that result from vague rules,[25] but it can reduce them by making the rules more precise.[26] For instance, a legal rule might provide that, for the purposes of the general prohibition on the possession of certain drugs, a person who is in possession of a suitcase that contains drugs is not in possession of the drugs if she does not know that the suitcase contains them. Lord Wilberforce appreciated this in *Warner*. His Lordship noted that, in connection with a borderline case, the law may have determined, or a judge may be required to determine, 'whether the given approximation is such that possession may be held sufficiently established to satisfy the relevant rule of law'.[27]

2.2.3 Variation

A person might have possession for the purposes of one legal rule but not for another. As Lord Parker CJ said in *Towers & Co v Gray*, 'the meaning of "possession" depends upon the context in which it is used'.[28] This becomes apparent

---

[22] *Warner v Metropolitan Police Commissioner* [1969] 2 AC 256 (HL).

[23] ibid 309.

[24] ibid.

[25] This was HLA Hart's view: see his *The Concept of Law* (3rd edn, OUP 2012) 126.

[26] For a general discussion see Hart (n 25) 130–32; TAO Endicott, 'Vagueness and Legal Theory' (1997) 3 LEG 37, 60–61.

[27] *Warner* (n 22) 309.

[28] [1961] 2 QB 351 (DC) 361 (cited with approval in *Warner* (n 22) 304 (Lord Pearce) and *Re Atlantic Computer Systems Plc* [1992] Ch 505 (CA) 531 (Nicholls LJ)).

when one considers the following question: can a person be in possession of a thing in English law notwithstanding that she has no knowledge of its existence? The question is problematic because of the unspecified reference to 'possession . . . in law'. A person who has no knowledge of a thing might be in possession of it for the purposes of some legal rules but not others. In *Warner v Metropolitan Police Commissioner*, the House of Lords considered whether the appellant had certain illicit drugs 'in his possession' contrary to section 1(1) of the Drugs (Prevention of Misuse) Act 1964.[29] The drugs were contained in a case that the appellant had collected and transported. The House of Lords held, inter alia, that where a person had physical control of a package or container, he was not 'in possession' of the contents for the purposes of section 1(1) of the 1964 Act if he had no knowledge of the contents and no reasonable opportunity to ascertain what they were.[30]

In contrast, if a person who has exclusive physical control of land has manifested an intention to exercise control over any chattels that might be on the land then, for the purpose of the rules concerning the acquisition of title by possession, he is in possession of chattels that are on the land, irrespective of whether he has any knowledge of their existence.[31] *Flack v National Crime Authority*,[32] an Australian case, provides a good illustration of this. The National Crime Authority (NCA) seized a bag containing money from premises occupied by Mrs Flack. Mrs Flack was unaware of the existence of the bag and money. No person was charged in connection with any offence and Mrs Flack asked the NCA to return the bag and money. The NCA submitted that Mrs Flack did not have a sufficient title to sue. The trial judge, Hill J, held that, for the purposes of the rules concerning the acquisition of title by possession, Mrs Flack was in possession of the bag and money, even though she was wholly unaware of them. Hill J accepted, while reviewing previous case law, that for the purposes of the statutory crime of being in possession of prohibited imports, a person could not be in 'possession' unless she had knowledge of the

---

[29] *Warner* (n 22). The Drugs (Prevention of Misuse) Act 1964 was repealed by the Misuse of Drugs Act 1971. Section 5(2) of the 1971 Act provides that, subject to certain exceptions, 'it is an offence for a person to have a controlled drug in his possession'. Section 28(3)(b)(i) of the 1971 Act provides that the accused shall be acquitted if 'he proves that he neither believed nor suspected nor had reason to suspect that the substance or product in question was a controlled drug'.

[30] *Warner* (n 22) 282 (Lord Reid), 305–06 (Lord Pearce), 310–11 (Lord Wilberforce). cf *R v McNamara* (1988) 87 Cr App R 246 (CA) 250–52 (Lord Lane CJ); *R v Lambert* [2001] UKHL 37; [2002] 2 AC 545 [16] (Lord Slynn), [61] (Lord Hope), [122] (Lord Clyde), [180]–[181] (Lord Hutton).

[31] *South Staffordshire Water Co v Sharman* [1896] 2 QB 44 (DC) 46–47 (Lord Russell CJ); *Parker v British Airways Board* [1982] QB 1004 (CA); *Waverley Borough Council v Fletcher* [1996] QB 334 (CA) 343–44 (Auld LJ).

[32] *Flack v National Crime Authority* (1997) 80 FCR 137 (FCA); *National Crime Authority v Flack* (1998) 86 FCR 16 (FCAFC).

chattels, but this did not assist 'at all in throwing light on what is necessary to establish a possessory title'.[33] An appeal against Hill J's decision was dismissed by the Full Court.[34]

2.2.4 Implications

The fact that a person may be in possession of chattels or land for the purposes of one rule but not for another, and that the courts, when considering what should count as 'possession' for the purposes of a particular rule, often consider the values that are promoted by the rule, led RWM Dias to conclude that 'possession is no more than a device of convenience and policy'.[35] However, this conclusion is not adequately supported by the premises of Dias's argument. The fact that 'possession' shifts its meaning from context to context, and that what constitutes possession for the purposes of one rule may not do so for the purposes of another, does not entail that, in a given context, what counts in law as possession is solely determined by 'policy and convenience'.

When a judge, for instance, is required to interpret a statutory provision or a binding judicial judgment that includes the term 'possession', she should consider what 'possession' means in the context of the provision or judgment; and when considering what 'possession' means in a particular context, she may be required to consider, among other things, any applicable general rules of interpretation, and any rules that specify the meaning of the particular term at hand. In a given context, the meaning of 'possession' may be, and frequently will be, readily apparent. It might be obvious, for instance, that the term means 'exclusive physical control'. It might also be clear that a given person does or does not have exclusive physical control of a thing.[36] The existence of borderline cases should not cause one to forget that there are many clear cases.

If the case before the court involves a borderline case of possession, and if the question as to where to place such a case is not settled for the judge by the law, the judge, in determining whether the case should fall on one side of the line or the other, should consider the considerations that underpin the law in question and other pertinent reasons for or against each view.[37]

---

[33] (1997) 80 FCR 137 (FCA) 148.

[34] *National Crime Authority v Flack* (1998) 86 FCR 16 (FCAFC). Foster J dissented on the ground that, in the circumstances, Mrs Flack had not been in possession of the bag and money.

[35] Dias (n 10) 285.

[36] cf Dias (n 10) 277.

[37] This point has been made by others, eg Harris (n 10) 72, 78–79; AES Tay, 'The Concept of Possession in the Common Law: Foundations for a New Approach' (1963–64) 4 Melbourne U L Rev 476, 493–97.

Lord Wilberforce recognised this in *Warner*.[38] His Lordship, having noted that the law had adopted 'varying solutions' to borderline cases of possession,[39] said:

> [t]hat the solution adopted ultimately depends upon the need justly and adequately to meet the requirements of the relevant legal rule is well shown in the words of Wills J in a case about finding on premises— 'a contrary decision would . . . be a great and most unwise encouragement to dishonesty'.[40]

Lord Wilberforce clearly thought this to be the right approach: he went on to consider how to 'justly and adequately' meet the requirements of the rule that was at the heart of the appeal in *Warner*. Thus, Lord Wilberforce recognised that what counts as 'possession' varies; a person might be in possession for the purposes of one rule but not for the purposes of another. His Lordship also rightly discerned that such variation is, in part, a consequence of the fact that the law has responded to the reasons that ground the assorted rules; and that the underlying reasons generally vary from rule to rule. When a judge is determining, in a borderline case, what should count as possession for the purposes of a legislative provision or a judicial precedent, she should be appropriately sensitive and responsive to the reasons upon which the rule is based, and any other applicable reasons, which may include reasons of policy and convenience. So, in some circumstances, policy and convenience may properly guide a judicial decision as to whether or not a person is in possession of a thing for particular purposes; but the ambiguity, vagueness, and variation that have been discussed in this section should not lead one to conclude that 'possession' is *no more than* a device of policy and convenience.

2.3 The Nature of Possession

We will see in Chapters 4 and 5 that, in order to understand the nature of the title acquired through possession, one must, among other things, consider the protection afforded to the possessor's title through the law of torts, particularly trespass to land, private nuisance, trespass to chattels, conversion, and property damage resulting from negligence.[41] The discussion of these torts in Chapters 4 and 5 aims to show that, by acquiring possession of land or chattels, a person

---

[38] *Warner* (n 22).
[39] ibid 310.
[40] ibid, citing *South Staffordshire Water Co v Sharman* [1896] 2 QB 44 (DC) 48 (Wills J).
[41] Chapter 4 (section 4.2.1); Chapter 5 (section 5.2.1).

acquires a right to exclude that grounds duties on others not to interfere with the land or chattels.[42] When considering what counts as 'possession' for the purposes of the acquisition of title by possession it is, therefore, appropriate—and, indeed, necessary—to consider how possession has been understood in the case law regarding the property torts.

In *Powell v McFarlane*,[43] Slade J considered the meaning of the term 'possession' in the statutory provisions concerning the doctrine of adverse possession.[44] His Lordship explained that, for the purposes of the doctrine of adverse possession, 'possession' bears 'the traditional sense of that degree of occupation or physical control, coupled with the requisite intention commonly referred to as *animus possidendi*, that would entitle a person to maintain an action of trespass in relation to the relevant land'.[45] This statement was subsequently endorsed by the House of Lords in *J A Pye (Oxford) Ltd v Graham*, which is the leading case on the nature of adverse possession.[46] Accordingly, this section's account of what generally counts as possession for the purposes of the acquisition of title is informed by, and based upon, the case law relating to adverse possession and the property torts. The fact that 'possession' has the very same meaning in these contexts is not surprising; as Chapters 4 and 6 explain, there is a close and significant connection between the rules concerning the acquisition of title through possession and the rules concerning the destruction of title by lapse of time.

How, then, does a person obtain possession for the purposes of the rules concerning the acquisition of title? The general rule is that, in order to obtain possession, one must have: (a) exclusive physical control of the land or chattel; and (b) an intention, in one's own name and on one's own behalf, to exclude the world at large from it. Hereinafter, this is referred to as 'the general possession rule'. Once a person has obtained possession by meeting the two conditions, she will remain in possession unless and until: (a) she voluntarily gives up possession; or (b) she is dispossessed by another.[47] The general possession rule and the authorities on which it rests are discussed in section 2.3.1. Section 2.3.2 briefly considers some of the special rules that modify or displace the general rule in certain circumstances.

---

[42] ibid.
[43] *Powell v McFarlane* (1977) 38 P & CR 452 (Ch).
[44] Limitation Act 1939, ss 5, 10. The relevant provisions are now contained in the Limitation Act 1980.
[45] *Powell* (n 43) 469. See also *Marsden v Miller* (1992) 64 P & CR 239 (CA) 242–43 (Scott LJ).
[46] *J A Pye (Oxford) Ltd v Graham* [2002] UKHL 30; [2003] 1 AC 419 [32] (Lord Browne-Wilkinson).
[47] *Pye* (n 46) [70] (Lord Hope); *Zarb v Parry* [2011] EWCA Civ 1306; [2012] 1 WLR 1240.

2.3.1 The General Possession Rule

In *J A Pye (Oxford) Ltd v Graham*,[48] Lord Browne-Wilkinson, giving the leading speech, explained that 'there are two elements necessary for legal possession': first, 'a sufficient degree of physical custody and control',[49] which must be 'exclusive';[50] and, secondly, 'an intention, in one's own name and on one's own behalf, to exclude the world at large'.[51] Lord Browne-Wilkinson was concerned with certain rules of land law, but it is clear that the same conditions must be met in order for a person to acquire a title to a chattel. In *Parker v British Airways Board*,[52] for example, the question was whether a person who found a gold bracelet in an airport lounge had a better title to it than British Airways, which occupied the lounge. The Court of Appeal ruled that, by taking possession, the finder acquired a title to the bracelet and British Airways did not have a better title. Eveleigh LJ said that, in order for a person to acquire a title by possession, 'the two elements of control and *animus possidendi* must co-exist'.[53] Similarly, in *Mainline Private Hire Ltd v Nolan*,[54] Arden LJ (with whom Sedley LJ and Sir Nicholas Wall P agreed) accepted that, upon obtaining possession of a chattel, a person is protected by the tort of conversion;[55] and that 'to have possession . . . a person must have not only the requisite degree of actual custody and control but also an intention to exercise that custody on his own behalf and for his own benefit'.[56] Her Ladyship went on to consider and apply Lord Browne-Wilkinson's analysis of these two features.[57]

2.3.1.1 Exclusive physical control

In order to obtain possession under the general possession rule, a person must have a sufficient degree of physical control.[58] The degree of physical control

---

[48] *Pye* (n 46).

[49] ibid [40].

[50] ibid [41]. See also *Allan v Liverpool Overseers* (1874) LR 9 QB 180 (QB) 191–92 (Blackburn J).

[51] *Pye* (n 46) [43], citing *Powell v McFarlane* (n 43) 471 (Slade J). See also *Buckinghamshire County Council v Moran* [1990] Ch 623 (CA) 636 (Slade LJ); *Zarb v Parry* (n 47) [37]–[38], [43]–[44] (Arden LJ), [71]–[75] (Lord Neuberger MR); *Greenmanor Ltd v Pilford* [2012] EWCA Civ 756 [25] (Etherton LJ). For a discussion of the origins of this conception of possession, and the influence of Savigny, Holmes, and Pollock, see Oliver Radley-Gardner, 'Civilized Squatting' (2005) 25 OJLS 727.

[52] *Parker* (n 31). See also *The Tubantia* [1924] P 78 (PDA) 88–91 (Sir Henry Duke P); *Marsden* (n 45); *Bocardo SA v Star Energy UK Onshore Ltd* [2010] UKSC 35; [2011] 1 AC 380 [29]–[31] (Lord Hope).

[53] *Parker* (n 31) 1019.

[54] *Mainline Private Hire Ltd v Nolan* [2011] EWCA Civ 189; [2011] CTLC 145.

[55] ibid [1].

[56] ibid [1].

[57] ibid[1]–[3], [30]–[42].

[58] *The Tubantia* (n 52) 89–90; *Powell* (n 43) 469–71; *Pye* (n 46) [40]–[41] (Lord Browne-Wilkinson); *Mainline Private Hire* (n 54) [1]–[3] (Arden LJ). cf Michael JR Crawford, *An Expressive Theory of Possession* (Hart 2020) ch 3. Crawford argues that 'possession', for the purposes of the rules concerning the acquisition of title, refers to 'those acts that function as recognised and accepted signals about one's

that suffices depends upon the circumstances; in particular, the nature of the thing. Insofar as land is concerned, the view advanced by Slade J in *Powell*,[59] and endorsed in *Pye*,[60] is that:

[e]verything must depend on the particular circumstances, but broadly . . . what must be shown as constituting factual possession is that the alleged possessor has been dealing with the land in question as an occupying owner might have been expected to deal with it and that no-one else has done so.

As this passage indicates, two important considerations when assessing whether a person has a sufficient degree of physical control are: (a) whether, as a matter of fact, she determines how the thing is dealt with—how it is kept, whether it is used and, if so, the manner in which it is used; and (b) whether her control is *exclusive*, ie whether others have used the thing without her permission, or whether she has effectively excluded others from it.[61]

What counts as effectively determining how a thing is dealt with depends, in part, upon the nature of the thing,[62] for divergent things admit of different forms and degrees of control. Pollock,[63] in a passage that was cited with approval by Lewison LJ in *Chambers v Havering London Borough Council*,[64] said:

it is not possible, as a matter of fact, to possess a house, a wood, or a field in the same manner as we possess the money in our pockets, or the owner of a cart and horse possesses them when he is driving the horse in the cart. There can only be a more or less discontinuous series of acts of dominion. What kind of acts, and how many, can be accepted as proof of exclusive use, must depend to a great extent on the manner in which the particular kind of property is commonly used.

intention to stake a claim to some object of property', and that, '[a]s long as the signal is clear and accepted, it does not matter that the possessor exerts no actual control over [it]': Crawford, 60, 85.

[59] *Powell* (n 43) 471.
[60] *Pye* (n 46) [41] (Lord Browne-Wilkinson).
[61] But there is no need for the control to be impregnable. As Pollock noted, 'exclusive occupation or control, in the sense of a real unqualified power to exclude others, is nowhere to be found. All physical security is finite and qualified': Pollock and Wright (n 2) 12.
[62] *Lord Advocate v Young* (1887) 12 App Cas 544 (HL) 556 (Lord FitzGerald); *The Tubantia* (n 52) 89–90 (Sir Henry Duke P); *Wuta-Ofei v Danquah* [1961] 1 WLR 1238 (PC) 1243 (Lord Guest); *Powell* (n 43) 470–71 (Slade J); *Pye* (n 46) [41] (Lord Browne-Wilkinson). See also Pollock and Wright (n 2) 13–14, 29–31.
[63] Pollock and Wright (n 2) 30.
[64] [2011] EWCA Civ 1576; [2012] 1 P & CR 17 [54].

In *Red House Farms (Thorndon) Ltd v Catchpole*,[65] for example, the Court of Appeal held that a person who had shot, and allowed others to shoot, over certain land for a number of years had obtained possession, since 'the only profitable use of [the] land was for shooting'.[66] In *The Tubantia*, the claimants were attempting to raise a sunken freighter and to recover anything of value when the defendants interfered.[67] The claimants maintained that they were in possession and sought damages for trespass. Sir Henry Duke P held that the claimants had obtained possession since, among other things, the claimants 'did with the wreck what a purchaser would prudently have done', and there was 'the use and occupation of which the subject matter was capable'.[68]

Generally speaking, land can be enclosed, and the means of access controlled; a person who encloses and exclusively controls the means of access will usually have a sufficient degree of physical control. In *Pye*,[69] for instance, the defendants maintained the land and used it for farming without the claimant's permission. Significantly, the land could be accessed only with a key that opened a padlocked road gate, as well as by foot over a public footway. The defendants held the key at all material times. Lord Browne-Wilkinson, having noted that the defendants had occupied and used the land and that the claimant 'was physically excluded . . . by the hedges and the lack of any key to the road gate', concluded without hesitation that the defendants had a sufficient degree of physical control.[70] *Pye* can be contrasted with *Boosey v Davis*,[71] in which Mr and Mrs Boosey, who claimed to be in adverse possession of certain waste land, had used the land for grazing but had not enclosed the land. The Court of Appeal concluded that they did not have possession.

The fact that a claimant has exercised some control over a chattel or certain land will not suffice if she has been unable, in general, to effectively exclude others from it. The case of *Marsden v Miller* illustrates this point.[72] The disputed land lay between the claimant's land and the defendants' land. It was used for a variety of purposes by both the claimant and the defendants for many years. In 1981, the claimant erected a fence around the land and also a notice

[65] [1977] 2 EGLR 125 (CA). See also *Umma v Appu* [1939] AC 136 (PC) 141–42; *Port of London v Ashmore* [2009] EWHC 954 (Ch) [22] (Stephen Smith QC), revd on other grounds [2010] EWCA Civ 30.

[66] [1977] 2 EGLR 125 (CA) 126 (Cairns LJ).

[67] *The Tubantia* (n 52).

[68] ibid 90.

[69] *Pye* (n 46).

[70] ibid [41]. For a further example of the significance of having exclusive control of the means of access, see *Buckinghamshire CC* (n 51).

[71] (1987) 55 P & CR 83 (CA).

[72] (1992) 64 P & CR 239 (CA). See also Pollock and Wright (n 2) 13, 35; *Simpson v Fergus* (1999) 79 P & CR 398 (CA). cf Crawford (n 58) 65.

board which stated that he claimed the ownership of the land. The defendants protested and removed the fence within twenty-four hours and, thereafter, the defendants used the land in the way they had previously. The claimant sought damages for trespass, a declaration that he had a right to possess, and an injunction. Despite the fact that the claimant had unequivocally expressed his intention to claim the land as his own, the Court of Appeal concluded that he had not obtained possession. The court accepted that, by erecting the fence and displaying the notice, the claimant had 'evinced the necessary *animus possidendi*'.[73] But the court also maintained that, since the claimant's actions were not 'effective to exclude' the defendants from the land,[74] he did not have a sufficient degree of physical control.[75]

2.3.1.2 The intention to possess

In order for a person to have possession of certain land or a particular chattel, she must have, in addition to a sufficient degree of physical control, an intention to possess.[76] In *Pye*, Lord Browne-Wilkinson said 'there is no doubt . . . that there are two separate elements in legal possession', and that it 'is crucial . . . to understand that, without the requisite intention, in law there can be no possession'.[77] His Lordship gave the example of a person who is 'in occupation of a locked house . . . as a friend looking after the house for the paper owner during his absence on holiday':[78] the occupier may have exclusive physical control, but she is not in possession because she does not have an intention to possess.

What is the intention to possess? The answer provided by Slade J in *Powell*,[79] and approved by the House of Lords in *Pye*,[80] is that it is 'the intention, in one's own name and on one's own behalf, to exclude the world at large, including the owner with the paper title if he be not himself the possessor, so far as it reasonably practicable and so far as the processes of the law will allow'. As this statement indicates, the requisite intention is not an intention to *own* the thing.[81] Moreover, one can be in possession notwithstanding that one is prepared to

---

[73] (1992) 64 P & CR 239 (CA) 243 (Scott LJ). The only other judge, Sir John Megaw, expressed his agreement with the order proposed, and the reasons given, by Scott LJ.

[74] ibid.

[75] But it does not follow, from the mere fact that it is physically *possible* for a person to gain access without the permission of the occupier, that the occupier does not have exclusive physical control: *Greenmanor* (n 51) [27] (Etherton LJ).

[76] *The Tubantia* (n 52) 89–90; *Powell* (n 43) 470–71; *Parker* (n 31) 1019 (Eveleigh LJ); *Pye* (n 46) [40], [43] (Lord Browne-Wilkinson), [70]–[71] (Lord Hope); *Mainline Private Hire* (n 54) [1]–[2] (Arden LJ).

[77] *Pye* (n 46) [40].

[78] ibid.

[79] *Powell* (n 43) 471–72. See also Pollock and Wright (n 2) 17.

[80] *Pye* (n 46) [43] (Lord Browne-Wilkinson).

[81] ibid [42] (Lord Browne-Wilkinson), [71] (Lord Hope).

give up possession, or to pay for possession, if asked by someone who has a better title.[82] It suffices that one intends, in one's own name and on one's own behalf, to exclude the world at large, including anyone who has a better title, 'for the time being and until [one] is evicted'.[83]

The fact that an intention to exclude the world 'for the time being' suffices explains how it is possible for one to have the requisite intention notwithstanding that one is willing, if asked, to relinquish control to another. Consider, for example, the position of a person who is occupying land in the mistaken belief that she is occupying the land with the permission of someone who has a better title. While the law on this point is unsettled,[84] it seems that such an occupier may have an intention to possess notwithstanding that she is prepared to vacate the land if asked by the person with a better title. In *Wretham v Ross*,[85] for instance, the court held that, where a person exercised exclusive physical control over a shed in the mistaken belief that he was permitted to do so under a licence agreement, the occupier had an intention to possess notwithstanding that he would have vacated the land if asked. David Richards J said that the occupier had 'an intention . . . to possess it to the exclusion of all other persons, including the owner, unless and until asked to give up possession'.[86] Such an occupier intends to exclude 'the owner' for the time being and until he is asked to leave.

It is more difficult to see how a lawful finder can have the requisite intention. A finder takes possession lawfully if she takes possession with the intention of keeping the chattel safe for the person or persons who are entitled to it.[87] Can it really be said that such a person intends to exclude the world, including the person or persons who have a better title? It is tempting to say that she has no such intention. Her actions are lawful precisely because she intends to keep the thing safe *for* the persons who are entitled to it. She intends, not to exclude those who are entitled to it, but to return the chattel to them if they appear. Of

---

[82] ibid [43], [46] (Lord Browne-Wilkinson), [78] (Lord Hutton). See also *Ocean Estates Ltd v Pinder* [1969] 2 AC 19 (PC); *Buckinghamshire CC* (n 51) 643 (Slade LJ).

[83] *Lambeth London Borough Council v Blackburn* [2001] EWCA Civ 912; (2001) 82 P & CR 494 [17] (Clarke LJ).

[84] See Stephen Jourdan and Oliver Radley-Gardner, *Adverse Possession* (2nd edn, Bloomsbury 2011) paras 9-48–9-51; *Ruoff & Roper: Registered Conveyancing*, vol 1, para 33.014 (2020).

[85] [2005] EWHC 1259 (Ch). See also *J Alston & Sons Ltd v BOCM Pauls Ltd* [2008] EWHC 3310 (Ch); [2009] 1 EGLR 93 [79]–[111] (Judge Marshall QC); *Malik v Malik* [2019] EWHC 1843 (Ch) [21], [36]–[37] (Falk J). cf *Clowes Developments (UK) Ltd v Walters* [2005] EWHC 669 (Ch); [2006] 1 P & CR 1 [39]–[41] (Hart J).

[86] [2005] EWHC 1259 (Ch) [44].

[87] *Isaack v Clark* (1614) 2 Bulst 306, 312; 80 ER 1143, 1148 (Coke CJ); *Hollins v Fowler* (1875) LR 7 HL 757 (HL) 766 (Blackburn J). See also Robin Hickey, 'Armory v Delamirie (1722): Possession, Obligation, and the Evolution of Relative Title to Goods' in Simon Douglas, Robin Hickey, and Emma Waring (eds), *Landmark Cases in Property Law* (Hart 2015) 133–38.

course, she may exercise control over the thing unless and until they appear, but she does not intend, even for a time, to keep them out. This suggests that, in the case of the lawful finder, at least, it suffices that she intends, in her own name and on her own behalf,[88] to exclude the world at large.

How can one prove that one had an intention to possess? Ordinarily, the question of whether a person had the requisite intention will be answered by assessing the person's conduct and determining whether an intention to possess can be inferred from that conduct,[89] though this is not the only way of establishing the intention.[90] Such an inference will often be drawn where a person has exclusive physical control,[91] but not if the person's acts in relation to the thing 'are equivocal and are open to more than one interpretation'.[92]

2.3.1.3 Possession through another

In *Bannerman Town v Eleuthera Properties Ltd*,[93] Lord Briggs, delivering the judgment of the Privy Council, said, '[p]ossession may be vicarious in the sense that A may occupy land on behalf of B, such that B rather than A is in possession of it . . . Vicarious possession may arise where, for example, A is the licensee, agent or agricultural contractor of B'.[94] Thus, Lord Briggs recognised that it is possible for A to have physical custody and for B to have possession. The general explanation of this is that B is exercising control of the thing through A; as Pollock put it, A is B's 'instrument for exercising [B's] power'.[95] B, not A, has the intention to possess. A does not intend to exclude the world in her own name and on her own behalf, but in the name of, and on behalf of, B.[96]

In some circumstances, the law will regard a person as holding a thing on behalf of another even though she actually intends to exercise control on her own behalf. Where, for example, A is B's employee or agent, and A finds and picks up a chattel in the course of her employment or agency, the law will regard B as acquiring possession through A *even if*, in truth, A intends to exercise control

---

[88] Of course, she acts for the benefit of those who have a better title, but she does not act as their representative.

[89] *Pye* (n 46) [40], [48], [58] (Lord Browne-Wilkinson), [76] (Lord Hutton).

[90] See, for example, *Marsden* (n 45) 243 (Scott LJ), where the occupier verbally expressed his intention to possess by displaying a notice. Oral evidence, provided by the alleged possessor in court, to the effect that he had an intention to possess is usually of limited evidential value: *Powell* (n 43) 476 (Slade J).

[91] See, eg *Pye* (n 46); *Buckinghamshire CC* (n 51).

[92] *Pye* (n 46) [76] (Lord Hutton). See also *Wretham v Ross* [2005] EWHC 1259 (Ch) [24] (David Richards J); *Port of London Authority v Mendoza* [2017] UKUT 146 (TCC) [22]–[29] (Judge Elizabeth Cooke).

[93] [2018] UKPC 27.

[94] ibid [54].

[95] Pollock and Wright (n 2) 18.

[96] See *Malik* (n 85) [34], [38] (Falk J).

on her own behalf and to exclude the world, including B.[97] Consequently, B, not A, will acquire a title to the chattel through possession.

2.3.1.4 Joint possession

Possession, in the present context, is exclusive: if a person or group has possession of certain land or a particular chattel, no one else can be in possession at the same time.[98] This follows from the fact that possession involves *exclusive* physical control. However, it is possible for two or more persons to have possession jointly.[99] Where this is so, the possessors exercise physical control over the thing on the basis of a common intention to exclude the rest of the world in the name of, and on behalf of, them both.

2.3.2   Special Possession Rules

Alongside the general possession rule, there are certain special rules that displace or modify the general rule in certain circumstances. Special rules apply to chattels that are on or under land.[100] First, it is a rule of English law that a possessor of land is in possession of chattels that are under or attached to the land.[101] A different rule applies to chattels that are found on, but not attached to, land.[102] The rule is that a possessor of land is in possession of chattels that are on the land if she has manifested an intention to possess chattels that may be on the land.[103] Consequently, it is not necessary for a possessor of land to show that she intended to possess, or was even aware of, a particular chattel; it suffices that she manifested an intention to possess any chattel that may be on the land.

[97] *M'Dowell v Ulster Bank* (1899) 33 ILT 225; *Crinion v Minister for Justice* [1959] Ir J Rep 15; *City of London Corp v Appleyard* [1963] 1 WLR 982 (QB) 988 (McNair J); *Parker* (n 31) 1017 (Donaldson LJ). For critical analysis, see OW Holmes Jr, *The Common Law* (Little, Brown and Co 1882) 227–28; McFarlane (n 18) 156–57; Robin Hickey, *Property and the Law of Finders* (Hart 2010) 135–39.

[98] *Pye* (n 46) [38] (Lord Browne-Wilkinson), [70] (Lord Hope).

[99] *Pye* (n 46) [38] (Lord Browne-Wilkinson), [70] (Lord Hope); *Bannerman Town* (n 93) [51]–[53], [59] (Lord Briggs).

[100] For discussion of these rules, see AL Goodhart, 'Three Cases on Possession' (1928) 3 CLJ 195; AES Tay, 'Possession and the Modern Law of Finding' (1962–64) 4 Syd LR 383; Hickey (n 97) ch 2; Crawford (n 58) ch 6.

[101] *Elwes v Brigg Gas Co* (1886) 33 Ch D 562 (Ch); *Hannah v Peel* [1945] KB 509 (KB); *Waverley Borough Council v Fletcher* (n 31). See also McFarlane (n 18) 157–59; Hickey (n 97) 46–53.

[102] It is highly doubtful that the distinction that the law has drawn between chattels that are on but unattached to land, and chattels that are attached to, or under the surface of, land is justified: see McFarlane (n 18) 157–59; Hickey (n 97) 47–50.

[103] *Parker* (n 31) 1014, 1017–19 (Donaldson LJ), 1020 (Eveleigh LJ), 1021 (Sir David Cairns). For a forceful critique of Donaldson LJ's reasoning, see Simon Roberts, 'More Lost Than Found' (1982) 45 MLR 683.

2.4 Possession of Estates and Interests

The account of possession set out in section 2.3 regards land and chattels as the subject matter of possession, not *interests* in land or chattels. One can be in possession of a piano, a car, or 221B Baker Street, but not in possession of a fee simple estate. The reason is that one can exercise physical control over the piano, the car, and 221B Baker Street, but not over a fee simple.

There is, however, a different view: one which maintains that it is quite possible to possess a proprietary interest, such as an estate in land. Mark Wonnacott QC has recently defended this view.[104] According to Wonnacott, in English land law, 'possession', in the 'proper, technical' sense, 'describes a relationship between a person and a corporeal estate in land (a fee simple, a lease, or, stretching the point, a profit à prendre) rather than the relationship between a person and any physical feature of the land'.[105] More specifically, it describes two types of relationship between a person and a corporeal estate. The first is a 'relationship of right': '[a] person has a *right to possess* an estate if he or she has acquired a title to it which is "vested in possession"'.[106] The second is a 'relationship of fact': 'when a person is, as a matter of observable fact, actually enjoying the rights and incidents of an estate in land'.[107] A person 'enjoys' the rights and incidents of an estate, for this purpose, if she exercises and uses them and has the benefit of them.[108] The second type of relationship, the 'relationship of fact', is particularly important for present purposes. For, according to Wonnacott, a person acquires, by virtue of this relationship, 'a presumptive title to an estate in land'.[109]

Lawyers frequently talk of persons being in 'possession of estates'; there are many examples of this usage in the law reports and statute books.[110] However, the authorities discussed in this chapter do not support the view that, in the modern law, the relevant question, for the purposes of determining whether a person, X, has acquired a title by possession, is 'was X in possession of an estate'? If Wonnacott's view is correct, when a court is required to decide whether X was in possession for such purposes, the court should consider whether X was enjoying the rights and other incidents of a particular kind of estate in the

---

[104] Mark Wonnacott, *Possession of Land* (CUP 2006) ch 1.
[105] ibid 1–2.
[106] ibid 2.
[107] ibid 3.
[108] ibid 2, fn 6 citing *Kenny v Preen* [1963] 1 QB 499 (CA) 511 (Pearson LJ).
[109] ibid 44.
[110] See, eg *Secretary of State for the Environment, Food and Rural Affairs v Meier* [2009] UKSC 11; [2009] 1 WLR 2780 [60] (Lord Neuberger MR); Land Registration Act 2002, sch 6.

land, say a fee simple or a term of years. To be able to properly answer this question, it is necessary to consider what the incidents of the various estates are, and whether the rights and other incidents of a particular kind of estate were 'enjoyed' by X.[111] But the law does not require the courts to reason in this way. If the general possession rule is applicable, the relevant question is 'did X have exclusive physical control of the land and an intention to possess it?' It is true that, when considering whether X had exclusive physical control of the land, the courts may consider whether X was dealing with the land as an occupying owner might have dealt with it;[112] and that the question as to whether X was dealing with the land as an occupying owner might have dealt with it is similar to the question as to whether X was 'enjoying' the rights and incidents of a fee simple estate. However, the assessment that the law requires into whether X was dealing with the land as an occupying owner might have dealt with it is part of an enquiry into whether X had *exclusive physical control of the land*, not an enquiry into whether X was in possession of an estate. These are different approaches, even if they reach the same outcome in some cases.

---

[111] How can one 'enjoy' a right that one does not have? The idea, presumably, is that one acts as though one had the right and obtains the benefits that the right serves to secure or promote.
[112] See section 2.3.1.1 above.

3

Possession and Title: Three Views

3.1 Introduction

'Possession', according to Lord Hoffmann, 'is in itself a good title against anyone who cannot show a prior and therefore better right to possession.'[1] Given that very many scholars and judges have made statements to this effect, it might appear that there is a general consensus regarding the acquisition of title by possessors at common law. In fact, there is no such consensus. On the contrary, there is, as we will see, much disagreement regarding the legal consequences of obtaining possession; and this disagreement is pervasive and persistent. One reason why there is a disconnect between how things are and how they may appear is that, as various scholars have explained,[2] the word 'title' has a number of different senses and, consequently, when several commentators assert that a possessor acquires a title, they may actually be advancing significantly different claims.

It is, therefore, important to identify the various senses of the term 'title'. In one of its senses, 'title' refers to what Tony Honoré described as 'the conditions of fact which must be fulfilled in order that a person may acquire a claim [ie a right] to a thing'.[3] These are sometimes called 'modes of acquisition or loss' or 'causative events',[4] and the laws governing such conditions have been called 'investitive' provisions.[5] In a second sense, the term 'title' is synonymous with 'right' or 'entitlement'. The word is also used to refer to specific kinds of right or interest: it is sometimes used to refer to rights to possess chattels or land;[6] or to

[1] *Alan Wibberley Building Ltd v Insley* [1999] 1 WLR 894 (HL) 898.
[2] Bernard Rudden, 'The Terminology of Title' (1964) 80 LQR 63, 65; AM Honoré, 'Ownership' in AG Guest (ed), *Oxford Essays in Jurisprudence* (OUP 1961) 107, 134–41; Robin Hickey, *Property and the Law of Finders* (Hart 2010) 165–66 (hereafter Hickey, *Law of Finders*).
[3] Honoré (n 2) 134. Harris used the term 'title' in this way (or in a very similar way): JW Harris, *Property and Justice* (Clarendon Press 1996) 39–40, 80–81. See also: Neil MacCormick, *Institutions of Law: An Essay in Legal Theory* (OUP 2007) 139: for a person, A, to have a real right 'there must be some particular title, some act, or event, or occurrence that has the effect in law of vesting the right in A'.
[4] Peter Birks, *Unjust Enrichment* (2nd edn, OUP 2005) chs 1–2. For Birks's account to be plausible, the term 'event' must be given a technical meaning, for some conditions of having a right or interest are not, in the ordinary meaning of the term, events.
[5] Joseph Raz, *The Concept of a Legal System* (2nd edn, Clarendon Press 1980) 175–83; MacCormick (n 3) 139.
[6] Honoré (n 2) 134; Rudden (n 2) 65.

Possession, Relative Title, and Ownership in English Law. Luke Rostill, Oxford University Press (2021). © Luke Rostill. DOI: 10.1093/oso/9780198843108.003.0003

legal estates in land;[7] or to what are sometimes called 'ownership interests' or 'general property interests' in respect of chattels.[8] In another sense of the term, a 'title' is a 'claim' to a right or interest.[9] Robin Hickey has asserted that title, in this sense, is 'purely a juridical notion, occupying a conceptual space between causative event and resultant right'.[10] Given that rights are acquired when the relevant 'causative events' occur, it might be thought that there is no conceptual space between 'causative events' and the acquisition of rights: either the relevant event occurs and a right is acquired or it does not. However, there is, as we will see, at least one intelligible account of the idea of a claim to a right or interest and, given a certain understanding of the law concerning the consequences of possession, the concept has a useful role to play in this area.

If it is true that, by taking possession of chattels or land, a person acquires a title, what is the nature of the possessor's title? The purpose of this chapter, and the following two chapters, is to examine how these questions have been, and should be, answered. The aim is not to examine every answer that has been given to these questions. Rather, the focus is on three views and some variations thereof. These three views have been selected because, taken together, they bring to light two important contrasts. The first is the contrast between those accounts that maintain that the law actually confers on a possessor an interest of some kind in the chattel or land, and those accounts that assert that the possessor must be *presumed* to have a certain interest in it. This distinction has been overlooked by some eminent writers.[11] Others have thought that the distinction is illusory or muddled.[12] It is argued in this chapter that the distinction is, in fact, both real and important.

The second contrast highlighted by the three views is the contrast between those accounts that maintain that the law confers on possessors merely possession-dependent, non-alienable rights, and those accounts that maintain that the law confers on possessors an alienable interest that is not possession-dependent; an interest that comprises certain rights, including a right to exclude. This distinction is significant. It represents the difference, as Honoré has explained,[13] between 'the protection of mere present possession' and the conferral of an alienable proprietary interest in a thing.[14]

---

[7] Rudden (n 2) 65.

[8] eg William Swadling, 'Property: General Principles' in Andrew Burrows (ed), *English Private Law* (3rd edn, OUP 2013) para 4.131 (hereafter Swadling, 'Property'); William Swadling, 'Ignorance and Unjust Enrichment: The Problem of Title' (2008) 28 OJLS 627, 640.

[9] eg HL Ho, 'Some Reflections on "Property" and "Title" in the Sale of Goods Act' (1997) 56 CLJ 571, 573.

[10] Hickey, *Law of Finders* (n 2) 165.

[11] See section 3.3.1 below.

[12] See sections 3.3 and 3.4 below.

[13] Honoré (n 2) 114–15.

[14] ibid 114.

The primary purpose of this chapter is to set up and clear the ground for the enquiry into the nature of a possessor's 'title' by undertaking three tasks. The first, which is the concern of section 3.2, is to expound, analyse, and compare the three views of the nature of a possessor's title. The second task, which is undertaken in section 3.3, is to evaluate and, ultimately, refute the claim that there is, in fact, no real difference between laws that *confer* an interest on a possessor or recognise that a possessor *has* an interest, on the one hand, and the law providing that courts are to *presume* that the possessor has an interest, on the other. The third task, undertaken in section 3.4, is to examine certain conceptual objections to the claim that a possessor of land or chattels is to be presumed to have an interest.

There are good reasons to consider the three views of a possessor's 'title' before discussing the law and the sources of the law, including the cases. Armed with a sound account of the main views and their similarities and differences, we will have a better understanding of what to look for in the legal sources; what is most relevant or important, and what turns on one interpretation or another. It also makes sense to consider at this point whether there is a genuine distinction between laws that confer or recognise an interest, and laws that provide that the courts are to presume that a person has an interest. For if there were no such distinction, it would not make sense to enquire into whether the legal authorities support the view that the law confers an interest on a possessor, or the view that a possessor is to be presumed to have an interest. Similarly, if the conceptual objections to the view that a possessor is to be presumed to have an interest are sound, then the rules of presumption that are thought, by some, to be part of English law would be rules that require the courts to invoke and rely on 'presumptions' that are conceptually impossible.

3.2 Three Views of Title by Possession

This section outlines three views of the nature of the 'title' that a person acquires by obtaining possession of land or chattels: the Possessory Right View, the Strong Proprietary Interest View, and the Presumed Property View.

3.2.1 The Possessory Right View

According to the Possessory Right View, when a person (X) obtains possession of certain land, or a chattel that is not unowned (res nullius), X acquires a possession-dependent, non-transferable right (or set of rights) over the land or chattel that binds the world at large. A right over certain land or a certain chattel is *possession-dependent* if it is a necessary condition of the right subsisting that the right-holder has possession of the land or chattel. Such a right is, therefore, extinguished if and when the right-holder ceases to be in possession. Accordingly, if the right that is acquired when X obtains possession of a chattel or certain land is possession-dependent, X will lose the right if and when X loses possession of the chattel or land.[15] Since the subsistence of a possession-dependent right is tied to the right-holder's possession, such a right will be called a 'right of possession'.[16]

A right is *non-transferable* if the right-holder does not have, and no other person has, a power that enables them to transfer the right to another person. To say that a right of possession cannot be transferred, is, of course, not to say that the possessor cannot effectively relinquish possession to another. For instance, if X is in possession of Blackacre, she might permit and facilitate the acquisition of possession by Y and, if the Possessory Right View is correct, then, when Y obtains possession, Y acquires a right of possession. In such circumstances, however, Y acquires, not X's right, but a new, independent right.

To say that X's right is a right *over* the land or chattel in X's possession is to say that the content of the right concerns the land or chattel. While there is some debate over the precise content of the right or rights acquired by taking possession of land or chattels, it is widely accepted that the possessor acquires what may be called a right to exclude: a right that others exclude themselves from, and do not interfere with, the land or chattels.[17]

What reasons, if any, support the view that a person who obtains possession of land or chattels should acquire a right to exclude? It is helpful, when seeking to answer this question, to consider a broader question: why should the law protect possession? It has long been recognised that there are various reasons for the law to protect possession.[18] Some of these considerations concern the

---

[15] It is consistent with the Possessory Right View to claim that, if X was dispossessed by Y, X is able to successfully sue Y. For, when Y interfered, X was in possession and had, therefore, a right of possession. When possession was taken by Y, X lost her right of possession, but she had a 'right of action' against Y, ie a right or power to obtain a remedy from Y.

[16] On the Possessory Right View, the right that one acquires by taking possession of land, or chattels that are not unowned, is similar to the right that is acquired by taking possession of a wild animal: see *Borwick Development Solutions Ltd v Clear Water Fisheries Ltd* [2020] EWCA Civ 578.

[17] See, eg RH Kersley, *Goodeve's Modern Law of Personal Property* (9th edn, Sweet & Maxwell 1949) 9, 23–25; Jonathan Hill, 'The Proprietary Character of Possession' in Elizabeth Cooke (ed), *Modern Studies in Property Law, Volume 1* (Hart 2000) 31–35; James Goudkamp & Edwin Peel, *Winfield & Jolowicz on Tort* (19th edn, Sweet & Maxwell 2014) paras 14-004–14-009, 18-010–18-011.

[18] Frederick Pollock and Robert Samuel Wright, *An Essay on Possession in the Common Law* (Clarendon Press 1888) 3; Frederick Pollock and Frederic William Maitland, *The History of English*

prevention of violence and, importantly, these provide a good explanation as to why a possessor should acquire, in particular, a legal right to exclude that is possession-dependent. According to Pollock and Maitland, 'to allow men to make forcible entries on land or to seize goods without form of law, is to invite violence'.[19] The concern is that, if the law were to fail to protect individuals who are in possession of goods or land, it is likely that others would seek to take possession of such things from them by force. Land and goods, as Donaldson LJ put it in *Parker v British Airways Board*, 'would be subject to a free-for-all in which the physically weakest would go to the wall'.[20]

The fact that the use of violence against a person is harmful is a reason for the law to take steps to discourage violent dispossessions; that is, the use of violence against a possessor to dispossess her.[21] Criminal prohibitions on such conduct, and laws conferring private rights on possessors, supplement the law governing the tort of trespass to the person and the crimes of assault and battery. There is, however, reason for the law to go further and to protect possessors from violent and non-violent dispossessions: such protection provides greater security and stability to possessors, and reduces the risk that situations will emerge that engender, or are conducive to, the use of violence. If non-violent dispossessions were lawful, people who have no legal entitlement to land and chattels that are in the possession of another would have an incentive to attempt to take possession without using force. But while the would-be dispossessor may not intend to use force when she sets out, there is a serious risk that the attempt to seize, and the possessor's attempt to resist the seizure, should she become aware of it, will lead to a violent struggle. In short, failing to protect possession may well lead, as Mitchell J said in *Anderson v Gouldberg*, to an 'endless series of unlawful seizures and reprisals'[22]; and attempts to seize, and attempts to resist such seizures, may lead to violence.[23] By conferring on

---

Law Before the Time of Edward I (2nd edn, CUP 1911) vol 2, 41; James Gordley, *Foundations of Private Law: Property, Tort, Contract, Unjust Enrichment* (OUP 2007) 53.

[19] Pollock and Maitland (n 18) 41.

[20] [1982] QB 1004 (CA) 1009.

[21] By virtue of s 6(1) of the Criminal Law Act 1977, it is an offence to use or threaten violence, without lawful authority, for the purpose of securing entry into any premises provided that there is someone present on the premises who is opposed to the entry and the person using or threatening the violence knows this. An exception is made for the 'displaced residential occupier' and the 'protected intending occupier': s 6(1A). For a detailed discussion of the elements and functions of this offence, see: Law Commission, *Report on Conspiracy and Criminal Law Reform* (Law Com No 76, 1976), paras 2.1–2.68; Dennis J Baker, *Glanville Williams' Textbook of Criminal Law* (4th edn, Sweet & Maxwell 2015), paras 38-038–38-051.

[22] (1892) 53 NW 636, 637.

[23] Savigny famously argued that protecting people from violence and remedying the consequences of violence underpinned the Roman law of possession: Friedrich Karl von Savigny, *Treatise on Possession* (Erskine Perry tr, 6th edn, S Sweet 1848) 27–28. Savigny's account was forcefully criticised by

a person who is in possession of goods or land a right to exclude—a right that grounds duties of non-interference on persons generally—the law instructs and incentivises others not to interfere.

A supporter of the Possessory Right View might argue that the fact that the rules which confer a right of possession on possessors are founded on a policy of discouraging violence explains why a possessor's rights are possession-dependent. The policy of discouraging individuals from taking, or attempt to take, land or chattels from the present possessor is served by conferring rights on possessors for so long as they remain in possession. The policy does not support conferring rights on persons who are not in possession.

Many legal scholars, including some who do not fully endorse the Possessory Right View, have accepted that the interest that a person acquires by taking possession of chattels is possession-dependent, unless the thing is unowned, in which case the possessor acquires the 'best title'. For instance, Roy Goode and Ewan McKendrick have averred that 'the holder of a purely possessory title [in respect of a chattel] loses his real right when he ceases to have possession, and his claim against the person who divested him of possession is a mere personal claim'.[24] Similarly, David Fox has claimed that, in general, 'a relative title to personal property . . . only survives so long as [the holder of the title] remains in possession of the chattel'.[25] This, on Fox's view, is to be explained by the fact that the doctrine serves to protect possession.[26] Fox adds, however, that the rule that a possessor's title will determine if the possessor ceases to be in possession is arguably subject to an important qualification, ie that a 'relative title' can be enforced against a defendant who derives her title from the original wrongdoer.[27]

Finally, it should be pointed out that some of those who have maintained that a possessor acquires an interest that is possession-dependent have nevertheless asserted that the interest can be alienated by the interest-holder.[28] This is puzzling, because if the interest can be alienated, the subsistence of the interest is

---

Jhering: see JM Lightwood, 'Possession in the Roman Law' (1887) 3 LQR 32; Henry Bond, 'Possession in the Roman Law' (1890) 6 LQR 259.

[24] Ewan McKendrick (ed), *Goode on Commercial Law* (5th edn, Penguin 2016) para 2.07. It should be emphasised that Goode and McKendrick's account does not wholly endorse the Possessory Right View because it maintains the interest that a possessor acquires *can* be transferred: see n 28 below.

[25] David Fox, 'Relativity of Title at Law and in Equity' (2006) 65 CLJ 330, 344 (hereafter, Fox, 'Relativity of Title').

[26] ibid 345.

[27] ibid 346ff. See also James Gordley and Ugo Mattei, 'Protecting Possession' (1996) 44 Am J Comp L 293, 327.

[28] eg McKendrick (n 24) paras 2.22, 2.48–2.50.

not conditional on the right-holder's possession. Suppose that X is in possession of a car under a 'possessory title'. X enters into a 'sale and leaseback' agreement with Y. Pursuant to this agreement, X's interest is transferred to Y by way of sale and X retains possession of the car under the lease agreement. It cannot be said that, in such circumstances, the existence of Y's interest is conditional on Y being in possession. For Y does not have possession. One response to this is to say that, following the transfer, the existence of the interest is conditional on the *transferor's* possession.[29] This response preserves, in an amended form, the right's 'possession-dependence'. But, if this response is correct, it is difficult to understand what the point of this condition is. Why should the existence of the interest be conditional on the interest-holder *or the interest-holder's predecessor in title* being in possession?

3.2.2 The Strong Proprietary Interest View

According to the Strong Proprietary Interest View, it is generally the case that, if and when a person, X, obtains possession of certain land or a certain chattel, X acquires a proprietary interest over the land or chattel that has certain features. An 'interest' is an interconnected set of rights, powers, liberties, and/or immunities.[30] X's interest is proprietary in that: (a) it comprises rights that are capable of 'running with' the thing—rights, in other words, that are capable of binding (ie grounding a duty on) a person who has, or subsequently acquires, an interest in respect of the thing; and (b) it comprises rights that ground duties on persons generally not to interfere with the thing.[31] According to the Strong Proprietary Interest View, the proprietary interest that is acquired through taking possession has the following additional features: it is not possession-dependent; and it comprises certain permissive and dispositive powers, including the power to permit others (conditionally or unconditionally) to interfere with the thing, the power to grant other kinds of proprietary interests over it, and the power to transfer the entire interest to another. On this view,

---

[29] See McKendrick (n 24) para 2.22.

[30] A similar, though slightly narrower, understanding of 'interests' has been advanced by Nicholas McBride, *The Humanity of Private Law Part I: Explanation* (Hart 2019) 74–78, 143–53. According to McBride, 'any given interest (INT*) in a particular item of property is constituted by a particular set (S) of rights and powers so that to have an INT* in P *is* to have S': (ibid. 78).

[31] This is not to say that all proprietary interests have both features. For discussion, see James Penner, 'Duty and Liability in Respect of Funds' in John P Lowry and Loukas Mistelis (eds), *Commercial Law: Perspectives and Practice* (LexisNexis Butterworths, London 2006); Ben McFarlane and Robert Stevens, 'The Nature of Equitable Property' (2010) 4 J of Equity 1.

therefore, a possessor acquires an interest that is more extensive and less fragile than a right of possession.

A number of distinguished legal scholars have endorsed this view. Among its most influential proponents are Oliver Wendell Holmes Jr and Frederick Pollock.[32] Holmes claimed that 'possessory rights', ie the rights that a person acquires by obtaining possession of chattels or land, 'pass by descent or devise, as well as by conveyance'.[33] Similarly, Pollock maintained that 'possession confers more than a personal right to be protected against wrongdoers; it confers a qualified right to possess, a right in the nature of property which is valid against every one who cannot show a prior and better right'.[34] The right is 'qualified', for it is subject to 'prior and better' rights and will be extinguished if the possessor is 'lawfully dispossessed'.[35] But it is a 'transmissible right';[36] and, as against strangers, it has 'the incidents of ownership'.[37] Accordingly, '[t]he possessor is in a relative sense an owner; possession, in our English phrase, is a root of title'.[38]

Pollock's claim that a possessor acquires an alienable right that has all the incidents of ownership was, and remains, controversial. Writing in 1940, AD Hargreaves criticised the 'fallacious conception that possession as such can be a good title'.[39] 'Mere possession' of land, he claimed, 'is never a title. At most it is evidence of seisin'.[40] More recently, James Gordley and Ugo Mattei have argued that the view that 'possession gives a kind of title' was 'invented' by Holmes and Pollock; and the consequences of the Holmes–Pollock view 'are more extreme than they or English or American courts would care for'.[41] Yet many scholars now regard the view endorsed by Holmes and Pollock—the Strong Proprietary Interest View—as correct.[42]

Among those who endorse the Strong Proprietary Interest View, there is some disagreement as to the exact nature of the proprietary interest that a

---

[32] Oliver Wendell Holmes Jr, *The Common Law* (Little, Brown and Co 1881) Lecture VI; Pollock and Wright (n 18) chs 1, 3.

[33] Holmes (n 32) 215.

[34] Pollock and Wright (n 18) 93.

[35] ibid 99.

[36] ibid 93.

[37] ibid 22.

[38] Frederick Pollock, *A First Book of Jurisprudence* (5th edn, Macmillan 1923) 189.

[39] AD Hargreaves, 'Terminology and Title in Ejectment' (1940) 56 LQR 376, 391.

[40] ibid.

[41] Gordley and Mattei (n 27) 294.

[42] eg Ben McFarlane, *The Structure of Property Law* (Hart 2008) 144–46, 647; Simon Douglas, *Liability for Wrongful Interferences with Chattels* (Hart 2011) 20–30; Swadling, 'Property' (n 8) paras 4.422–4.428; Stuart Bridge, Elizabeth Cooke, and Martin Dixon (eds), *Megarry & Wade: The Law of Real Property* (9th edn, Sweet & Maxwell 2019) para 7-004. See also: Hickey, *Law of Finders* (n 2) 107–11, 122–24, 164.

possessor acquires. With respect to land, one view is that X acquires, when X obtains possession, a fee simple absolute in possession.[43] Among those who take this view, there is some debate as to the scope in the rule and, in particular, whether it applies only to adverse possessors.[44] According to another version of the Strong Proprietary Interest View, a possessor of land acquires, not a fee simple estate, but a more limited kind of alienable proprietary interest, sometimes referred to as a 'possessory interest'.[45]

Discussions of the nature of the proprietary interest that is, allegedly, acquired by a person who obtains possession of chattel are hindered by the lack of a stable terminology for referring to proprietary interests in chattels. Ben McFarlane calls the interest that is acquired through obtaining possession of a chattel 'an Ownership'.[46] William Swadling calls it 'a right to exclusive possession forever' or, more simply, 'title'.[47] Other commentators have called it a 'possessory title',[48] or 'special property'.[49] It is suggested in Chapter 5 that the interest should be called a 'general property interest'.

If the Strong Proprietary Interest View is correct, there can be numerous interests of the same kind in certain land or a particular chattel. Consider the following example (*Stolen Car*):

> X was in possession of a car. Y, desiring the car for herself, took it without X's consent. Later, Z took the car without the permission of Y or X. A short time later, Y demanded the return of the car and Z refused to return it.

Suppose that, in *Stolen Car*, each of X, Y, and Z had possession of the car in turn. When X obtained possession, X acquired, according to the Strong Proprietary Interest View, an alienable proprietary interest that is not possession-dependent, and which comprises a right to exclude along with various powers. When Y acquired possession, Y also acquired the very same kind of interest, as did Z when Z acquired possession. How do their interests compare? According to those who are committed to the Strong Proprietary Interest View, the rights

---

[43] eg Bridge, Cooke, and Dixon (n 42) paras 7-004, 7-070; McFarlane (n 42) 647.

[44] Compare, eg JM Lightwood, *Possession of Land* (Stevens & Sons 1894) 123–25, 270–72; McFarlane (n 42) 647; Bridge, Cooke, and Dixon (n 42) paras 7-004–7-013, 7-070.

[45] See, eg *Hawdon v Khan* (1920) 20 SR (NSW) 703 (NSWSC) 712–13 (Ferguson J); *Allen v Roughley* (1955) 94 CLR 98 (HCA) 145 (Taylor J).

[46] McFarlane (n 42) 140. See also Hickey, *Law of Finders* (n 2) 122–24, 164; Douglas (n 42) 26.

[47] Swadling, 'Property' (n 8) para 4.131.

[48] eg Michael Bridge, *Personal Property Law* (4th edn, OUP 2015) 30–31, 43–45, 53–54; Norman Palmer, 'Possessory Title' in Ewan McKendrick and Norman Palmer (eds), *Interests in Goods* (2nd edn, LLP 1998).

[49] See, eg Nicholas Curwen, 'General and Special Property in Goods' (2000) 20 LS 181, 182.

that one acquires with respect to a thing by obtaining possession bind persons generally, but not anyone with a better interest in the thing.[50] The various interests are prioritised or ranked according to rules of priority.[51] These rules partly determine who is bound by the rights that are part of the interest. The basic rule is that an interest has priority over later, but not earlier, interests.[52] Accordingly, X's interest, which arose before Y's and Z's, is better than theirs; and, Y's interest is better than Z's. The result is that, other things being equal, X's right to exclude binds Y and Z; Y's right to exclude binds Z but not X; and Y's binds persons in general but not X or Y.

On this view, then, the doctrine of relative title is, in part, about the priority of competing interests of the same kind, and about the bindingness of the rights that are partly constitutive of those interests. Significantly, on this view, there is, in principle, no limit on the number of 'titles' that may exist with respect to a particular thing; several persons might have the *very same type of interest* in land or chattels. X, Y, and Z, for instance, might each have, the very same kind of interest in the car.

It was said above that the law may confer rights of possession on possessors in order to discourage violence and civil unrest, but these considerations do not explain why a possessor should acquire a more extensive interest such as a fee simple.[53] Accordingly, if, as Chapters 4 and 5 argue, the Strong Proprietary Interest View is correct, one important question is: what are the legal grounds of the rules that confer a proprietary interest on a possessor? Chapter 6 will seek to answer this question.

3.2.3 The Presumed Property View

According to the Presumed Property View, English law provides that if a person, X, is (or has been) in possession of a chattel, the courts, in certain circumstances, are to presume that X has (or had) ownership of it; and, similarly, if a person, X, is (or has been) in possession of certain land, the courts, in certain circumstances, are to presume that X holds or held the land for an estate in fee simple.

---

[50] See, eg McFarlane (n 42) 146; Swadling, 'Property' (n 8) para 4.427.
[51] McFarlane (n 42) 146; Douglas (n 42) 24–27.
[52] McFarlane (n 42) 146; Swadling, 'Property' (n 8) paras 4.423, 4.427.
[53] See Robin Hickey, 'Possession as a Source of Property at Common Law' in Eric Descheemaeker, *The Consequences of Possession* (Edinburgh UP 2014) 92.

A rule requiring a court to presume that a possessor is the owner of a chattel, or holds land for an estate in fee simple, must be distinguished from a rule that confers a proprietary interest, such as ownership or a fee simple, on a possessor.[54] Consider *Stolen Car* again. Suppose that Y brings an action in conversion against Z and that, since Y was in possession of the car when it was taken by Z, the court is required to presume that Y is the owner of it for the purposes of his action against Z. In such circumstances, Y is not the owner but the court, for the purposes of resolving the dispute, will treat Y as though she were.

Many legal commentators have thought that there is some such rule of presumption in English law. For instance, Fox has claimed that, where X has a valid paper title to land under an unregistered fee simple estate and Y squats on the land, Y acquires, by virtue of his possession, a 'title' and '[a]n evidential presumption applies under which [Y] is to be treated as holding a fee simple estate in the land'.[55] Similarly, if Y takes possession of a lost chattel that belongs to X, Y acquires a 'possessory title' to the chattel and 'would be presumed against a wrongdoer to have an ownership interest in it'.[56]

It is sometimes said that possession gives rise, in cases concerning chattels, to what has been described as a 'title' or 'claim' to the ownership of the chattel; and, in cases involving land, to 'title' or 'claim' to a fee simple estate. These descriptions appear to be problematic. After all, anyone might *claim* to have a freehold estate in Blackacre or to be the owner of a particular car. What does it mean to say that the possessor acquires a claim to an interest? The Presumed Property View provides a way of making sense of these descriptions. One who is committed to this view may say that the statements 'X has a title to the ownership of the car' and 'X has a title to a fee simple estate in Blackacre' mean, not that X can merely *make a claim* to the ownership of the car and the fee simple in Blackacre, but that if X claims to be the owner of the car, or to have a fee simple estate in Blackacre, the courts will be required, in certain circumstances, to accept and uphold that claim. When the courts are required, by virtue of the rules of presumption, to proceed on the basis that that X is the owner of the car, or that X holds Blackacre for an estate in fee simple, the courts will be required to accept that X has the interest that she claims to have. Interpreted in this way, X has a title to the ownership of the car if it is the case that, in certain

---

[54] The distinction between having a proprietary interest and being treated as though one had a proprietary interest has been recognised by the courts when interpreting construction contracts: see *Re Cosslett (Contractors) Ltd* [1998] Ch 495 (CA) 506–07 (Millett LJ).

[55] Fox, 'Relativity of Title' (n 25) 331. See also: Mark Wonnacott, *Possession of Land* (CUP 2006) 40–42; Stephen Jourdan & Oliver Radley-Gardner, *Adverse Possession* (2nd edn, Bloomsbury 2011) paras 20-016–20-041.

[56] Fox, 'Relativity of Title' (n 25) 342.

circumstances, the courts will be required to accept that X is the owner of the car. This title—this claim to the ownership—might be better or worse than another title to the ownership. In *Stolen Car*, for instance, Y's title is 'good against' Z but it is not 'good against' X; therefore, Y is to be deemed (other things being equal) to be the owner of the car against Z but not against X. Relativity of title, on this view, does not presuppose that multiple proprietary interests of the same kind (eg multiple fees simple or multiple ownership interests) can exist concurrently in respect of a given thing; rather, it presupposes that there can be multiple claims to the ownership of a chattel, or to the fee simple in certain land.

3.2.4 Combining the Three Views

Many scholars have adopted just one of the three views and rejected, explicitly or implicitly, the other two. However, one could logically embrace both the Possessory Right View and the Presumed Property View: it could be that the law confers a right of possession on a possessor and provides that she is to be presumed, for certain purposes, to have a fee simple estate over the land or ownership of the chattel (as the case may be). Furthermore, one could largely embrace both the Strong Proprietary Interest View and the Presumed Property View, for the law could confer a strong proprietary interest on a possessor and also provide that she is to be presumed, for certain purposes, to have the best such interest. And while one could not logically endorse, in full, the Possessory Right View and the Strong Proprietary Interest View, one could accept some central elements of both views while also largely accepting the Presumed Property View. One might claim, for instance, that possession gives rise to a right of possession; that a possessor will be presumed, for certain purposes, to have a certain interest (for example, the best fee simple, in cases concerning land); and that wrongful (or 'adverse') possession will give rise to a strong proprietary interest, such as a fee simple estate. The three views have been individuated in order to highlight some important distinctions, but this should not lead one to think that elements of them cannot be combined.

3.3 The Importance of Distinguishing the Three Views

It is apparent that the legal rules that are thought to exist, respectively, by those who endorse the Possessory Right View, and those who endorse the Strong Proprietary Interest View, differ considerably from one another, and that the differences are of practical significance. On the Strong Proprietary Interest View, X, by obtaining possession of land or chattels, acquires an interest that comprises a right to exclude persons in general from the land or the chattels, and a variety of powers, including the power to grant licences and the power to alienate her entire interest *inter vivos* or in her will. On the Possessory Right View, X acquires no such powers. She acquires a right that merely protects her present possession; a right that will be lost if she is dispossessed or if she discontinues her possession.

When one compares the Strong Proprietary Interest View with the Presumed Property View, on the other hand, it might be thought that these views are, in substance, the same; or that, if they are genuinely different, it does not matter, in practice, which is correct. It is argued in this section that such thoughts are mistaken. The Strong Proprietary Interest View and the Presumed Property View are genuinely and importantly different.

3.3.1 Distinguishing Rules of Acquisition from Rules of Presumption

The fundamental difference between the Strong Proprietary Interest View and the Presumed Property View is that the former maintains that English law contains certain acquisition rules, whereas the latter maintains that it contains particular rules of presumption. This is a genuine distinction: rules that confer an interest on a person are not the same as rules that provide that the courts are to presume in certain circumstances that a person has an interest.

Unfortunately, some commentators and judges have overlooked this distinction. For example, AD Hargreaves, in a seminal contribution, asserts that the fact that a person is in possession of land is evidence, or gives rise to a presumption, that the possessor is seised and '[i]t is only when this evidence [or presumption] is not rebutted that possession can *create* a title by investing the tenant with a freehold estate derived from seisin'.[57] This assertion rests on a mistaken understanding of the effect of rules of presumption and the effect of court judgments. For Hargreaves, the occupier cannot have a freehold estate derived from seisin unless she was seised. But the fact that a court is required to presume that a particular person was seised of land does not make it the case that she really was seised.

---

[57] Hargreaves (n 39) 391. See also *Re Atkinson and Horsell's Contract* [1912] 2 Ch 1 (CA) 9 (Cozens-Hardy MR), 17 (Fletcher Moulton LJ).

Where a court is required, by a rule of presumption, to take some proposition—such as the proposition that X has a fee simple in Blackacre—as true, the court is required to proceed, for the purpose of deciding the case, on the basis that the proposition is true.[58] The fact that the court proceeds in this way, and the fact that the court makes a decision on this basis, does not, without more, mean that the proposition really is true. Whether X really has a fee simple in Blackacre depends, not on whether a court presumes, or decides a case on the basis that, X has a fee simple in Blackacre, but on whether, so far as X and Blackacre are concerned, the legal conditions for the ascription of a fee simple have been met. Such rules are examples of rules of acquisition (or 'investitive' rules).[59] Once one recognises the distinction between rules of presumption and rules of acquisition, it seems obvious that a court may decide a case on the basis that a person holds land for a freehold estate without thereby making it the case that the person actually holds the land for such an estate.

Fox's influential account of title by possession does not acknowledge the distinction between a person having an interest in land or chattels and a person being presumed by a court to have such an interest.[60] It is fruitful to consider Fox's view because it brings to light certain jurisprudential theses that may well provide the motivation, and an ostensible basis, for rejecting the distinction between a person having an interest in land or chattels and a person being presumed by a court to have an interest.

Fox maintains that, if X has an unregistered fee simple estate in Blackacre and a second party, Y, squats on the land and dispossesses X, the courts will presume, for the purposes of an action brought by Y against a third party, Z, that Y has a fee simple estate in Blackacre.[61] Similarly, according to Fox,[62] if B finds and takes possession of A's chattel, the courts will presume, if B brings an action against a third party who interferes with B's possession, that B has an ownership interest in the chattel. Now, Fox appears to think that, by virtue of these rules of presumption, when Y takes possession of the land, Y actually has a fee simple estate in Blackacre; and, correspondingly, that when B takes possession of the chattel, B actually has an ownership interest in the chattel. In other words, it seems that Fox would reject the distinction between a person

---

[58] See section 3.4 below.
[59] Raz (n 5) 175–83; MacCormick (n 3) 139.
[60] Fox, 'Relativity of Title' (n 25). See also David Fox, 'Enforcing a Possessory Title to a Stolen Car' (2002) 61 CLJ 27 (hereafter Fox, 'Enforcing a Possessory Title').
[61] Fox, 'Relativity of Title' (n 25) 331–32.
[62] ibid 340–44.

having an interest in land or chattels and a person being presumed by a court to have such an interest.

A strong reason for thinking that this is Fox's view is that, if the distinction is sound, his account of the law appears to be internally inconsistent. Fox states that the doctrine of relative title is about the priority of competing 'interests' and the 'claims' to which they give rise.[63] However, there is a tension between this view of the doctrine of relative title and Fox's account of the law regarding title by possession. This tension can be illustrated by considering his analysis of a case in which one person, B, finds and takes possession of a lost chattel which belongs to another person, A. According to Fox, in an action in trespass or conversion against C, who wrongfully interferes with B's possession, B is presumed to have an ownership interest in the chattel and, accordingly, a 'claim' to possess. Fox does not say that, apart from the rule(s) providing for this 'presumption of ownership', there are any rules that would confer on B an 'ownership interest' in the chattel. It is clear that A, the holder of the 'best title' to the chattel, actually has an 'ownership interest' in the chattel. B, however, is, for the purposes of the action against C, merely presumed to have an 'ownership interest' (and hence a 'claim' to possess). Now, if this is right, then, *pace* Fox, there are not in fact two competing 'ownership interests'; there is in fact only one 'interest', ie A's. And if there is just one 'interest', then the situation is not one in which the priority of competing interests can arise.

If each of two or more parties to an action claim to be the owner of a particular chattel, and if these claims can be assessed, relative to one another, as 'better' or 'worse', then it may make sense to talk of the 'priority' of competing claims to the ownership of a chattel; a claim, one might say, takes 'priority' over another claim if it is better than the other. But clearly this kind of priority dispute is not a dispute about the priority of *competing ownership interests*; it is, rather, a dispute as to the priority of competing *claims to* the ownership interest. Therefore, if, like Fox, one regards the doctrine of relative title as a doctrine that serves to determine the priority of competing proprietary interests, the doctrine does not apply to the case involving A, B, and C, which really involves just one proprietary interest. Far from demonstrating the breadth of the principle of relative title, Fox's account leads to the conclusion that the principle does not apply to what he terms 'the core case of relativity of title'.[64]

This provides a reason for believing that Fox would not accept the distinction between a person having an interest in a thing and a person being presumed by

---

[63] ibid 331, 333–38.
[64] ibid 330.

a court to have an interest. Some of Fox's statements provide additional support for this interpretation. For example, when contrasting the 'absolute title' of the *dominus* in classical Roman law with the 'title' of an estate-holder in English law, Fox says, 'English law . . . freely permits *the possibility of more than one fee simple estate existing concurrently* in the same land. As has been seen, it applies a *presumption* in favour of the person in possession of land that he holds it under a fee simple estate'.[65]

If Fox has rejected the distinction, why has he done so? It is not clear, but there are some indications that Fox's account is committed to, or premised on, a predictive theory of legal rights according to which a person, X, has a legal right if a court will, or is likely to, make a remedy available to X if X claims that his right has been infringed.[66] If this theory were correct, the distinction between a court presuming that X has a right and X actually having a right would collapse, at least if, and insofar as, a court will, or is likely to, make a remedy available to a person who is presumed by the court to have an interest. The very fact that the court will, or probably will, make a remedy available to X (as a result of the presumption) makes it the case, on this view, that X has the interest.

There are, however, powerful reasons to reject predictive theories of legal rights. In *The Concept of Law*, HLA Hart explained how predictive theories of law, if understood as jurisprudential theories about the nature of law, have absurd implications and cannot account for important features of law.[67] Hart's objections to predictive theories of law apply to predictive accounts of the nature of legal rights and legal obligations.[68] Suppose that a claimant submits before a court that the defendant has violated one of her rights and that, therefore, she (the claimant) ought to receive a remedy. In its deliberations about whether to accept the claimant's submission, the court asks itself: 'does the claimant have the right that the defendant allegedly violated?' It would be absurd and extremely strange for the court to answer the question thus: 'the claimant has the right if we award a remedy in response to her claim, so the only question

---

[65] ibid 335 (emphasis added). Fox adds that 'the presumption allows what are, *in effect*, multiple fees simple to be created in the same land' (emphasis added). Is this an acknowledgement that, if the law is what he maintains it is, the law does not really allow multiple fees simple? If so, where does this leave his account of the doctrine of relative title?

[66] See, eg Fox, 'Enforcing a Possessory Title' (n 60) 29: 'To say that [the claimant] *had* a relative ownership interest in the car when he lacked possession *simply expresses the conclusion that* the court, for pragmatic reasons, was willing [to] allow him an action in conversion against the [defendant]. As has long been true of common law actions, *the availability of the remedy determined the existence of* [the claimant's] substantive right, not the right of the remedy' (emphases added). See, also, Fox, 'Relativity of Title' (n 25) 335.

[67] HLA Hart, *The Concept of Law* (3rd edn, OUP 2012) 83–85, 104–05, 136–48.

[68] For further discussion, see PMS Hacker, 'Sanction Theories of Duty' in AWB Simpson (ed), *Oxford Essays in Jurisprudence (Second Series)* (Clarendon Press 1973) 131, 142–48.

is: will we award a remedy?' If the court concludes that the claimant is entitled to a remedy on the basis that defendant violated one of the claimant's rights, the assertion that the claimant had the right 'constitutes not a prophecy of but part of the *reason* for [its] decision'.[69]

Since predictive theories of legal rights are untenable, they can provide no support for the view that we should reject the distinction between a person having an interest and a court presuming that a person has an interest.

3.3.2 Is the Distinction Important?

It might be thought that it does not matter whether the Strong Proprietary Interest View or the Presumed Property View is correct because the outcomes of cases do not depend upon which view is correct.[70] If, as this claim presupposes, the importance of the distinction turns solely on whether the outcomes of cases depend on which view is correct, then the question undoubtedly matters. This is demonstrated by the fact that, on the Presumed Property View, the presumption that applies to possessors can, in some circumstances, be rebutted.[71]

In any case, one should reject the view that the sole criterion of whether it matters is whether the outcomes of cases turn on which view is correct. It is important to consider not only the outcome of a case, but also the court's reasons for making the decision that it made. For, unless one considers the court's reasons, one cannot identify the grounds of the decision and, without knowing the grounds, one cannot determine the content of the ratio decidendi, or whether the decision was justified. Accordingly, even if the three views led to exactly the same outcomes in all cases, it would be a mistake to say that it does not matter which view is correct. The three views advance different accounts of the reasons why a given claimant would win or lose (eg because the claimant had, or did not have, a right of possession; or because the claimant had, or did not have, a strong proprietary interest; or because the court did, or did not, presume that the claimant is the owner or the holder of the legal fee simple). Therefore, the correctness (or otherwise) of the Possessory Right View, the Strong Proprietary Interest View, and the Presumed Property View matters.

---

[69] Hart (n 67) 105.

[70] This claim does not appear to have been advanced in any published texts. However, the claim has frequently been advanced by legal scholars in oral discussions of this topic.

[71] See Chapter 4 (section 4.2.2.1) and Chapter 5 (section 5.3).

3.4 Conceptual Objections to Presumptions of Property

According to the Presumed Property View, the law requires the courts to presume, in certain circumstances, that a person who was in possession of a piece of land or a particular chattel has (or had) a certain interest in it. This section is concerned with certain conceptual objections to this view: objections to the very idea of a presumption of property.

William Swadling has claimed that the statement 'the fact of possession gives rise to a presumption of ownership' involves a misnomer; it rests on a misunderstanding as to the true nature of presumptions.[72] He has advanced two arguments in support of this claim. First, '[p]resumptions properly-so-called'—or 'true presumptions'—'are methods of proof of facts, and no fact is here in issue, merely a legal inference from facts proved by evidence.'[73] This argument seeks to establish that there can be no such as thing as a presumption of ownership, because presumptions prove facts, and whether the claimant is the owner is not an issue of fact. If this is correct, the view that there is such a presumption involves a conceptual muddle. Robin Hickey has advanced a similar argument. He has claimed that where the claimant has actually proven, before the court, that she was in possession, the issue to be settled concerns:

> the legal inference to be drawn from facts *already proven* by evidence. In these circumstances, it is not technically possible for a claimant to benefit from any presumption, and it seems analytically more accurate to regard possession as the source of a definite legal relation.[74]

Swadling's second argument is that 'the "presumption" [of ownership] cannot be displaced by adducing evidence showing ... that the claimant is not the "owner". The "presumption" is irrebuttable, and an irrebuttable presumption ... is nothing but a rule of substantive law.'[75] Whereas the first argument maintains that there can be no such thing as a presumption of ownership, the second argument maintains that the so-called 'presumption of ownership' is irrebuttable and there can be no such thing as an irrebuttable presumption.

Senior members of the judiciary have thought that, in certain circumstances, possessors of chattels are to be presumed to have ownership and, similarly, that possessors of land are to be presumed in certain circumstances to

---

[72] Swadling, 'Property' (n 8) para 4.426.
[73] ibid.
[74] Hickey, *Law of Finders* (n 2) 110.
[75] ibid.

have a legal fee simple estate.[76] If Hickey and Swadling are right, these judges have embraced a position that is nonsensical and must, therefore, be dismissed. Nevertheless, supporters of the Hickey–Swadling view may well add that judicial statements that support the Presumed Property View should be re-interpreted in a way that is consistent with the Strong Proprietary Interest View. It is necessary, therefore, to consider whether Hickey and Swadling are right. The remainder of this section seeks to show that Hickey and Swadling's arguments are not sound and that, therefore, they have not established that the very idea of a presumption of ownership is confused. If this is right, the Presumed Property View cannot be discarded on the ground that it is conceptually flawed; in order to determine whether it is correct, one must examine the authorities.

3.4.1 The First Argument

The premises of the first argument are: (a) presumptions are necessarily methods of proof of facts; and (b) whether or not a person has ownership of a chattel (or holds land for an estate in fee simple) is not a matter of fact. It is argued here that premise (a) is false.

3.4.1.1 Presumptions and rules of presumption

The terms 'presume' and 'presumption' are used in ordinary speech and in legal discourse in various ways.[77] It is not necessary to provide a survey of these various uses here. The aim is not to provide an account of how the word 'presume' is used, but, first, to provide an account of a particular concept that plays a central role in practical reasoning, and which is invoked by the Presumed Property View. This concept frequently is—and can appropriately be—called the concept of a presumption.[78] The second aim is to consider whether, given this account of presumptions, presumptions are methods of proof of facts (in the relevant sense of 'fact').

In order to understand the nature and role of presumptions in the law, it is necessary, as JB Thayer recognised in his celebrated chapter on presumptions, to distinguish presumptions from rules of presumption.[79] A *rule of*

---

[76] See Chapter 4 (section 4.2.2.1) and Chapter 5 (section 5.3).

[77] Daniel Mendonca, 'Presumptions' (1998) 11 Ratio Juris 399, 400–01.

[78] The act of presuming that is described below may be called 'deeming'. Note, however, that while these terms sometimes are regarded as interchangeable, 'deeming' is also used in other ways.

[79] JB Thayer, *A Preliminary Treatise on Evidence at the Common Law* (Little, Brown 1898) 339.

presumption provides that, in certain circumstances, such as where a particular fact has been proved, a certain proposition must be taken as true by the rule-subjects (eg legal officials).[80] To take a proposition as true is to include the proposition among one's premises in one's reasoning as to what to do or think, irrespective of whether one believes the proposition or has reason to believe it. Accordingly, where a rule of presumption applies to a judge, the judge's reasoning, qua judge, must proceed, according to the rule, on the basis that a certain proposition, *q*, is true. The judge, according to the rule, should adopt *q* as a premise of her reasoning when reaching a decision in the case. Suppose, for example, that a rule of law provides that, if it is proved in a court of law that a certain person has not been known to be alive for a period of at least seven years, the court must presume that this person is dead.[81] If, in a particular case, it is proved before a court to which this rule applies that a certain person, X, has not been known to be alive for more than seven years, the court must take as true the proposition that X is dead, ie it must adopt the proposition 'X is dead' as one of its premises when deciding the case. So, as Thayer said, presumptions 'are aids to reasoning and argumentation, which assume the truth of certain matters for the purpose of some inquiry', and the study of them is part of the study of 'legal reasoning'.[82]

Rules of presumption do not require the rule-subjects to *believe* that the presumed fact is true. As Edna Ullmann-Margalit has said, the rule requires 'one to hold *q* as true for the purpose of concluding one's practical deliberation on the impeding issue; it neither requires nor entitles one to believe that *q*'.[83] Where one is required by a rule of presumption to take *q* as true, *q* might or might not be true and one might take *q* as true without believing *q*.

There are three particularly important respects in which rules of presumption may differ. First, a rule of presumption may provide that *q* is to be taken as true by the rule-subjects only if some other proposition, *p*, is proved. Where this is so, *p* is typically called the 'basic fact' or the 'primary fact' and *q* is called the 'presumed fact'. It is often asserted that rules of presumption, by their very nature, are conditional in just this way; that a rule is not a rule of presumption unless it provides that the rule-subjects may or must take a proposition as true

---

[80] See Edna Ullmann-Margalit, 'On Presumption' (1983) 80 J of Philosophy 143, 148: '[A presumption rule] instructs its subjects to hold a certain proposition as true so as to have a foothold (as it were) for action. Put somewhat differently, the instruction is this: given *p*, make *q* a premise in the rest of the pertinent piece of your practical reasoning'. It is not necessary, for present purposes, to discuss whether rules of presumption include rules that provide that rule-subjects *may* take a certain proposition as true.
[81] This example is based on an actual rule of English law: see the Presumption of Death Act 2013, ss 1–3.
[82] Thayer (n 79) 314.
[83] Ullmann-Margalit (n 80) 149.

only if a basic fact is proved.[84] While many rules of presumption provide that the 'presumed fact' is to be taken as true by the rule-subjects only if a 'basic fact' is proved, it is doubtful that this is an essential ingredient of rules of presumption. For a rule may require a rule-subject to take a certain proposition as true, not on the condition that a basic fact is proved, but from the outset of a case. Rules requiring courts, in criminal cases, to presume that the defendant is innocent unless it is established that she is guilty are examples of such rules.[85]

Secondly, some rules of presumption provide that the presumption is rebuttable; others provide that the presumption is irrebuttable. This point, which is controversial, is discussed further below. Thirdly, with respect to rules of presumption that give rise to rebuttable presumptions, the conditions that must be met in order for the presumption to be rebutted vary. For example, a rule of presumption may require the rule-subjects to take a certain proposition as true unless evidence to the contrary is produced, or unless a certain party establishes (relative to a certain standard) that the proposition is false. In English law, for example, there is a distinction between 'evidential presumptions' and 'persuasive presumptions'. A rule concerns an 'evidential presumption' if, following proof of the basic fact, 'the presumed fact must be taken to be established in the absence of evidence to the contrary' and an evidential burden is placed upon the opponent of the presumed fact.[86] A rule concerns a 'persuasive presumption' if, 'after proof of the basic fact, the presumed fact must be taken to be established unless the trier of fact is persuaded to the appropriate standard to the contrary'.[87]

Richard Glover has asserted that '[t]he theoretical basis for recognizing presumptions' is that the presumed fact would usually 'flow naturally from' the basic fact 'so that there is such a strong rational connection between the two that it is unnecessary to require evidence of the presumed fact in the absence of unusual circumstances'.[88] While this may well be the basis of some rules of presumption, it is, as Thayer recognised,[89] a mistake to think that this is, or should be, the basis of all such rules. A rule of presumption requiring,

[84] See, for example, Richard Glover (ed), *Murphy on Evidence* (15th edn, OUP 2017) 152–53; Roderick Munday, *Cross & Tapper on Evidence* (13th edn, OUP 2018) 136.

[85] It has been claimed that these rules are not 'true' rules of presumption, because they 'are really no more than expressions of the incidence of the burden of proof in such cases': Glover (n 84) 153. While, within the law of proof, there is an important distinction between Glover's 'true' rules of presumption and rules that require the court to take a proposition as true without proof of a primary fact, all these rules can be said to concern presumptions for they concern the act of taking a proposition as true.

[86] Munday (n 84) 136. See also Glover (n 84) 153.

[87] Munday (n 84) 136–37. See also Glover (n 84) 153.

[88] Glover (n 84) 152.

[89] Thayer (n 79) 314.

say, the rule-subjects to take q as true might be justified on the ground that, in the circumstances, a rule of presumption is needed in order to facilitate decision making and there are practical (ie value-related) reasons to prefer q being taken as true by the rule-subjects rather than not-q. One important function of rules of presumption in the law is to facilitate decision making (principally by courts and tribunals) where: (a) the law requires a decision on some matter to be made by the decision-maker; (b) the decision depends on whether a certain proposition is true; and (c) the question of whether this proposition is true remains unresolved at the time of the decision. Rules of presumption can, in other words, function as what Ullmann-Margalit described as 'a method of extrication . . . from unresolved deliberation processes' by supplying 'a procedure for decision by default'.[90] In supplying such a procedure, rules of presumption, in effect, select one solution to the problem over another: the rule requires the decision maker to take, say, q as true rather than not-q. Now, a rule requiring the decision maker, if a certain basic fact is proved, to take q as true may be justified on the basis that, where the basic fact is established, it is likely that q is true. Importantly, however, the rule might be justified, not because it is likely in such circumstances that q is true, but on the basis that there are practical reasons to prefer a rule requiring q to be presumed over a rule requiring not-q to be presumed. Since, for example, it is morally worse to convict an innocent person than to acquit a guilty person, a rule requiring courts to presume that defendants in criminal cases are innocent unless the state proves that they are guilty is to be preferred to a rule requiring courts to presume that defendants in criminal cases are guilty unless they prove that that they are innocent.

3.4.1.2 Presumptions, facts, and the law of proof

Suppose that a law ('L1') provides that if, in judicial proceedings, the claimant (C) establishes that she was in possession of a tangible chattel (T) when it was taken by the defendant (D), the court, for the purposes of C's action, is to take as true the proposition that C is the owner of T unless D establishes that some other person is the owner. No one has claimed that there could not be such a law, and it is difficult to conceive of a convincing argument for such a claim. Presumably, Swadling would insist that L1 is not a rule of presumption because rules of presumption prove *facts*. This presupposes, of course, that the proposition that is taken as true where a rule of presumption applies must be a proposition of fact. In order to determine whether this argument is sound, we need to know what propositions of fact are.

---

[90] Ullmann-Margalit (n 80) 155.

The term 'proposition of fact' is ambiguous, and it is not entirely clear how we should interpret it in the context of Swadling's argument. Sometimes 'proposition of fact' is used broadly to mean 'a true proposition'. If a 'proposition of fact' is simply a proposition that is true, then all of the following propositions, if true, are propositions of fact: 'the Battle of Hastings took place in 1066'; 'it is wrong to intentionally kill an innocent person'; 'in the absence of exceptional circumstances, it is unreasonable to drive a motor vehicle at a speed of 70 mph in a residential area'. It is clear that Swadling's argument should not be regarded as employing the term 'proposition of fact' in this broad sense. For, among other things, the statement 'in law, C is the owner of T' could be true and, where this is so, the proposition 'in law, C is the owner of T' is, on the broad definition, a proposition of fact.

We get closer, it would seem, to Swadling's conception of a proposition of fact when we recognise that, in the present context, 'proposition of fact' designates a contrast class: 'propositions of fact' are contrasted with 'propositions of law'. How do these differ? When considering this question, it is helpful to examine the distinction that specialists in the law of evidence draw between 'issues of fact' and 'issues of law'. Consider, for instance, the following passage from Ian Dennis's textbook on evidence:

> [t]he division of issues in legal proceedings into questions of fact and questions of law is fundamental. It represents the distinction, in Zuckerman's words, between 'the question of what happened and the legal consequences of that which happened'. Official adjudication of disputes is founded on the assumption that facts of cases exist independently of the law. Accordingly, it is conceived to be part of the function of the legal process to 'find' the facts . . . This must be done before the law, which states normative rules for certain fact-situations, can be applied to the particular facts of the dispute.[91]

Taking, as one's point of departure, Dennis's claim that 'facts' (in the relevant sense) exist independently of the law, and drawing on Joseph Raz's discussion of legal statements,[92] one can usefully draw a general distinction between two kinds of proposition: legal propositions and non-legal propositions. Legal propositions are propositions, the truth conditions of which include the existence or non-existence of laws. Non-legal propositions are propositions, the truth

---

[91] Ian Dennis, *The Law of Evidence* (7th edn, Sweet & Maxwell 2020) para 4-003, citing Adrian Zuckerman, *The Principles of Criminal Evidence* (Clarendon Press 1989) 22.

[92] Raz (n 5) 49–50, 217–18; Joseph Raz, *Practical Reason and Norms* (OUP 1999) 171–77.

conditions of which do not include the existence or non-existence of laws. For instance, whereas 'the peak of Mount Everest is 8848m above sea level' is a non-legal proposition, 'sexual assault is a criminal offence in English law' is a legal proposition.

Should we maintain that, in the context of Swadling's argument, a 'proposition of fact' is a non-legal proposition? It is not entirely clear. Assuming, however, that Swadling's understanding of 'facts' (ie 'propositions of fact') is broadly in line with that of evidence lawyers, this definition of 'proposition of fact' appears to be too broad. For it seems that, on this account, not all legal propositions are excluded from the category of propositions of fact; excluded are legal propositions of the *relevant* legal system, ie propositions whose truth conditions include the existence or non-existence of laws of the legal system to which the relevant courts belong. If this is right, Swadling may be interpreted as accepting the claim that where, in a given legal system (*LS*), a legal rule of presumption applies to a court, a proposition that, by virtue of this rule, is to be taken as true by the court must be a proposition of fact, not a proposition whose truth conditions include the existence or non-existence of laws belonging to *LS*.

In light of the discussion so far, one might advance the following reconstruction of Swadling's first argument:

(1) A rule of presumption is a rule that requires a court to take a proposition of fact as true.

(2) Since the proposition 'in English law, P is the owner of C' is, so far as English courts are concerned, a proposition of law, the proposition is not a proposition of fact.

(3) Therefore, a rule of presumption cannot require a court to take as true the proposition 'in English law, P is the legal owner of C'.

This argument raises a number of questions. Most importantly, is it really the case that all rules of presumption necessarily require a court to take as true a proposition of fact? If so, why? It might be thought that the answer is that legal rules of presumption are part of the law of proof, and the law of proof is about the establishment of facts. This may well be Swadling's answer, for he has maintained that '[p]resumptions properly-so-called form part of the law of proof'.[93] If the law of proof is about the establishment of facts, this may well support the contention that a rule of law, such as L1, that requires the courts to

---

[93] William Swadling, 'Explaining Resulting Trusts' (2008) 124 LQR 72, 74.

take as true the proposition 'C is the owner of T' is not part of the law of proof. But it does *not* follow from this that the rule is not a rule of presumption at all. For this to follow, an additional premise is needed, ie that all legal rules of presumption form part of the law of proof. But what considerations support this premise? The answer cannot be that legal rules of presumption necessarily concern proving facts by way of presumption, for this is a circular argument.

The view that the courts may be required, by virtue of a rule of presumption, to take as true a proposition of fact *or* a proposition of law is supported by two considerations. First, no argument has been put forward to establish that propositions which rules of presumption oblige courts to take as true must be propositions of fact. Secondly, legal practice, and the general usage of the term 'presumption', are fully compatible with, and provide support for, the contention that the proposition that is to be taken as true by a court may well be a proposition of law. Rules establishing presumptions of innocence, for example, require courts to take as true certain propositions of law, eg the proposition that the defendant, D, has not committed the criminal offence that D has been charged with. There is, moreover, a plethora of examples in the law reports of courts applying and following rules requiring them to take as true such propositions as 'C is the owner of T', and 'C holds T for an estate in fee simple'. In *Jeffries v Great Western Railway Co*, for instance, Lord Campbell CJ said, 'in truth the presumption of law is that the person who has possession [of goods] has the property'.[94] In *Metters v Brown*, Channell B, giving the judgment of the Court of Exchequer, said:[95]

> [i]t appeared that the plaintiff's mother in her lifetime was in possession of the land ... There was, therefore, evidence from which it would be presumed that she was seised in fee, unless her title was cut down or explained. It was necessary for the plaintiff to rebut the presumption of a seisin in fee.

There are very many more cases in which judges have invoked or relied on presumptions of ownership or presumptions of estates.[96] In such circumstances, the burden is on those who maintain that rules of presumption necessarily concern propositions of fact to advance an argument in support of this contention.

Importantly, it is possible to account for the role of presumptions as a mechanism for proving facts without confining presumptions to that role. We can

---

[94] *Jeffries v Great Western Railway Co* (1856) 5 El & Bl 802, 806; 119 ER 680, 681 (cited with approval in *The Winkfield* [1902] P 42 (CA) 55 (Collins MR)).

[95] (1863) 1 H & C 686, 692; 158 ER 1060, 1062.

[96] See Chapter 4 (section 4.2.2.1) and Chapter 5 (section 5.3).

say that presumptions involve taking propositions as true, and the proposition that is taken as true by a court might be a proposition of fact or a proposition of law. If judicial presumptions are not confined to the role of proving propositions of fact, then it seems there is nothing to prevent us from concluding that a rule requiring courts to presume that a person in possession of chattels has ownership is a rule of presumption. The rule operates in the same way as those rules of presumption that concern propositions of fact; it requires, when the rule applies, the rule-subjects (ie the courts) to take a certain proposition as true.

Interestingly, Thayer argued against the view that rules of presumption belong solely to the law of proof. Presumptions, he said:[97]

> are ordinarily regarded as belonging peculiarly to [the law of proof]. This appears to be an error; they belong rather to a much larger topic, already briefly considered, that of legal reasoning, in its application to particular subjects . . . Presumptions are aids to reasoning and argumentation, which assume the truth of certain matters for the purpose of some given inquiry.

The objection advanced by Swadling and Hickey to the notion of a presumption of ownership incorporates the claim that what is 'assumed' when a presumption is in play *must* be a proposition of fact. But Swadling and Hickey have failed to establish that the concept of a presumption must be so confined. Legal practice and the ordinary usage of the term 'presumption' in legal discourse support the view that it is not.

3.4.2 The Second Argument

The second argument that Swadling has advanced in support of his claim that 'presumption of ownership' is a misnomer is that the '"presumption" cannot be displaced by adducing evidence showing . . . that the claimant is not the "owner". The "presumption" is irrebuttable, and an irrebuttable presumption . . . is nothing but a rule of substantive law'.[98] Now, most scholars who are committed to the Presumed Property View would deny that the 'fee simple presumption' and the 'presumption of ownership' are irrebuttable. We cannot determine whether the (alleged) presumptions are rebuttable without

---

[97] Thayer (n 79) 314.
[98] Swadling, 'Property' (n 8) para 4.426

considering the authorities and, accordingly, this question will not be pursued here.[99] The point to be defended at this stage is that, in any case, Swadling's second argument is not sound. For there can be irrebuttable presumptions. A rule of law might provide that, in certain circumstances, the courts are to take a proposition, q, to be conclusively true. There is no reason, and Swadling provides no reason, to think that there can be no such law. Since the rule provides that the rule-subjects are to take p as true in certain circumstances, it is a rule of presumption.

Neither of Swadling's conceptual objections to presumptions of ownership should be accepted. Swadling has not established that the very idea of a (rebuttable or irrebuttable) presumption of ownership is conceptually wrong-headed or that talk of 'presumptions of ownership' and 'presumed fees simple' is nonsensical. The pertinent question is, then, not a conceptual question; it is a doctrinal question, ie whether English law actually contains such rules of presumption. The debate can be settled only by examining the content of the law.

3.5 Conclusion

This chapter has sought to set up and clear the ground for the enquiry that is to follow into the nature of a possessor's title by examining and contrasting three views. And, with a view to ensuring that this enquiry will not cause further confusion in this area, the chapter has analysed the distinction between a person having an interest in land or chattels and a person being presumed by a court to have an interest; it has defended the claim that this distinction is real and important; and it has explained why certain conceptual objections to the idea of a presumption of ownership should be dismissed. With this work complete, it is time to turn to the legal sources.

---

[99] See Chapter 4 (section 4.2.2). and Chapter 5 (section 5.3).

4

Possession and Title to Land

4.1 Introduction

Frederick Pollock's well-known claim that '[p]ossession is a root of title' was advanced in 1888.[1] This claim has been endorsed by the authors of many modern textbooks,[2] but it was, and still is, controversial. According to AWB Simpson, the traditional view is that 'mere possession is not a root of freehold title.'[3] The acquisition of possession was contrasted with the acquisition of seisin.[4] Suppose that A was seised of Blackacre for an estate in fee simple until 1800, when he was disseised by B.[5] By virtue of the disseisin, B (the disseisor) acquired the fee simple.[6] Conversely, A (the disseisee) lost the estate and acquired a right of entry.[7] He ceased to be seised of the land in fee simple, although he was entitled to be seised in fee simple. His right of entry enabled him to recover the land in ejectment, but this right could not be alienated *inter vivos* or devised by will (though it could be inherited).[8]

In 1896 Charles Sweet claimed that there is a 'fundamental difference between the seisin of a disseisor and the possession of a wrongful or adverse possessor': whereas the disseisor has 'a title in fee simple by wrong which continues until put an end to by the act of the disseisee', the possessor has an interest that

---

[1] Frederick Pollock and Robert Samuel Wright, *An Essay on Possession in the Common Law* (Clarendon Press 1888) 22, 93.

[2] eg Ben McFarlane, *The Structure of Property Law* (Hart 2008) 647; Stuart Bridge, Elizabeth Cooke, and Martin Dixon (eds), *Megarry & Wade: The Law of Real Property* (9th edn, Sweet & Maxwell 2019) paras 7-004–7-013, 7-070; William Swadling, 'Property: General Principles' in Andrew Burrows (ed), *English Private Law* (3rd edn, OUP 2013) para 4.422.

[3] AWB Simpson, *A History of the Land Law* (2nd edn, OUP 1986) 154.

[4] For discussion of the nature of seisin, see Joshua Williams, *The Seisin of the Freehold* (Sweet & Maxwell 1878); Simpson (n 3) 37–44.

[5] For discussion of what constitutes a 'disseisin', see JM Lightwood, *Possession of Land* (Stevens & Sons 1894); 42–56.

[6] ibid 42–43, 270–71; Williams (n 4) 7–8, cited with approval in *Leach v Jay* (1878) 9 Ch D 42 (CA) 44–45 (James LJ); Richard Preston, *Abstracts of Title* (2nd edn, J & W T Clarke 1824) vol 2, 284–85.

[7] FW Maitland, 'The Mystery of Seisin' (1886) 2 LQR 481, 482 (hereafter Maitland, 'Mystery'); Lightwood (n 5) 42, 274.

[8] A right of entry could not be alienated *inter vivos* before 1 October 1845: Real Property Act 1845, s 6. And it could not be devised by will before 1 January 1838: Wills Act 1837, s 3. For discussion of these matters, see Maitland, 'Mystery' (n 7) 483–85.

Possession, Relative Title, and Ownership in English Law. Luke Rostill, Oxford University Press (2021). © Luke Rostill. DOI: 10.1093/oso/9780198843108.003.0004

is 'only co-extensive with his actual possession'.[9] AD Hargreaves, writing in the 1940s, claimed that, while seisin creates a title, possession 'is not a title and gives no such right of action in ejectment as it does in trespass', though a possessor will benefit from a presumption of title in the absence of contrary evidence.[10] The view that possession is not a root of title, but that a possessor of land will benefit from a presumption of freehold title in the absence of contrary evidence, has been defended by modern writers.[11] In a judgment handed down in 2010, Lord Neuberger MR asserted that 'a claimant's previous possession is evidence of his title (or, strictly speaking, of his prior seisin) but it is rebuttable evidence, and if rebutted by other evidence, the right to claim possession dissolves'.[12]

Given all this, it is perhaps unsurprising that the authors of an influential practitioner text on adverse possession state that there are two 'quite different' explanations of the consequences of possession:[13] one is that 'possession itself confers a freehold title'; the other is that 'possession acts as evidence of a lawful title'. This suggests that there are two inconsistent lines of authority and that, as SA Wiren maintained in 1925, 'we can only await . . . the considered and exhaustive judgment of some high tribunal'.[14] This chapter argues, however, that while the law has been persistently debated, it is largely settled and certain. A person actually acquires, through taking possession, a legal fee simple estate. The Strong Proprietary Interest View is, therefore, correct so far as land is concerned. The chapter seeks to marshal new arguments in support of this position and to identify the sources of doubt and error that have led so many eminent lawyers astray. Its primary strategy, pursued in section 4.2, is to examine the incidents of the interest acquired by a possessor with a view to determining whether the interest has the core features of a fee simple estate. We will see that it does, and that the contrary view, defended by 'traditionalists', is plausible only if one relies on historical precedents and ignores the manner in which, and the reasons why, the law developed in the latter half of the 19th century. Section 4.3 considers a number of objections to the view that a possessor of land acquires a fee simple and concludes that these are not convincing. Section 4.4 examines the scope of the acquisition rule and the impact of the registration statutes. We

---

[9] Charles Sweet, 'Seisin' (1896) 12 LQR 239, 249. It appears that Sweet thought that the possessor's interest would cease to be possession-dependent if it was 'perfected' by the expiry of the limitation period.

[10] AD Hargreaves, 'Terminology and Title in Ejectment' (1940) 56 LQR 376, 397.

[11] eg Mark Wonnacott, *Possession of Land* (CUP 2006) ch 3; Nicholas Curwen, 'The Squatter's Interest at Common Law' [2000] Conv 528.

[12] *Mayor of London v Hall* [2010] EWCA Civ 817; [2011] 1 WLR 504 [25] (emphasis added).

[13] Stephen Jourdan and Oliver Radley-Gardner, *Adverse Possession* (2nd edn, Bloomsbury 2011) para 20-16.

[14] SA Wiren, 'The Plea of The *Ius Tertii* in Ejectment' (1925) 41 LQR 139, 158.

will see that the rule is not confined to cases involving adverse possession, and that it applies irrespective of whether there is a registered title to the land.

4.2 The Incidents of a Possessor's Interest

The aim of this section is to establish that the interest acquired by a possessor of land has the core incidents of a legal fee simple estate (ie a fee simple absolute in possession). A legal fee simple estate has four core incidents. First, it comprises: (a) a right to exclusive possession;[15] and (b) what is usually called a right to 'use and enjoy' the land,[16] unless these rights have been acquired by another (as where a fee simple is burdened by a term of years that has taken effect in possession).[17] The right to exclusive possession grounds duties on other persons not to physically interfere with the land.[18] As Lord Templeman said in the context of a discussion of leases,[19] '[a] tenant armed with exclusive possession can keep out strangers and keep out the landlord', though not anyone who has a better right. Similarly, the holder of a fee simple estate, which is not subject to a term of years that has taken effect in possession, is entitled to 'keep out strangers'; that is to say, all the world except those persons, if any, who have a better right.

The second incident is absence of term: the estate is capable of lasting forever.[20] This is what distinguishes a fee simple from a term of years.[21] While a fee simple will determine in a limited set of circumstances, the subsistence of a fee simple is not dependent upon possession. This is the third feature of fee simple estates: they are not possession-dependent. The fourth is that the estate-holder has certain powers of disposition. She can, subject to certain

---

[15] This right may be called a 'right to exclude': see, eg Simon Douglas and Ben McFarlane, 'Defining Property Rights' in James Penner and Henry E Smith (eds), *Philosophical Foundations of Property Law* (OUP 2013). The term 'right to exclusive possession' is used here because it is used in the legal sources, but, in this book, the terms are generally treated as interchangeable.

[16] *Williams v Network Rail Infrastructure Ltd* [2018] EWCA Civ 1514; [2019] QB 601 [40] (Sir Terence Etherton MR). For further discussion of this right, see section 4.2.1 below.

[17] Where the estate holder has been deprived of these rights, the law protects him from 'injury to [his] reversionary interest': *Baxter v Taylor* (1832) 4 B & Ad 72, 76; 110 ER 382, 384 (Parke J). See also *Mayfair Property Co v Johnston* [1894] 1 Ch 508 (Ch). For the purposes of s 1(1)(a) of the Law of Property Act 1925 (LPA 1925), a fee simple that is burdened by a lease still counts as a fee simple absolute in possession: LPA 1925, ss 95(4), 205(1)(xix).

[18] See Simon Douglas, 'The Content of a Freehold: A "Right to Use" Land?' in Nicholas Hopkins (ed), *Modern Studies in Property Law, Volume 7* (Hart 2013) 367.

[19] *Street v Mountford* [1985] AC 809 (HL) 816. See also Susan Bright, 'Leases, Exclusive Possession and Estates' (2000) 116 LQR 7.

[20] Bridge, Cooke, and Dixon (n 2) para 3-008.

[21] Importantly, a fee simple is only *potentially* perpetual: see Ian Williams, 'The Certainty of Term Requirement in Leases: Nothing Lasts Forever' (2015) 74 CLJ 592.

restrictions, convey it to another in her lifetime,[22] or devise it by will.[23] And she can create lesser proprietary interests over the land, including a term of years, an easement, or a restrictive freehold covenant.

The remainder of this section attempts to show that the interest acquired by a possessor of land has these four features. The first is discussed in section 4.2.1; the second, third and fourth in section 4.2.2.

4.2.1 Possession and Rights

The aim of this subsection is to establish that a possessor of land is protected by the law of torts, *not* on the basis of a rule of evidence or presumption, but because a possessor actually acquires, through taking possession, a right to exclusive possession and a right to 'use and enjoy' the land. To achieve this objective, it is clearly necessary to consider the law of torts and, in particular, the law concerning trespass to land, private nuisance, and liability in negligence for damage to property.

The tort of trespass to land consists of the infringement of a duty, owed to another, not to intentionally interfere,[24] physically and directly, with certain land.[25] An interference is 'direct' if it is an immediate result of the defendant's conduct.[26] Since directness is a matter of degree, it is difficult to draw a clear line between 'direct' and 'indirect' interferences. Consequently, the directness criterion has been criticised for being too uncertain.[27] Nevertheless, the law remains, it seems, that an interference with land will amount to a trespass only if the interference is direct.[28]

---

[22] Statute of Westminster the Third (Quia Emptores) 1290; Bridge, Cooke, and Dixon (n 2) para 3-012.

[23] Wills Act 1837, s 3; Bridge, Cooke, and Dixon (n 2) paras 3-012, 13-002.

[24] The interference with the land must be intentional. It is irrelevant whether the duty-ower intends to interfere with another's rights or knows, or should know, that she is doing so. Accordingly, the duty-ower may breach the duty notwithstanding that she reasonably believes that she is permitted to enter the land: *Conway v George Wimpey & Co Ltd* [1951] 2 KB 266 (CA) 273–74 (Asquith LJ); *Jolliffe v Willmett & Co* [1971] 1 All ER 478 (QB).

[25] It seems that, at the present time, an unintentional interference with land may amount to trespass to land if the interference is a direct result of the defendant's negligence: *National Coal Board v J E Evans & Co (Cardiff) Ltd* [1951] 2 KB 861 (CA); *Network Rail Infrastructure Ltd v Conarken Group Ltd* [2010] EWHC 1852 (QB); [2010] BLR 601 [65]–[67] (Akenhead J). But the law is in a state of flux, and the more principled view is that trespass is confined to intentional interferences, and negligent interferences give rise to liability only if they satisfy the conditions of the tort of negligence: *Letang v Cooper* [1965] 1 QB 232 (CA); Simon Douglas, *Liability for Wrongful Interferences with Chattels* (Hart 2011) ch 6 (hereafter Douglas, *Liability*).

[26] *Reynolds v Clarke* (1725) 2 Ld Raym 1399; 92 ER 410.

[27] Thomas W Merrill, 'Trespass, Nuisance, and the Costs of Determining Property Rights' (1985) 14 JLS 13, 33; Douglas, *Liability* (n 25) 100.

[28] *Esso Petroleum Co Ltd v Southport Corp* [1953] 3 WLR 773 (Assizes) 776 (Devlin J); [1954] 2 QB 182 (CA) 195–96 (Denning LJ), 204–05 (Morris LJ); [1956] AC 218 (HL) 241–42 (Lord Radcliffe), 244–45

A long line of cases supports the proposition that trespass to land protects a possessor.[29] In *Cary v Holt*, decided in 1745, the claimant brought trespass and, according to the report, the King's Bench held that the case 'stands upon the plaintiff's possession, which is enough against a wrong-doer'.[30] In 1764, Lord Mansfield CJ, giving the judgment of the King's Bench in *Harker v Birkbeck*, asserted that '[w]hoever is in possession, may maintain an action of trespass, against a wrong-doer to his possession'.[31]

It does not follow from the proposition that a possessor can successfully sue in trespass that a person acquires a legal right by taking possession of land. To determine whether the latter proposition is true, one must consider why a possessor is able to sue. Is it because a person acquires, by taking possession, certain legal rights? Or is it because possession gives rise to a presumption that the possessor has a right in respect of the land? Some legal commentators have given an affirmative answer to the latter question,[32] as have certain judges.[33] However, the proposition that possession is sufficient in trespass, because proof that the claimant was in possession gives rise to a presumption that the claimant has a proprietary interest, is incompatible with a number of cases.

In *Graham v Peat*,[34] for instance, the King's Bench held that, where a person was in possession of land under a void lease, the possessor could maintain trespass *quare clausum fregit* against a stranger. The defendant contended that possession was merely 'prima facie evidence of title' and that, as the claimant entered the land under a void lease, there was contrary evidence before the court.[35] Lord Kenyon CJ rejected this submission. His Lordship averred that '[a]ny possession is a legal possession against a wrong-doer'.[36]

(Lord Tucker). There is disagreement among legal scholars over whether there are good reasons to retain the 'directness' criterion: see, eg Douglas, *Liability* (n 25) 97–110; Christopher Essert, 'Nuisance and the Normative Boundaries of Ownership' (2016) 52 Tulsa Law Rev 85, 113–114; Arthur Ripstein, *Private Wrongs* (HUP 2016) 47–48.

[29] Jonathan Hill, 'The Proprietary Character of Possession' in Elizabeth Cooke (ed), *Modern Studies in Property Law, Volume 1* (Hart 2001) 30–33. A controversial question is whether it is a necessary element of trespass that the claimant is in possession at the time of the alleged wrong. It seems that the law has not wholly abandoned the possession requirement, but the exceptions have almost swallowed the rule: see Charles Mitchell and Luke Rostill, 'Making Sense of Mesne Profits: Causes of Action' (2021) 80 CLJ (forthcoming).

[30] (1745) 2 Strange 1238; 93 ER 1154.

[31] (1764) 3 Burr 1556, 1563; 97 ER 978, 982.

[32] eg JP Taylor, *A Treatise on the Law of Evidence* (JB Matthews and GF Spear eds, 11th edn, Sweet & Maxwell 1920) vol 1, 130–31; Adam Baker, '*Bruton*, Licensees in Possession and a Fiction of Title' [2014] Conv 495, 500–06. (hereafter Baker, '*Bruton*').

[33] eg *Brest v Lever* (1841) 7 M & W 593, 595; 151 ER 904, 905 (Parke B).

[34] *Graham v Peat* (1801) 1 East 244; 102 ER 95.

[35] (1801) 1 East 244, 244–45.

[36] ibid 246.

Lord Kenyon's view was endorsed in *Chambers v Donaldson*.[37] In this case, the claimant brought trespass *quare clausum fregit* against the defendants, who had entered the claimant's dwelling house without the claimant's consent. The defendants pleaded that a third party, Mr Portman, had a freehold title in the house, and that they entered the premises as his servants and by his command. The claimant admitted that the house was Portman's 'soil and freehold', but denied that the defendants were Portman's servants and had entered by his command. The defendants contended that this admission amounted to a concession that the claimant had 'no title to maintain the action'.[38] In response, Bayley J asked: 'Is not actual possession sufficient to maintain the action against a wrong-doer?'[39] The defendants answered that actual possession was sufficient only if, and insofar as, it gave rise to a presumption of title.[40] The King's Bench rejected the defendants's argument. Lord Ellenborough CJ thought it was settled that 'trespass may be maintained by a person in possession against a wrong-doer'.[41] The defendant could not establish that he had not committed the tort simply by showing that a third party had a better title; 'he must also shew that he had the authority of that other'.[42]

In *Graham v Peat* and *Chambers v Donaldson*, the reason that the claimants succeeded was not that the court *presumed* that they had a legal estate in the land, such as a fee simple.[43] The reason the claimants succeeded was because, when the claimants acquired possession, people generally came under a duty not to intentionally interfere, directly and physically, with the land. This reasoning has been accepted and affirmed in many later cases.[44]

The cases also make clear that, in addition to the duty not to physically and directly interfere with land imposed by the law of trespass, people in general are under a duty not to physically damage land in another's possession by failing to take reasonable care.[45] In *The Aliakmon*, Lord Brandon explained that a person is able to 'claim in negligence for loss caused to him by reason of

---

[37] *Chambers v Donaldson* (1809) 11 East 65; 103 ER 929.

[38] (1809) 11 East 65, 67.

[39] ibid.

[40] ibid 67–68.

[41] ibid 74.

[42] ibid 75. See also *Harper v Charlesworth* (1825) 4 B & C 574, 593; 107 ER 1174, 1181 (Holroyd J); *Jones v Chapman* (1849) 2 Exch 803, 154 ER 717; 18 LJ Ex 456.

[43] cf *Harper* (n 42), 585–86 (Bayley J), 593–94 (Holroyd J), 594–95 (Littledale J).

[44] eg, *Harper* (n 42); *Allan v Liverpool Overseers* (1874) LR 9 QB 180 (QB) 191–92 (Blackburn J); *Bristow v Cormican* (1878) 3 App Cas 641 (HL) 651 (Lord Cairns LC), 657 (Lord Hatherley), 660–61 (Lord Blackburn); *Adams v Naylor* [1944] KB 750 (CA) 755 (Scott LJ); *Delaney v TP Smith Ltd* [1946] KB 393 (CA) 397 (Tucker LJ); *National Provincial Bank Ltd v Ainsworth* [1965] AC 1175 (HL) 1232 (Lord Upjohn).

[45] *Leigh & Sullivan Ltd v Aliakmon Shipping Co Ltd (The Aliakmon)* [1986] AC 785 (HL); *Jan De Nul (UK) Ltd v Axa Royale Belge SA* [2002] EWCA Civ 209; [2002] 1 Lloyd's Rep 583.

loss of or damage to property' if, and only if, he 'had either the legal ownership of or a possessory title to the property concerned at the time when the loss or damaged occurred'.[46] Where a person is in possession of chattels or land, 'he is entitled, by virtue of his possessory title . . . to sue in tort for negligence' a person who has damaged the thing by failing to exercise reasonable care.[47]

The law regards the duties owed by the rest of the world not to physically interfere with the land as rights-based, that is, as grounded by the possessor's right to exclusive possession. Consequently, the duty-ower, by breaching one of the duties, infringes the possessor's right.[48] In *Bristow v Cormican*, for instance, Lord Blackburn said: '[a]ctual possession in the *locus in quo* would have been not merely evidence of title, but actually a title against wrongdoers'.[49] More recently, Lord Hoffmann maintained in *Alan Wibberley Building Ltd v Insley* that '[p]ossession is in itself a good title against anyone who cannot show a prior and therefore better right to possession'.[50] Furthermore, it has long been clear that a claimant in ejectment is required to establish that he has, as against the person in possession of the land, a right to possess it and he is required to establish this because the possessor has, by virtue of his possession, a right to exclude the world except those who have a better right. As Lord Mansfield explained in *Roe d Haldane and Urry v Harvey*, 'possession gives the defendant a *right* against every man who cannot shew a good title'.[51] Accordingly, a person acquires, upon obtaining possession of land, a right to exclusive possession as against people generally, but not against a person who has a better right.[52]

A possessor also acquires what is commonly, though somewhat misleadingly,[53] called a right to 'use and enjoy' the land. The fact that a possessor acquires such a right is made clear by the case law concerning the tort of private nuisance. Committing the tort of private nuisance, or at least one subspecies of private nuisance,[54] involves infringing a duty not to unreasonably impair the utility (or 'usability') of the right-holder's land.[55] Such a duty is undoubtedly

---

[46] *The Aliakmon* (n 45) 809.

[47] ibid 812.

[48] cf Baker, '*Bruton*' (n 32) 503–06.

[49] *Bristow* (n 44) 660. See also *Harper* (n 42) 593 (Holroyd J).

[50] [1999] 1 WLR 894 (HL) 898.

[51] (1769) 4 Burr 2484, 2487; 98 ER 302, 304 (emphasis added). See also *Danford v McAnulty* (1883) 8 App Cas 456 (HL) 460–61 (Lord O'Hagan), 462 (Lord Blackburn), 464–65 (Lord FitzGerald).

[52] *Jones* (n 42).

[53] See Donal Nolan, 'The Essence of Private Nuisance' in Ben McFarlane and Sinéad Agnew (eds), *Modern Studies in Property Law, Volume 10* (Hart 2018) 73 (hereafter Nolan, 'Essence').

[54] For present purposes, it is not necessary to determine whether every private nuisance involves impairing the usability of land.

[55] *Hunter v Canary Wharf* [1997] AC 655 (HL) 696 (Lord Lloyd), 706 (Lord Hoffmann); *Williams v Network Rail* (n 16) [40]–[43] (Sir Terence Etherton MR); Donal Nolan, '"A Tort Against Land": Private

owed to a person who is in possession of land.[56] In *Foster v Warblington Urban District Council*, the claimant, who was in possession of certain oyster ponds that were situated upon the foreshore, contended that the defendant, by discharging sewage into the sea near the ponds, had committed the tort of private nuisance.[57] The defendant submitted that the claimant did not have an interest in the ponds that was protected by the law of nuisance. The Court of Appeal held that, since the claimant was in possession of the ponds, the defendants owed him a duty not to unreasonably interfere with the claimant's 'use and enjoyment' of the land, and that the defendants had breached this duty.

Foster was approved by the House of Lords in *Hunter v Canary Wharf*.[58] The law lords held that a private nuisance is a wrong against a person who has a proprietary interest in land, and that the interest that is acquired by obtaining possession of land is protected by the tort. According to Lord Hoffmann, 'only a person with an interest in the land can sue' in private nuisance,[59] and since possession is a root of title, 'the person in possession is entitled to sue in trespass and in nuisance'.[60] Lord Hope and Lord Lloyd also endorsed these propositions.[61] Lord Lloyd, for example, said: 'it is the owner, or the occupier with the right to exclusive possession, who is entitled to sue' in private nuisance;[62] and '*Foster v Warblington Urban District Council* was decided on the basis that the plaintiff's occupation was such that he had the exclusive right to possession'.[63]

It might be argued that, where a private nuisance is committed, the tortfeasor necessarily infringes, not a right to usability, but a right to exclude.[64] However, a right to exclude is infringed only if a duty-ower physically interferes with land; for instance, by intentionally entering and walking there. And, as Christopher Essert and Donal Nolan have claimed,[65] a person may commit the tort of private nuisance *without* physically interfering with land. A person may, for instance, commit private nuisance by carrying out excavations on her

---

Nuisance as a Property Tort' in Donal Nolan and Andrew Robertson (eds), *Rights and Private Law* (Hart 2011); Nolan, 'Essence' (n 53).

[56] *Foster v Warblington Urban DC* [1906] 1 KB 648 (CA); *Hunter* (n 55) 688–89 (Lord Goff), 697 (Lord Lloyd), 703 (Lord Hoffmann), 724 (Lord Hope); *Pemberton v Southwark LBC* [2000] 1 WLR 1672 (CA).
[57] [1906] 1 KB 648 (CA).
[58] *Hunter* (n 55).
[59] ibid 706.
[60] ibid 703.
[61] ibid 723–24 (Lord Hope).
[62] ibid 695.
[63] ibid 697.
[64] See Merrill (n 27) 13–20; Douglas and McFarlane (n 15) 230–32.
[65] Essert (n 28) 94–98; Nolan, 'Essence' (n 53) 79–85.

land that cause her neighbour's undeveloped land to collapse.[66] Where such a nuisance is committed, the tortfeasor does not infringe a right to exclude; she infringes the victim's right to usability (ie the right to 'use and enjoy' the land).

It follows that, according to the common law, when a person obtains possession of certain land, she acquires a right to exclusive possession and a right to 'use and enjoy' the land. The right to exclusive possession grounds duties not to intentionally interfere, physically and directly, with the land and duties not to bring about, through negligence, physical damage to the land. The right to 'use and enjoy' grounds duties not to unreasonably impair the utility of the land. These duties are owed by persons generally.

Of course, to say that a person acquires, upon obtaining possession of land, a right to exclusive possession and a right to 'use and enjoy' the land is not the same as saying that a person acquires, upon obtaining possession of land, a fee simple absolute in possession. And it might be thought that some of the cases discussed in this section are not only consistent with, but actually support and illustrate, the view that there is an important distinction between the rights acquired through possession and estates in land. In *Hunter*, for example, Lord Goff drew a distinction between a person who is in actual possession of land 'either as the freeholder or tenant' and 'a person who is in exclusive possession of land [who] may sue [in private nuisance] even though he cannot prove title to it'.[67] Is this distinction defensible? To work out whether it is, we need to consider whether the possessor's interest is alienable and capable of lasting forever.

4.2.2 Possession-dependence and Alienability

The primary aim of this subsection is to establish that a possessor of land acquires, not mere rights of possession, but an estate in the land, that is, an alienable interest that comprises a right to exclusive possession, and which is not possession-dependent. We have already seen that this has long been—and, to a lesser degree, still is— a controversial claim. One reason for this is that, historically, the rights acquired by a mere possessor of land were possession-dependent. This is demonstrated by the early 19th-century case law concerning who was entitled to recover possession of land in ejectment (from which the modern action to recover possession of land derives). These historical precedents have been invoked to support the claim that, in the modern law, '[m]ere

---

[66] *Hunt v Peake* (1860) Johnson 705; 70 ER 603; *Dalton v Angus & Co* (1881) 6 App Cas 740 (HL).
[67] *Hunter* (n 55) 688.

possession is not a title, and gives no such right of action in ejectment as it does in trespass'.[68] The problem with this view is that it overlooks how the law has changed. The courts eventually accepted, for reasons that will be explained, that a possessor does not have a mere right of possession; he has an estate in the land. Tracing these developments is crucial to understanding the modern law relating to the acquisition of title to land by possession.

4.2.2.1 Possession and ejectment

The late 18th- and early 19th-century case law concerning the recovery of land in ejectment shows that possession was not a source of freehold title. To see this, it is necessary to first understand the nature of ejectment. The action originated in the 14th century as a form of the writ of trespass, which became known as the writ of *ejectione firmae*,[69] and protected lessees of land. By the start of the 16th century, it was established that a successful plaintiff in *ejectione firmae* should recover, if the term had not expired, not merely damages for trespass, but possession of the land.[70]

Ejectione firmae was devised in order to provide greater protection for lessees, but it eventually became 'a new and final common form for the trial of freehold titles'.[71] One driving force behind this development was that, while a freeholder was protected by the real actions, these actions had many undesirable features.[72] Litigants sought to recover land by other means and, in the 17th century, the courts facilitated such manoeuvres by inventing, as Blackstone put it, 'a new and more easy method of trying titles by writ of ejectment';[73] a method that 'entirely depends on a string of legal fictions'.[74] The new practice, which has been attributed to Rolle CJ,[75] involved the courts permitting the possessor to defend the action only if he conceded that the claimant had leased the land to a nominal tenant (usually called 'John Doe'), that the tenant had entered onto the land, and that John Doe was ousted by the nominal defendant (typically called 'John Roe').[76] If the possessor refused to defend the action on

---

[68] Hargreaves (n 10) 397.

[69] John Baker, *An Introduction to English Legal History* (5th edn, OUP 2019) 318 (hereafter, Baker, *English Legal History*); Simpson (n 3) 74–77.

[70] John Baker, *Baker and Milsom's Sources of English Legal History: Private Law to 1750* (2nd edn, OUP 2010) 200(hereafter Baker, *Sources*); Simpson (n 3) 74–75, 92–93, 144–45.

[71] SFC Milsom, *Historical Foundations of the Common Law* (2nd edn, Butterworths 1981) 161. For an example, see *Gerrarde v Worseley* (1580) Dyer 374a; 73 ER 839.

[72] FW Maitland, *Equity; also The Forms of Action at Common Law: Two Courses of Lectures* (CUP 1910) 351–52 (hereafter Maitland, *Equity*); Simpson (n 3) 44–46, 144–45.

[73] 3 Bl Comm 202.

[74] ibid 203.

[75] ibid 202–03.

[76] *Anon* (1652) Style 368; 82 ER 784; 3 Bl Comm 203–04; Maitland, *Equity* (n 72) 353.

behalf of the nominal tenant, judgment would be entered against the nominal tenant by default, with the result that the true defendant would be ousted from the land. At the trial, the claimant was required, as Blackstone explained, 'to make out a clear title, otherwise his fictitious lessee [Doe] cannot obtain judgment to have possession of the land for the term supposed to be granted'.[77] Indeed, as a result of the fictions, the only issue raised at the trial was whether the (true) claimant had a good freehold title as against the defendant.

The law concerning ejectment and the old real actions was reformed by the Real Property Limitation Act 1833 and the Common Law Procedure Act 1852. The 1833 Act was enacted following the publication of the *First Report of the Real Property Commissioners*.[78] The commissioners maintained that '[m]uch perplexity and confusion have ... been occasioned by ... the incongruous variety of remedies allowed for the recovery of real property'.[79] The commissioners proposed that the action of ejectment 'alone, with some improvements, should be retained and extended to all cases'.[80] This recommendation was implemented by section 36 of the 1833 Act, which abolished all real and mixed actions except two writs of dower, *quare impedit*, and ejectment. The Common Law Procedure Act 1852 abolished the fictions in ejectment and introduced a new procedure: section 168 of the Act required a writ to be issued, 'directed to the Persons in Possession by Name, and to all Persons entitled to defend the Possession of the Property claimed, which Property shall be described in the Writ with reasonable Certainty'. The claimant was required to state in the writ that he or she was entitled 'to the possession' of the land and 'to eject all other Persons therefrom'.[81] In 1875 the action of ejectment was, strictly speaking, supplanted.[82] As Lord Denning MR has explained: '[b]y the Supreme Court of Judicature Act 1875, the old action of ejectment was replaced by an action for the recovery of land: but the practice remained the same, although the machinery was different.... The judgment was, as before, that the plaintiff "do recover" possession'.[83]

---

[77] 3 Bl Comm 204.

[78] *First Report made to His Majesty by the Commissioners appointed to inquire into the Law of England respecting Real Property* (1829) House of Commons Papers (Paper No 263) Volume X, 1 (hereafter *First Report*). The Real Property Commissioners were established as a result of Henry Brougham's renowned six-hour speech on the state of the common law: HC Deb 7 February 1828, vol 18, cols 128–258; HC Deb 29 February 1828, vol 18, cols 834–923.

[79] *First Report* (n 78) 8.

[80] ibid 40.

[81] Common Law Procedure Act 1852, s 169, sch A.

[82] Maitland, *Equity* (n 72) 355.

[83] *McPhail v Persons, Names Unknown* [1973] Ch 447 (CA) 458. For a discussion of the 'machinery' that was introduced in 1875, see *Gledhill v Hunter* (1880) 14 Ch D 492 (Ch) 495–500 (Jessel MR).

Prior to the 19th century reforms, it was clear that a claimant who maintained that he had, as against the possessor, a good freehold title to land would succeed in ejectment only if established that he had a right of entry.[84] The reason for this, as John Baker has explained, is that '[t]he fictions enabled the plaintiff to take a short cut only where, on the facts, he could have chosen to go the long way'; and 'since a valid lease could only be granted by a person entitled to enter, the apparatus could not be set up if the real plaintiff had no right of entry'.[85]

There are three important points to be made about rights of entry. First, a right of entry arose in various ways, such as upon an ouster of a freeholder by disseisin.[86] Secondly, a right of entry was enforced either by entry (that is, by entering onto the land) or by action.[87] Thirdly, a right of entry was 'tolled' (ie taken away) in certain circumstances, such as upon a descent cast or discontinuance.[88] A right of entry was also lost upon the expiration of the limitation period under James I's Statute of Limitations.[89] Prior to the abolition of the real actions, a claimant who had lost a right of entry, and thus the ability to recover the land in ejectment, may have been entitled to recover the land by bringing a real action. So, as Maitland pointed out, while 'the man with the better right (the true owner) generally has a right to enter', this was not always the case, because there were situations in which a person with a freehold title 'was entitled to the possession of land but could not bring an action of ejectment for it'.[90] This was the position until 1833 when, as we have seen, almost all of the old real actions were abolished. Since ejectment could not be brought without a right of entry, ejectment could not satisfactorily replace the old actions unless the rules that tolled rights of entry were also amended. Accordingly, section 39 of the Real Property Limitation Act 1833 abrogated the rule that a right of entry is tolled upon a descent cast or discontinuance.

Where a plaintiff in ejectment sought to establish that he had a right of entry derived from a freehold estate, he could provide evidence that he, or his predecessor in title, was formerly in possession of the land. The reason for this is

---

[84] *Roe d Haldane* (n 51); *Berrington d Dormer v Parkhurst* (1811) 13 East 489, 494–95; 104 ER 460, 463 (Lord Hardwicke CJ); *Danford v McAnulty* (n 51) 464–65 (Lord FitzGerald); Maitland, *Equity* (n 72) 354; Simpson (n 3) 146, 149.

[85] Baker, *English Legal History* (n 69) 322.

[86] 3 Bl Comm 175–80.

[87] ibid 175–76.

[88] Simpson (n 3) 151; Milsom, *Historical Foundations* (n 71) 159. For an example, see *Makepiece v Fletcher* (1734) 2 Com 457; 92 ER 1158.

[89] Statute of Limitations 1623 (21 Jac 1, c 16); Simpson (n 3) 150.

[90] Maitland, *Equity* (n 72) 354.

that, as numerous cases decided in the 19th century make clear,[91] proof that a person was in possession of land, or had received rent from an apparent tenant or exercised other 'acts of ownership', even for a short period, was regarded as prima facie evidence that the possessor was seised of the land for a freehold estate; and, in the absence of evidence indicating that the plaintiff had a lesser freehold estate, it was regarded as evidence that the plaintiff was seised for an estate in fee simple.

There is, of course, a distinction between, on the one hand, treating the fact that a person was in possession of land as *evidence* that he was seised of the land for a freehold estate and, on the other, regarding possession of land as giving rise to a *rebuttable presumption* that the possessor was seised of the land for a freehold estate. In the latter case, but not the former, where it is proved that a person is in possession, the trier of fact *must* conclude that the possessor was seised of a freehold estate unless the defendant rebuts the presumption.[92] Unfortunately, however, this distinction has been overlooked by some commentators[93] and has not always been adequately acknowledged by the courts.

Notwithstanding these complications, it does appear to have been established in the first half of the 19th century that, whereas proof that a person had been in possession of land, or had performed other 'acts of ownership', for twenty years or more ('long possession') would give rise to a rebuttable presumption that the possessor was seised in fee,[94] proof that a person had been in possession, or exercised other 'acts of ownership', for a shorter period ('short possession') was merely 'prima facie evidence' that the possessor was seised for a freehold estate.[95] In *Doe d Harding v Cooke*,[96] for instance, the claimant proved that he and his father had let the premises and received the rent for twenty-three years. The defendant proved that he had been in possession since 1819. The court held that, in these circumstances, it would be presumed that the claimant was seised in fee.[97] Tindal CJ said that the 'presumption ... *must*

---

[91] eg *Peaceable d Uncle v Watson* (1811) 4 Taunt 16; 128 ER 232; *Doe d Hall v Penfold* (1838) 8 Car & P 536, 537; 173 ER 607, 608; *Doe d Smith and Payne v Webber* (1834) 1 Ad & El 119; 110 ER 1152; *Doe d Humphrey v Martin* (1841) Car & M 32; 174 ER 395; *Whale v Hitchcock* (1876) 34 LT 136 (DC).

[92] See Chapter 3 (section 3.4).

[93] eg Lightwood (n 5) 114–16, 121.

[94] *Jayne v Price* (1814) 5 Taunt 326, 128 ER 715; *Doe d Harding v Cooke* (1831) 7 Bing 346; 131 ER 134; *Metters v Brown* (1863) 1 H & C 686; 158 ER 1060.

[95] *Doe d Smith and Payne v Webber* (n 91); *Doe d Humphrey v Martin* (n 91); *Whale v Hitchcock* (n 91). Dixon CJ and Kitto J distinguished the effects of 'long possession' and 'short possession' in *Allen v Roughley* (1955) 94 CLR 98 (HCA) 108–09 (Dixon CJ), 139–40 (Kitto J).

[96] *Doe d Harding v Cooke* (n 94).

[97] (1831) 7 Bing 346, 347 (Tindal CJ), 348 (Park J). Bosanquet and Alderson JJ agreed.

prevail till a better title is shown'.[98] Similarly, Park J stated that the presumption 'throws the Defendant upon establishing, if he can, a title of a higher description'.[99]

Doe d Harding v Cooke can be contrasted with *Doe d Humphrey v Martin*.[100] Humphrey brought ejectment to recover possession of five houses and proved at trial that he had received rent in respect of the houses for four or five quarters. Lord Denman CJ, in summing up for the jury, stated that Humphrey 'has given sufficient evidence for me to leave to you, and you are to consider whether this evidence satisfies you, that the lessor of the plaintiff is the owner of this property'.[101]

Where a claimant proved that he was in possession for twenty years or more, the court was required to conclude that the claimant was seised in fee unless there was sufficient evidence to the contrary. In *Metters v Brown*,[102] for example, the claimant brought ejectment in his capacity as the administrator of his mother's estate. The claimant's mother had been in possession of the land from 1819 until her death in 1848. The defendant submitted that, in such circumstances, 'the legal presumption followed that she was seised in fee' and that, consequently, her title passed to her heir, not the claimant.[103] The claimant maintained that his mother had acquired, by a deed of assignment, the residue of a lease of ninety-nine years; that she went into possession under the lease; and that the lease had passed to him, as administrator. The court concluded that, as there was 'clear evidence' that the mother was in possession under a lease, the claimant had rebutted the presumption that his mother had a fee simple.[104]

The discussion above supports the conclusion that, whereas a person in possession of land has long been protected by the law of trespass, a claimant in ejectment had to establish that he had a lease that entitled him to possession or a right of entry derived from a freehold estate. Possession did not, by itself, give rise to a freehold estate, but proof of possession was evidence of, or gave rise to a presumption that, the possessor had such an estate. Accordingly, there was an important distinction between trespass and ejectment. This was recognised by Holroyd J in *Harper v Charlesworth*:

---

[98] (1831) 7 Bing 346, 348 (emphasis added).
[99] ibid.
[100] *Doe d Humphrey v Martin* (n 91). See also *Doe d Hall v Penfold* (n 91).
[101] (1841) Car & M 32, 33.
[102] *Metters v Brown* (1863) 1 H & C 686; 158 ER 1060; (1863) 32 LJ Ex 138.
[103] (1863) 32 LJ Ex 138, 139.
[104] ibid 141 (Channell B).

[t]he plaintiff took no legal estate from the Crown . . . and he could not, therefore, maintain an action of ejectment . . . . The action of ejectment, and the action of trespass are very different in their nature. It is clearly established with respect to private property, that trespass may be brought by a person in the actual possession against a wrong doer.[105]

The same point was made by Patteson J in *Doe d Carter v Barnard*.[106] In His Lordship's view, proof that the claimant had been in possession for thirteen years could suffice in ejectment, but:

[t]he ground however for saying so would not be that possession alone is sufficient in ejectment (as it is in trespass) to maintain the action; but that such possession is prima facie evidence of title and, no other interest appearing in proof, evidence of seisin in fee.[107]

Holroyd J and Patteson J recognised that, according to the law of the early 19th century, a person acquired, simply by taking possession, certain rights of possession. But possession did not give rise to an estate in the land. This analysis fits with what the courts regarded as the primary justification for protecting possession through the law of trespass. This was that such protection served the interests of possessors, and the public interest, by discouraging violence.[108] The protection afforded to possessors was regarded as 'an extension of that protection which the law throws around the person'.[109] Consequently, the possessor was protected for so long as he remained in possession. His rights, in other words, were mere rights of possession.

4.2.2.2 The emergence of a new rule
In the final decades of the 19th century, a number of eminent legal commentators put forward accounts of the law that are markedly different from the law described in section 4.2.2.1. Oliver Wendell Holmes Jr,[110] Frederick Pollock,[111]

---

[105] (1825) 4 B & C 574, 592; 107 ER 1174, 1180.

[106] (1849) 13 Ad & El (NS) 945; 116 ER 1524.

[107] (1849) 13 Ad & El (NS) 945, 953; 116 ER 1524, 1527.

[108] See eg *Cholmondeley v Clinton* (1821) 4 Bligh 1, 75; 4 ER 721, 747 (Lord Redesdale); *Jeffries v Great Western Railway Co* (1856) 4 El & Bl 802, 805; 119 ER 680, 681 (Lord Campbell CJ).

[109] *Rogers v Spence* (1844) 13 M & W 571, 581; 153 ER 239, 243 (Lord Denman CJ). See also *Beckham v Drake* (1849) 2 HLC 579, 613; 9 ER 1213, 1225 (Cresswell J).

[110] Oliver Wendell Holmes Jr, *The Common Law* (Little, Brown and Co 1881) Lecture VI.

[111] Pollock and Wright (n 1) 22, 91–100; for further discussion of Pollock's account, see James Gordley and Ugo Mattei, 'Protecting Possession' (1996) 44 Am J Comp L 293, 300–05; Robin Hickey, *Property and the Law of Finders* (Hart 2010) 106–10 (hereafter Hickey, *Law of Finders*); Robin Hickey,

and JM Lightwood,[112] for instance, all claimed that possession was a source of title. According to Pollock, 'possession confers more than a personal right to be protected against wrongdoers; it confers a qualified right to possess, a right in the nature of property which is valid against every one who cannot show a prior and better right'.[113] This right is 'transmissible' and capable of being inherited, devised or conveyed.[114] In short, '[p]ossession is a root of title'.[115] James Gordley and Ugo Mattei have argued that the 'doctrine that possession gives a kind of title was in fact invented' by Holmes and Pollock.[116] It is argued here that this claim is false. The rule was accepted and applied by the courts many years before Holmes and Pollock published their works. Holmes and Pollock— and Lightwood, too—simply acknowledged that the law had changed. To understand how possession became a source of title, it is necessary to examine *Davison v Gent* and *Asher v Whitlock*. These cases are milestones in the history of title by possession.

4.2.2.2.1 Davison v Gent

Mr and Mrs Coates held certain land (a house and three closes) under a lease for twenty-one years, which was granted by the Dean and Chapter of Durham.[117] Mr and Mrs Coates sublet the land to Davison, who took possession of two closes before he was forcibly turned out of possession by Gent, the defendant. Davison sought to recover possession in an action of ejectment. The defendant provided evidence that, before the purported commencement of Mr and Mrs Coates's lease, the Dean and Chapter of Durham had demised the premises to another party, Sherwood, for a term of twenty-one years, which had not yet expired.

The claimant advanced two points in response. The first was that he was in possession of the land at the time of the defendant's entry and this sufficed to enable him to recover the land from a 'mere wrongdoer'.[118] The second was that Sherwood had surrendered his lease, prior to the demise, to Mr and Mrs

---

'Possession as a Source of Property at Common Law' in E Descheemaeker (ed), *The Consequences of Possession* (Edinburgh UP 2014) 77, 87–91 (hereafter Hickey, 'Possession').

[112] Lightwood (n 5) 111, 123–25, 270–75.
[113] Pollock and Wright (n 1) 93.
[114] ibid 22, 93.
[115] ibid.
[116] Gordley and Mattei (n 111) 294.
[117] (1857) 1 H & N 744; 156 ER 1400; (1857) 3 Jur (NS) 342; (1857) 26 LJ Ex 122; (1857) 28 LTOS 291.
[118] (1857) 3 Jur (NS) 342, 343 citing *Allen v Rivington* (1670) 2 Saund 111; 85 ER 813; *Doe d Hughes v Dyeball* (1829) Mood & M 346; 173 ER 1184. It seems that these authorities do not actually support the submission advanced by the claimant in *Davison*: see Peter Sparkes, 'Title in Ejectment' [2014] Conv 123, 130–32.

Coates.[119] The defendant conceded that 'mere possession is sufficient against a mere wrongdoer' but contended that 'if the [claimant], instead of relying upon his possessory title, attempts to set up a true one, and fails, he cannot recover by force of the possession', at least not where the claimant, in attempting to set up a true title, discloses a 'title in a third party'.[120]

The Court of Exchequer rejected the defendant's arguments. It held that the evidence justified the finding that the prior lease had been surrendered but that, even if it did not, the claimant could rely simply on his possession. According to the report in *The Jurist*, Pollock CB said:[121]

> the fact, that, in addition to his possession, [the claimant] brings forward evidence which fails to make out a perfect title cannot interfere with his right to sue: for a man may have two strings to his bow—he may set up a title in law and also a title by possession.

Similarly, Bramwell B maintained that proof of Davison's 'prior possession' was sufficient against a person who did not have a better title.[122]

There are, for present purposes, three important points to be made about *Davison v Gent*. The first is that the court accepted that, since the claimant was in possession until he was evicted by the defendant, the claimant was entitled to recover the land in ejectment, unless the defendant could establish that he had a better right to possession. The claimant had, in other words, a 'title by possession' that was good as against the defendant,[123] who was a mere 'wrongdoer'.[124] Importantly, the claimant's ability to recover on the basis of his possession was *not* a result of the rule that possession is 'prima facie evidence' of a freehold title. The claimant did not attempt to rely on such a rule. This is not surprising, for the claimant took possession following the purported grant of a lease to him by Mr and Mrs Coates, and he sought to establish a leasehold title. The claimant argued, and the court accepted, that if he did not have a good leasehold title, he was nonetheless entitled to succeed, because his possession gave him a title that could be enforced in ejectment against a person who had wrongfully turned him out. This aspect of the decision has been criticised by

---

[119] (1857) 3 Jur (NS) 342, 343.

[120] ibid.

[121] ibid 344. See also (1857) 26 LJ Ex 122, 125; (1857) 1 H & N 744, 750.

[122] (1857) 26 LJ Ex 122, 125; (1857) 1 H & N 744, 750. The report in *The Jurist* does not state that Bramwell B used the words 'prior possession', but it does allege that Bramwell B said that Davison's 'possession [was] good against' Gent unless Gent established that he had a better title: (1857) 3 Jur (NS) 342, 344.

[123] (1857) 3 Jur (NS) 342, 344 (Pollock CB).

[124] (1857) 1 H & N 744, 750; (1857) 26 LJ Ex 122, 125 (Pollock CB).

commentators. Hargreaves disapproved of it on the ground that a claimant in ejectment *must* establish a right of entry derived from a freehold title, or a right to possession under a chattel interest (eg a term of years)—nothing less will do.[125] Similarly, Peter Sparkes has commented that, while 'prior possession' was a 'pointer to title when adverse or otherwise unexplained', it was itself 'never a title in ejectment', for it failed to demonstrate a title 'sufficient to grant the fictional lease to Doe'.[126]

The second point is that the court, as Sparkes has explained,[127] rejected the contention that a defendant in ejectment can defeat the claimant's claim by invoking the better title of a third party (*jus tertii*). Pollock CB accepted that the claimant's 'title by possession' was sufficient against the defendant.[128] Bramwell B maintained that the claimant, in answer to the defendants' argument, could say, 'it is not for you to set up [a third party's] title against me'.[129] Watson B said that, even if the third party had a better title than the claimant, 'the defendant does not shew a connexion between himself and it'.[130]

Sparkes has contrasted *Davison v Gent* with *Doe d Carter v Barnard*.[131] In *Barnard*, the claimant was in possession of land until the defendant, who did not have a better title, turned her out. The claimant's action in ejectment did not succeed. Patteson J, giving the judgment of the court, maintained that 'possession is prima facie evidence of . . . seisin in fee'; and that, since the claimant had established that her husband was in possession before her for eighteen years, that the husband died in possession, and that he had several children, she had 'by her own shewing proved the title to be in another', namely the husband's heir.[132] Clearly, this reasoning is not compatible with the proposition, which was endorsed in *Davison v Gent* and in numerous later cases,[133] that the dispossessee actually has a right to exclusive possession that can be enforced in ejectment against a dispossessor. Once it is recognised that the dispossessee has such a right—and does not, therefore, need to rely upon a rule of evidence or a rule of presumption—it is obvious that, so far as the claimant's action to recover possession from the defendant is concerned, it is irrelevant

---

[125] Hargreaves (n 10) 391–93.
[126] Sparkes (n 118) 132.
[127] ibid 141–42.
[128] (1857) 3 Jur (NS) 342, 344.
[129] ibid.
[130] ibid.
[131] Sparkes (n 118) 140–42; *Barnard* (n 106).
[132] (1849) 13 Ad & El (NS) 945, 953; 116 ER 1524, 1527. In *Perry v Clissold* [1907] AC 73 (PC) Lord Macnaghten, delivering Their Lordships' judgment, maintained (at 79) that it is 'difficult, if not impossible, to reconcile [*Barnard*] with the later case of *Asher v Whitlock*'.
[133] eg *Asher v Whitlock* (1865) LR 1 QB 1, 5–6 (Cockburn CJ); *Allan v Liverpool Overseers* (n 44) 191–92 (Blackburn J).

that a stranger has a better title. The mere fact that a stranger has a better title has no bearing on the rights of the parties *inter se*: the claimant is entitled to possession as against the defendant, notwithstanding that the stranger is entitled to possession as against the claimant. This is why, as Watson B explained, the defendant needs to show a connection between himself and the third party's right, such as where he defends with the authority of the third party, or derives his own title from the third party.[134] Fortunately, the courts confirmed, in many subsequent cases, that in the absence of such a connection, the fact that a person who is not a party to the action has a better title than the claimant will not prevent the claimant from recovering possession.[135]

The third point is that *Davison v Gent* appears to be incompatible with the view that, by obtaining possession of land, a person acquires 'possessory rights', which will endure only for so long as she remains in possession. Clearly, if A is dispossessed by B and A thereby acquires a right to recover possession from B, A has a right in respect of the land that is *not* possession-dependent. Now, a supporter of the Possessory Right View may well concede this and add that it necessitates only a minor amendment to her view. The possessor's rights, she might say, are *in general* possession-dependent, but if the possessor is wrongfully dispossessed, the possessor has a right to recover possession *from the dispossessor*.[136]

JM Lightwood argued in 1894 that *Davison v Gent* stands for a much broader principle:

> [t]he right of possession . . . rests now on mere possession, and not on seisin alone. This is the real principle which underlies *Davison v Gent*. To say, as was there said, that a plaintiff is entitled to rely on possession as against a mere wrongdoer, is equivalent to giving him a right of possession against strangers, and this right of possession ranks . . . as a species of property. In other words, it is a possessory title which is capable of devise, and which, if not devised, will in general devolve upon the heir.[137]

---

[134] See, eg *Roberts v Tayler* (1845) 1 CB 117, 126; 135 ER 481, 485 (Cresswell J); *Jones v Chapman* (n 42).

[135] eg *Perry v Clissold* (n 132); *Oxford Meat Co Pty v McDonald* [1963] 63 SR (NSW) 423; *Ezekiel v Fraser* [2002] EWHC 2066 (Ch). It is arguable that, where a claimant seeks to recover damages in respect of a tortious interference with land, the defendant should be able to invoke the better title of a stranger in order to diminish the claimant's damages: compare the position in relation to chattels, which is discussed in Chapter 5 (section 5.3.2). This, however, has not been recognised by the courts: see, eg *Nicholls v Ely Beet Sugar Factory* [1931] 2 Ch 84 (Ch) 86–87 (Farwell J).

[136] cf Gordley and Mattei (n 111) 327.

[137] Lightwood (n 5) 124.

Lightwood thought, therefore, that *Davison v Gent* was an authority for the Strong Proprietary Interest View. But this is a mistake, for the court was not asked to consider, and did not consider, whether the rights acquired by a possessor are transmissible. This question was, however, considered by the Queen's Bench in another case cited by Lightwood: *Asher v Whitlock*.[138]

4.2.2.2.2 Asher v Whitlock

Asher v Whitlock is widely regarded as a landmark case, and as the leading decision in this area; but, for various reasons, it is actually a weak authority for the Strong Proprietary Interest View.[139] The case was decided in the Queen's Bench by three judges (Cockburn CJ and Mellor and Lush JJ); only two of the judges provided reasons and, although they were in agreement as to the result, their reasoning is significantly different.[140] The reports tell us that the third judge, Lush J, simply 'concurred'. Moreover, although the Chief Justice's judgment does support the claim that possession gives rise to an estate in the land—a transmissible interest that comprises a right to exclusive possession—his Lordship simply asserted that this was so and did not establish, or even attempt to establish, that this claim was justified as a matter of authority or principle. The scope and justificatory basis of the rule has been debated ever since. Nevertheless, the case has been remarkably influential, and it has been cited with approval by judges in the appellate courts on numerous occasions.[141]

Mr and Mrs Asher brought ejectment against Whitlock to recover possession of certain land that included a cottage and garden. The disputed land had been enclosed, by a Mr Williamson, from the waste of a manor. He enclosed part of it in 1842 and the rest in 1850. Mr Williamson occupied the land until his death in 1860 and devised it, by his will, to his wife for so long as she remained unmarried and, upon her death or second marriage, whichever should occur first, to his only child, Mary Anne Williamson. Following Mr Williamson's death, his widow remained in possession with the daughter and, in 1861, married Mr Whitlock. The three of them occupied the land until, in 1863, Mary Williamson died. The widow died later the same year, and Mr Whitlock continued to occupy the land. In 1865 Mary Williamson's heir-at-law, Mrs Asher, and her husband issued a writ. At the trial, it was proved that a certain person had a better title to all the land at the time of Mr Williamson's

---

[138] (1865) LR 1 QB 1; (1865) 35 LJQB 17; (1865) 11 Jur (NS) 925.

[139] See Hickey, 'Possession' (n 111) 84–87.

[140] Hickey, *Law of Finders* (n 111) 104.

[141] eg *Perry* (n 132) 79; *St Marylebone Property Co v Fairweather* [1962] 1 QB 498 (CA) 529 (Pearson LJ); *Hunter* (n 55) 703 (Lord Hoffmann); *Alan Wibberley* (n 50) 898 (Lord Hoffmann).

death, and that he still had a better title to the part that was enclosed by Mr Williamson in 1850. Nevertheless, the judge, Cockburn CJ, directed a verdict for Mr and Mrs Asher, with leave for the defendant to move to enter a verdict in his favour on the ground that the testator had no devisable interest in the land.

The case came before the Queen's Bench in 1865. Markby, on behalf of Mr and Mrs Asher, made two submissions. First, that a possessor has an interest capable of being inherited, devised, or conveyed.[142] Secondly, that the claimants were not required to establish a title as against the defendant because he had entered by the daughter's permission and was therefore estopped from disputing her title.

Merewether, on behalf of the defendant, submitted that the defendant was not estopped from disputing the claimant's title, and that 'the case is that of two trespassers, and in such a case, the one last in possession is entitled to keep the land until the person having title ejects him; and the devise of the first confers no title on his devisee'.[143]

The Queen's Bench decided that the claimants were entitled to recover possession as against the defendant. Mellor J reasoned as follows:[144]

(1) 'the fact of possession is prima facie evidence of seisin in fee';[145]

(2) the testator, Mr Williamson, was in possession;

(3) therefore, Mr Williamson was, prima facie, seised in fee;

(4) if it were shown that the testator was not seised in fee (because, say, he was a mere tenant at will) the prima facie evidence of seisin in fee would be defeated and the defendant would have succeeded;[146]

(5) but the defendant did not defeat the evidence or presumption of seisin in fee;

(6) therefore, the court is to proceed on the basis that the testator was seised of the land for an estate in fee simple; (7) the testator's interest, his fee simple estate, was, of course, devisable and inheritable;

(8) the fee simple estate was acquired by Mary Williamson when the testator's widow remarried;

(9) Mrs Asher is Mary Williamson's heir-at-law;

(10) therefore, Mrs Asher is entitled to the land for an estate in fee simple and, accordingly, she has a good title as against the defendant.[147]

---

[142] (1865) LR 1 QB 1, 2–3.

[143] ibid 4.

[144] This account combines the steps in Mellor J's reasoning that are articulated in the judgment with a number of propositions that were implicitly accepted.

[145] (1865) LR 1 QB 1, 6; (1865) 11 Jur (NS) 925, 926.

[146] ibid.

[147] (1865) LR 1 QB 1, 6–7.

It should be emphasised that Mellor J's reasoning is consistent with the case law discussed in section 4.2.2.1 of this chapter and, thus, with the rejection of the Strong Proprietary Interest View.

Cockburn CJ took a different approach. His Lordship advanced the following argument:

(P1) Possession gives rise to a title that is 'good against all the world except the person who can show a better title'.[148]

(P2) The possessor 'has a right to devise that estate, which the law gives him against all the world but the true owner'.[149]

(P3) Mr Williamson's title passed under his will to his widow; when the widow remarried, it passed to his daughter; and, upon the daughter's death, it passed to her heir, Mrs Asher.

(P4) Therefore, Mrs Asher has a better right to possession than Mr Whitlock.

The Chief Justice thought P1 was 'clearly established'.[150] His Lordship opined that in *Doe d Hughes v Dyeball* it was decided that one year's possession was 'good against a person who came and turned him out; and there are other authorities to the same effect'.[151] If the defendant, Whitlock, had taken possession of the land when the testator, Mr Williamson, had been in possession of it, 'ejectment could have been maintained by the [the testator] against the defendant'.[152] Thus, his Lordship accepted, in line with *Davison v Gent*, that if A is in possession of land until B takes possession, and A then brings ejectment against B, A can establish that she has a right to recover the land from B simply by proving that she (A) was in possession when B entered.

It is true, as we have seen, that the pre-1865 cases support the proposition that a possessor acquires certain rights, including a right to exclusive possession. By accepting P2, however, the Chief Justice went beyond the trespass cases discussed in section 4.2.1, beyond *Davison v Gent*, and well beyond anything that might be justified by a policy of discouraging dispossessions. His Lordship did not explain why the testator's interest was transmissible. He simply asserted that there 'can be no doubt that a man has a right to devise that estate, which

---

[148] (1865) 35 LJQB 17, 20. See also: (1865) LR 1 QB 1, 5; (1865) 11 Jur (NS) 925, 926.

[149] (1865) LR 1 QB 1, 6. See also: (1865) 35 LJQB 17, 20; (1865) 11 Jur (NS) 925, 926.

[150] (1865) LR 1 QB 1, 5.

[151] ibid, citing *Doe d Hughes v Dyeball* (1829) Mood & M 346, 173 ER 1184. For a fuller report of the case, see: *Doe d Hughes v Dyball* (1829) 3 Car & P 610; 172 ER 567. Cockburn CJ's account of what was decided in *Dyeball* (or *Dyball*) is inaccurate: see Sparkes (n 118) 131–32.

[152] ibid.

the law gives him against all the world but the true owner'.[153] But this is too quick. If the possessor's rights are justified by a concern to protect peaceable possession and discourage violence, it would seem to follow that the right is possession-dependent: the right is lost if and when the possessor ceases to be in possession, though, in the case of a dispossession, the dispossessee has a right to recover possession from the dispossessor in ejectment. If this is an accurate description of the nature and basis of the possessor's interest, why should the right be transmissible? Cockburn CJ did not answer this question.

As we have seen, the jurisprudence of the 18th and early 19th centuries is incompatible with the view that *mere possession* gave rise to an estate in the land. A disseisor, in contrast, acquired a fee simple estate in the land.[154] The Chief Justice referred, both in argument and in his judgment, to the 'old law' of disseisin and noted that 'the disseissor's title was good against all but the disseisee'.[155] It was not argued that the testator in *Asher* was a disseisor, and the court did not decide that he was.[156] The defendant's counsel, in response to the Chief Justice's references to seisin and disseisin, asserted that '[t]his is not the case of a disseisor'.[157] However, the fact that the Chief Justice drew an analogy between possession and the 'old law' of disseisin, and his assertion that a 'possessor' has a 'good title against all the world' except a person with a better title and the 'right to devise [his] estate', show that the Chief Justice thought that possession had become a source of freehold title.

Gordley and Mattei have contended that Cockburn CJ's judgment was not as radical as it appears to be. The Chief Justice, they claim, did not subscribe to 'a theory of relativity of title', but merely 'thought that the possessor could recover in ejectment against one who dispossessed him'.[158] Based, in part, on this reading of Cockburn CJ's judgment, they assert:

> *Asher v Whitlock* . . . established . . . that even the prior possessor who clearly did not have title could recover *against a dispossessor*; that it did not matter if he was dispossessed by force or by occupation of the property without force; and that the rights of the prior possessor could pass by will, and presumably, by contract.[159]

---

[153] ibid 6.
[154] See section 4.1 above and section 4.3.1.2 below.
[155] (1865) LR 1 QB 1, 4, 5.
[156] cf Lightwood (n 5) 111, 124–25.
[157] (1865) LR 1 QB 1, 4.
[158] Gordley and Mattei (n 111) 327.
[159] ibid 326 (emphasis added).

This interpretation of *Asher v Whitlock* is an important part of their argument for the claim that '[i]n no case . . . has an English court allowed a prior possessor, on the strength of his prior possession alone, to recover against a later possessor who neither dispossessed him nor claims the land through someone who did';[160] as well as the associated claim that the doctrine of relative title is an 'invention' of textbook writers and commentators.[161]

The main problem with Gordley and Mattei's interpretation of *Asher v Whitlock* is that, on the facts, there was no dispossession. The testator, Williamson, was not dispossessed: the defendant did not enter until after Williamson had died. The testator's daughter, Mary, was not dispossessed: she was in possession with the testator's widow and the widow's husband, Whitlock, until she died. And Mary's heir, Mrs Asher, was not dispossessed: she had never been in possession and could not, therefore, have lost possession. The better view, therefore, is that Cockburn CJ meant what he said: the testator had a right to possession that was 'good against *all the world* except the person who can shew a good title'; this right passed to the testator's daughter and, thereafter, it was inherited by the daughter's heir, Mrs Asher. So, Mrs Asher, who had never been in possession, acquired a right to possession that was 'good against all the world except the person who can shew a good title.' If this is right, it is obviously a mistake to claim that Mrs Asher acquired a right that bound only the dispossessor and those who claimed through him.

While Gordley and Mattei's interpretation of the case is unsatisfactory, it is true that the claim that possession of land gives the possessor an estate in the land was advanced by just one of the judges, Cockburn CJ; and His Lordship did not consider the justificatory basis of the purported rule, its scope, or the exact nature of the interest acquired.[162] Moreover, the court's decision is arguably compatible with the orthodox view of the law. As we have seen, Mellor J reached the same conclusion as Cockburn CJ by invoking the long-established rule that possession is 'prima facie evidence' of seisin in fee. This explains why Wiren thought that *Asher v Whitlock* is 'quite consistent . . . with the decisions that possession is prima facie evidence of title . . . The only difficulty is a certain wideness of language in the judgment of Lord Cockburn.'[163] Hargreaves put the point in stronger terms. He contrasted Mellor J's 'unexceptionable statement of the law' with Cockburn CJ's 'completely misleading' account.[164] The

---

[160] ibid 327.
[161] ibid 294, 301, 319–20.
[162] See Hickey, 'Possession' (n 111) 85.
[163] Wiren (n 14) 156.
[164] Hargreaves (n 10) 387.

accuracy of these descriptions may be debated, but the remarkable truth, which Hargreaves did not acknowledge, is that the creative reasoning of Cockburn CJ ultimately superseded the 'unexceptionable' reasoning of Mellor J.

4.2.2.3 Alienability and possession-dependence: the modern law

Cockburn CJ's view that possession gives rise to an alienable interest in land, which comprises a right to exclusive possession that binds everyone except those who have a better title, was accepted and applied in many subsequent cases.[165] In *Clarke v Clarke*,[166] for example, a testator had devised lands to his son, A, subject to the proviso that, if A took up with a Roman Catholic or died without a lawful heir, the lands were to go to B. A took up with a Roman Catholic and died without a lawful heir and, after his death, B brought eject-ment against A's devisee, C. It was submitted by B that A had no devisable in-terest, but the court rejected this. Lord Whiteside CJ, delivering the judgment of the court, said: 'the case of *Asher v Whitlock* proves that a person in pos-session of land, without any other title than such as [A] had, after condition broken, has a devisable interest'.[167]

Rosenberg v Cook is an even stronger authority for Cockburn CJ's view.[168] The claimant entered into a contract of sale with the defendant whereby the claimant agreed to purchase certain 'freehold building land' from the de-fendant. The defendant had purchased the land from a railway company, which had no power to sell it. The contract of sale between the claimant and de-fendant contained a number of conditions of sale, including that the claimant should send any objections that he might have to the defendant's title within seven days from the delivery of the abstract. The claimant made no objection in respect of the title until after the expiration of seven days, when he objected that the conveyance was void because the defendant's predecessor in title (the railway company) had no power to sell. The claimant brought an action to re-cover the deposit.

The defendant argued in the Court of Appeal that the claimant was barred by the conditions of sale from objecting to the title after seven days had ex-pired.[169] The claimant, on the other hand, contended that the 'conditions as to

---

[165] eg *Clarke v Clarke* (1868) IR 2 CL 395 (QB); *Ex p Winder* (1877) 6 Ch D 696 (Ch) 700–01 (Hall VC); *Rosenberg v Cook* (1881) 8 QBD 162 (CA); *Dalton v Fitzgerald* [1897] 2 Ch 86 (CA) 90–91 (Lindley LJ); *Mount Carmel Investments Ltd v Peter Thurlow Ltd* [1988] 1 WLR 1078 (CA) 1086. See also: *Perry* (n 132); *Hawdon v Khan* (1920) 20 SR (NSW) 703 (NSWSC) 707 (Cullen CJ), 712–13 (Ferguson J); *Wheeler v Baldwin* (1934) 52 CLR 609 (HCA); *Allen* (n 95).
[166] *Clarke* (n 165).
[167] ibid 401.
[168] *Rosenberg* (n 165).
[169] ibid 164.

time apply to objections as to the degree of the title: here there is a want of title altogether, and a total failure of consideration'.[170] The defendant purported to sell 'freehold land ... quite ready for building operations', but only had a 'revocable licence'.[171]

The Court of Appeal rejected the claimant's argument. It held that the claimant's objection was within the scope of the relevant condition of sale, because it was an objection to the defendant's title and, therefore, the claimant was not entitled to recover the deposit. Sir George Jessel MR said:

> the title of the disseisor is in this country a freehold title, and therefore, although the vendor had a very bad title, and a title liable to be defeated, he had still a title good against all the world, except against those who might be proved to have a better one.[172]

We have already seen that, historically, a disseisor acquired a freehold estate. But the Court of Appeal did not decide that the defendant in *Rosenberg v Cook* was a disseisor. Brett LJ thought that 'the defendant had more than an easement or a recoverable licence. He had possession of all the land above the tunnel'.[173] His Lordship added that it was 'not necessary to decide' whether time was running in the defendant's favour, against the railway company, under the limitation statutes.[174] What mattered was that the defendant 'had a possession of some kind, and he assumed to sell it [ie his possession] by a right *similar to* that of a disseisor or trespasser'.[175] Therefore, the objection 'was an objection to title, and was taken too late'.[176] Cotton LJ's reasoning was, in all material respects, the same as Brett LJ's.[177] It is not entirely clear whether Jessel MR's analysis differs from Brett and Cotton LJJ's. For, while Jessel MR pointed out that a disseisor obtains a 'freehold title', he also said that the defendant had 'only bare possession' and 'a fair sale of that possession is perfectly good'.[178] These remarks suggest that Jessel MR, like Cockburn CJ in *Asher v Whitlock*, thought that an analogy could be drawn between the consequences of possession and the consequences of disseisin.

---

[170] ibid.
[171] ibid.
[172] ibid 165.
[173] ibid.
[174] ibid 166.
[175] ibid (emphasis added).
[176] ibid.
[177] ibid.
[178] ibid 165.

The judgments in *Rosenberg* do not illuminate the nature of the vendor's interest as well as they might have done. What is clear is that all three judges thought that the vendor, who had taken possession of the land under a void conveyance from the railway company, had an interest in the land that could be, and was, conveyed to the purchaser, and that the purchaser's objection was an objection to the vendor's 'title'. The case is clearly an authority, therefore, for the proposition that possession gives rise to an alienable interest in the land.

The case law that illustrates that a possessor has an alienable interest also supports the contention that the interest acquired by possession is not possession-dependent. Consider *Asher v Whitlock*.[179] If, as Cockburn CJ maintained, Williamson, by taking possession of the land, acquired an interest in the land that passed to his widow, then to his daughter, and then to the claimants, the interest could not have been possession-dependent. The claimants acquired the interest notwithstanding that they were not, and never had been, in possession. They did not have a mere right of possession.

The question as to whether the interest acquired by a possessor is possession-dependent was considered by the High Court in *Ezekiel v Fraser*.[180] Ryehurst Ltd was the registered proprietor of a freehold estate in 17 Wingfield Street, London. The company was dissolved in 1998 and, thereupon, its estate vested in the Crown. The claimants had been in possession of the land for approximately sixteen years, ending in February 1999. Thereafter, it was occupied by various squatters. In October 2000, Fraser went into possession and undertook substantial work at a cost of £50,000. Shortly after Fraser had made the premises habitable, the claimants brought possession proceedings against various parties, including Fraser. Master Moncaster gave summary judgment for the claimants and the defendants appealed. HHJ Rich QC, having considered a number of authorities, including *Asher v Whitlock*, maintained that the claimants 'are entitled to rely on their prior possession as entitling them to claim to be restored to possession against an intruder with no right, and the *jus tertii* of the Crown ... is irrelevant'.[181] His Honour did 'not see how the possibility, as a matter of fact, that the claimants had already been dispossessed by squatters could make any difference'.[182]

Regrettably, Judge Rich went on to allow the defendants' appeal. His Honour maintained that the claimants' claim should be treated 'as a claim in trespass'; that, if Fraser obtained possession, 'the presumption [of title] favours him'; and

---

[179] *Asher* (n 138).
[180] *Ezekiel* (n 135). See also *Hawdon* (n 165).
[181] *Ezekiel* (n 135).
[182] ibid.

that the question as to whether Fraser obtained possession as a result of the claimants having stood by while Fraser carried out works, was a question of fact which should be tried.[183] This aspect of Judge Rich's reasoning is highly problematic. It is difficult to see how it is consistent with the proposition, accepted earlier in the judgment, that, even if the claimants had been dispossessed by squatters before Fraser entered, the claimants' 'prior possession gives them a better right to possession than the defendant could claim when he took possession'.[184] If the claimants' prior possession gave them a better right, it should not matter, for the purposes of the claimants' claim to recover possession, whether Fraser had obtained possession as a result of the claimants' failure to intervene at an earlier stage; nor should it matter whether the claimants would have been able to recover damages for trespass. As Master Moncaster recognised, the relevant question was whether the claimants could 'prove a better title', and 'earlier possession is a better title'.[185]

4.2.3 The Incidents of a Possessor's Interest: Conclusions

The main conclusion of this section is that, as a result of judicial innovation in the second half of the 19th century, the interest acquired by a possessor of land has the four core features of a legal fee simple estate. It comprises a right to exclusive possession, and the concomitant right to 'use and enjoy' the land. It is capable of lasting forever and will not automatically determine if and when the interest-holder ceases to be in possession. And it can be conveyed *inter vivos* or devised by will. Given all this, it is not surprising that a number of judges in the senior courts have asserted that a possessor acquires a legal estate: a fee simple absolute in possession. In *Central London Commercial Estates Ltd v Kato Kagaku Co Ltd*, for example, Sedley J said 'a squatter's title is a freehold'.[186] In *Turner v Chief Land Registrar*, Roth J decided that, if an adverse possessor had an estate in the land, it could only be an 'estate in fee simple absolute in possession';[187] and that, since section 15(3) of the Land Registration Act 2002 provides that no caution against first registration 'may be lodged . . . by virtue of ownership of . . . a freehold estate', an adverse possessor could not lodge a

---

[183] ibid.
[184] ibid.
[185] ibid.
[186] [1998] 4 All ER 948 (Ch) 951. See also *Fairweather v St Marylebone Property Co Ltd* [1963] AC 510 (HL) 535 (Lord Radcliffe).
[187] [2013] EWHC 1382 (Ch); [2013] 2 P & CR 12 [13].

caution against first registration. It was not necessary for Roth J to determine whether the adverse possessor actually had a legal estate in the land (for the registrar conceded that he did), but Roth J expressed his approval of the view that the squatter had a fee simple absolute in possession.[188] This view has also been endorsed by the Law Commission,[189] and certain provisions of the Land Registration Act 2002 appear to presuppose its correctness.[190]

It should not be thought, however, that a universal consensus has been reached. The failure of certain judges in the senior courts to appreciate the legal significance of the developments that occurred in the latter part of the 19th century has caused much confusion. The judgment in *Ezekiel v Fraser*, discussed above,[191] provides one example of this.[192] Eminent judges have continued to deny that, through taking possession, the possessor actually acquires a legal fee simple estate.[193] It is necessary, therefore, to examine the arguments that might lead one to reject the claim that possession is a source of freehold estates.

4.3 Objections to the Strong Proprietary Interest View

This section examines four objections to the claim that a possessor acquires a fee simple absolute in possession. It contends that none of the objections provide a sufficiently strong reason for rejecting this claim.

4.3.1 The Illegitimate Judicial Innovation Objection

One objection to the contention that possession is a source of freehold title is that the legal authorities on which the claim is based departed, without good reason, from foundational and well-established legal principles. Hargreaves, for example, objected to the view that mere possession gives rise to a freehold title on the ground that it is not compatible with 'principles which are the foundations of our law and from which we depart at our peril'.[194] Nicholas Curwen

---

[188] [2013] 2 P & CR 12 [14]–[20].
[189] Law Commission, *Land Registration for the Twenty-First Century: A Consultative Document* (Law Com No 254, 1998) para 10.22.
[190] eg Land Registration Act 2002, sch 6(9)(1).
[191] section 4.2.2.3.
[192] For another example, see *Re Atkinson and Horsell's Contract* [1912] 2 Ch 1 (CA) 9 (Cozens-Hardy MR), 17 (Fletcher Moulton LJ).
[193] eg *Hawdon* (n 165) 712–13 (Ferguson J); *Mayor of London* (n 12) [25] (Lord Neuberger MR).
[194] Hargreaves (n 10) 397–98.

claimed that the view that a possessor acquired a new fee simple estate in the land and that, consequently, there could be more than one such estate in the same land 'overlooks the survival of the old law and substitutes complexity for simplicity'.[195]

A satisfactory response to these critics must explain why there was a need for judicial innovation of the kind illustrated by Cockburn CJ's judgment in *Asher v Whitlock*. It is argued below that the legal changes brought about by the courts in the latter part of the 19th century were necessitated by, and intended to further, purposes that Parliament had embraced when, and through, enacting the Real Property Limitation Act 1833 and the statutes that superseded it.

4.3.1.1 The Limitation Acts

The 1833 Act was enacted following the publication of the *First Report of the Real Property Commissioners*.[196] The commissioners concluded that the law of limitation as it applied to land was 'very unsystematic and very defective'.[197] The commissioners' chief complaint was that the various actions for the recovery of real property were subject to different limitation periods. Accordingly, the commissioners maintained that the period of limitation should be twenty years, subject to a small number of exceptions.[198]

Many of the commissioners' recommendations regarding actions for the recovery of land and the limitation of such actions were implemented by the Act of 1833. Section 2 established the general rule that an action to recover land must be brought within twenty years from the moment the right to bring the action accrued. A number of the Act's provisions concerned the determination of the date of accrual of rights to make an entry, or to bring an action to recover land.[199] It is not necessary to fully consider these provisions here. It is sufficient to note that section 3 of the Act provided, among other things, that where a person with an estate or interest was in possession until he was dispossessed, his right of action shall be 'deemed to have first accrued' at the time of the dispossession.

What consequences followed upon the expiration of the statutory limitation period? Importantly, the commissioners had recommended that 'wherever by the provisions aforesaid all remedy is barred, the right shall be considered as

---

[195] Curwen (n 11) 547.
[196] *First Report* (n 78).
[197] ibid 39.
[198] ibid 42, 44–45, 77–78.
[199] For discussion of how the date of accrual of the right to make an entry or bring an action under the Real Property Limitation Act 1833 (as amended) was determined, see Lightwood (n 5) 180–247.

extinguished to the party out of possession, and absolutely vested in the party in possession'.[200] However, this recommendation was not fully implemented. The Act of 1833 did not provide that, upon the expiration of the limitation period, 'the right'—or, as the Commissioners called it elsewhere in the report, 'the title'[201]—of the person against whom time had run would be 'absolutely vested in the party in possession'. Rather, section 34 provided that, at the end of the limitation period, the 'Right and Title' of the person against whom time has run 'shall be extinguished'.

The scheme introduced in 1833 is still with us, though it has been amended in various respects. Section 1 of the Real Property Limitation Act 1874 replaced the period of twenty years in the general limitation rule with a period of twelve years. The Real Property Limitation Acts were repealed by, and replaced with, the Limitation Act 1939.[202] The 1939 Act contained provisions that were similar to those outlined above.[203] But there is an important difference between the 1939 Act and the earlier Acts: the 1939 Act used the term 'adverse possession' and adopted, in sections 10(1) and 10(2), a principle that had long been recognised at common law;[204] namely that, in order for the statutory limitation period to run against a right-holder, there must be a person 'in whose favour or for whose protection the Act could operate'.[205]

The Limitation Act 1939 was itself repealed by, and replaced with, the Limitation Act 1980, which contains provisions that are materially the same as those in the 1939 Act.[206] The modern equivalent of section 34 of the 1833 Act is section 17 of the 1980 Act, which states that 'at the expiration of the period prescribed by this Act for any person to bring an action to recover land . . . the title of that person to the land shall be extinguished'.[207]

The Land Registration Act 2002 radically altered the law of adverse possession so far as registered land is concerned.[208] One notable difference between the rules discussed above and the rules that apply to registered land is that, under the latter, a form of statutory transfer takes place.[209] Where a person is

---

[200] *First Report* (n 78) 81.
[201] ibid 52.
[202] Limitation Act 1939 (LA 1939), sch.
[203] LA 1939, ss 4–5, 16.
[204] *M'Donnell v M'Kinty* (1847) 10 Ir LR 514; *Agency Co Ltd v Short* (1888) 13 App Cas 793 (PC); *Moses v Lovegrove* [1952] 2 QB 533 (CA) 539 (Sir Raymond Evershed MR).
[205] *M'Donnell v M'Kinty* (n 204) 526 (Blackburne CJ).
[206] Limitation Act 1980 ss 15, 17, sch 1.
[207] This is subject to the rules in s 18, which concern trusts of land and settled land. Before the commencement of the Land Registration Act 2002 (LRA 2002), s 17 was also subject to s 75 of the Land Registration Act 1925.
[208] LRA 2002 ss 96–98, sch 6.
[209] LRA 2002, sch 6(4), (5)(1), (7), (9).

in 'adverse possession' of land as against the registered proprietor of an estate, time does not run in the possessor's favour under the Limitation Act 1980.[210] Instead, after at least ten years' adverse possession, the possessor can apply to the registrar to be registered. If the application is successful, the possessor is entered in the register as the 'new proprietor of the estate'; the possessor thereby takes the place of the original proprietor, and the title that the possessor acquired through possession is destroyed.[211] Thus, the 2002 Act transformed the law of adverse possession in relation to registered land. With regard to unregistered land, however, the law of adverse possession has not fundamentally changed since 1833.

4.3.1.2 The source of a squatter's title

In connection with unregistered land, a central objective of the doctrine of adverse possession—and, in particular, the rule that extinguishes a person's title at the end of the statutory limitation period—is to provide greater certainty as to who has a good title to land and greater security to proprietors.[212] When the Bill that became the 1833 Act was passing through Parliament, Lord Lyndhurst informed the House of Lords that the principle on which the Bill was founded 'owed its origin to the necessity, or at least the convenience, of quieting titles to property';[213] and that it was necessary or convenient to quieten titles to land because, among other things, 'evidence of title to property, however good that title was, might be lost', and 'the witnesses required to prove it might die'.[214] Moreover, the Bill would 'give security in possession, and, consequently, ease in letting, and facility in conveying, property'.[215] For these objectives to be achieved, it is not enough to simply destroy the title of the person against whom time has run. The law must, in addition, confer a title on one or more others. There can be no doubt that Lord Lyndhurst appreciated this, for his Lordship told the House that the Bill was 'founded on [the] principle . . . that a long period of adverse possession should *give* an indefeasible right to the property'.[216] How, then, does a person who is an adverse possessor of unregistered land acquire a 'right to the property'?

---

[210] LRA 2002, s 96.

[211] LRA 2002, sch 6(4), (5)(1), (7), (9).

[212] *First Report* (n 78) 39, 41; Martin Dockray, 'Why Do We Need Adverse Possession?' [1985] Conv 272.

[213] HL Deb 14 June 1833, vol 18, col 790.

[214] ibid.

[215] HL Deb 14 June 1833, vol 18, col 792.

[216] HL Deb 14 June 1833, vol 18, col 790 (emphasis added).

For some time after the enactment of the 1833 Act, a number of eminent lawyers accepted, or appeared to accept, what is called the 'parliamentary conveyance theory'.[217] On this view, upon the expiration of the statutory limitation period, the estate of the person against whom time has run is automatically conveyed, by operation of the statute, to the person in possession. This theory was, however, forcefully rejected by the Court of Appeal in *Tichborne v Weir*, on the ground that it is not compatible with the statute.[218] Lord Esher MR said, '[t]he effect of the statute is not that the right of one person is conveyed to another, but that the right is extinguished and destroyed'.[219] This has been endorsed and reaffirmed by the courts on many occasions.[220]

Moreover, as AWB Simpson has said, 'there was nothing in the statute of 1833 or in any later statute which expressly abrogated the old common-law rule that mere possession is not a root of freehold title'.[221] This led many commentators to assert that possession is not itself a source of an estate in the land; and that, since a disseisor acquires an estate in fee simple,[222] a possessor will acquire such an estate if she was a disseisor, but not if she was a mere possessor.[223] This view has not disappeared. Curwen, for instance, claimed in 2000 that 'the essence of the old [ie pre-1833] scheme survives': the act of disseisin gives the disseisor the existing fee simple, and the disseisee retains merely a 'title to the estate' and a right of entry.[224] Upon the expiration of the limitation period, the disseisee's title and right of entry are 'extinguished'.[225] The fee simple is not extinguished; by virtue of the disseisin, it is vested in the disseisor.

A major objection to Curwen's view is that, while seisin played a fundamental role in the law of real property for many centuries,[226] it is now obsolete.[227]

---

[217] See, eg *Doe d Jukes v Sumner* (1845) 14 M & W 39, 42; 153 ER 380, 381 (Parke B); AC Meredith, 'A Paradox of Sugden's' (1918) 34 LQR 253, 255–57; JCW Wylie, 'Adverse Possession: An Ailing Concept' [1965] NILQ 467, 471–75; Una Woods, 'Adverse Possession of Unregistered Leasehold Land' (2001) 36 IJNS 304, 305.

[218] (1892) 67 LT 735 (CA).

[219] ibid 737.

[220] eg *Dalton* (n 165) 89–90 (Lindley LJ); *Re Atkinson* (n 192) 9 (Cozens-Hardy MR), 17 (Fletcher Moulton LJ); *Fairweather* (n 186) 535 (Lord Radcliffe), 544 (Lord Denning), 553 (Lord Morris). If a person is in adverse possession as against a lessee, upon the expiry of the limitation period, the lease is extinguished as against the squatter, but not as against the landlord: *Fairweather* (n 186); *Chung Ping Kwan v Lamb Island Developments Co Ltd* [1997] AC 38 (PC).

[221] Simpson (n 3) 154.

[222] See Lightwood (n 5) 42–44, 72–73, 108, 270–71; *Leach* (n 6).

[223] eg Hargreaves (n 10).

[224] Curwen (n 11) 529–31, 535–47. Curwen defines a 'title to an estate' as a 'claim to an estate supported by appropriate evidence': Curwen (n 11) 530.

[225] ibid 531.

[226] Simpson (n 3) ch 2; Baker, *English Legal History* (n 69) 247–58; John Hudson, *The Oxford History of the Laws of England, Volume II: 871–1216* (OUP 2012) chs 14, 23, 24.

[227] Sweet (n 9). Sweet concluded that, for all purposes bar two, seisin is 'obsolete in everything but name': Sweet (n 9) 251. The two exceptions concerned conveyances of land by feoffment and curtesy.

Curwen concedes that '[a]lmost all the important legal consequences which flowed from seisin seem to have been abolished'.[228] He claims, however, that seisin 'survives as an empty shell', and that '[i]ts sole surviving function' is to determine who holds the fee simple in cases involving squatters: the squatter will acquire the fee simple if her entry amounts to a disseisin.[229] This gives rise to three significant problems. First, it overlooks the post-1833 case law, which, as we have seen,[230] supports the proposition that *possession*—irrespective of seisin—gives rise to an estate in the land. A second problem, related to the first, is that Curwen's account of the role that seisin plays in the modern law presupposes that two (or more) fees simple cannot exist concurrently in the same land. Curwen does not overlook this point: indeed, he argues that it is correct.[231] He notes that Bernard Rudden has claimed that, in the modern law, two or more fees simple may exist in respect of the same land.[232] Rudden's central point is that the content of the interest retained by an ousted freeholder changed over the course of the 19th century.[233] Historically, a desseisee was left with a mere right of entry that could not be devised or conveyed.[234] Today, however, a freeholder who has been dispossessed retains her estate. She retains a right to exclusive possession that is capable of lasting forever, and it can be conveyed *inter vivos*, or devised by will. Curwen's response to this is that such a change could not occur without 'an express statutory reform to that effect'.[235] This might strike one as confused; as Rudden explained,[236] the nature of an ousted freeholder's interest *was* expressly amended by Acts of Parliament. It seems that, for Curwen, it is not enough for Parliament to alter the content of the interest: it must actually state that there can be two fees simple in the same land. But this is mistaken. If, as a result of statutory and judicial reforms, the dispossessor and the dispossessee each hold an interest that has the constitutive features of a fee simple estate,[237] it follows, logically, that the effect of those reforms is that more than one fee simple may exist in respect of the same land.

Curtesy has been abolished. And it has not been possible to convey land by feoffment since 1925: Law of Property Act 1925, s 51(1).

[228] Curwen (n 11) 536.
[229] ibid.
[230] section 4.2 above.
[231] Curwen (n 11) 535–36.
[232] Bernard Rudden, 'The Terminology of Title' (1964) 80 LQR 63, 66–72.
[233] ibid 66–68.
[234] See section 4.1 above.
[235] Curwen (n 11) 536–37.
[236] Rudden (n 232) 67.
[237] Of course, one might object that, even after the statutory reforms, some essential element of a fee simple estate, such as tenure, is missing. Tenure is considered in greater detail below: see section 4.3.2.

A third problem is that the Real Property Limitation Act 1833 provided that the claimant's right to recover the land must be exercised within a certain number of years from the moment when the defendant (or his predecessor) acquired *possession*. Therefore, the running of time and, consequently, the extinction of title, depend upon possession; whether the defendant obtained seisin was, and is, irrelevant.[238] If seisin were the basis of the squatter's title, there would be a disconnect between the rules concerning the extinction of title by adverse possession and the rules concerning the acquisition of title by squatters. A related point is that one of the objectives of the 1833 Act was to '[render] useless the vast mass of technical learning connected with' the real actions,[239] which were founded on seisin. This aim would not have been achieved if the acquisition of title by a squatter depended upon seisin.

If the rules of seisin are not to be invoked to explain the acquisition of title by an adverse possessor, a point made earlier resurfaces: the statutory scheme would not have worked as it was intended to—the 1833 Act's objectives would not have been achieved—unless, in one way or another, the law conferred a new title. Since the 1833 Act did not confer a title on the possessor—or, for that matter, on anyone else—the Act, as Sparkes has pointed out, created a 'vacuum' that needed to be filled.[240] Cockburn CJ and the judges that followed him filled the statutory lacuna by recognising that possession is a root of title: a squatter acquires an estate in the land when she obtains, and by virtue of obtaining, possession of the land. Whatever its imperfections, a real advantage of this approach is that it provides a solution to the problem created by the Act, and facilitates the achievement of the Act's objectives, without invoking the anachronistic doctrine of seisin. It gives effect to Lord Lyndhurst's view that 'a long period of adverse possession should give an indefeasible right to the property'. The squatter, through taking possession, acquires a fee simple estate in the land. Consequently, the statute, by 'extinguishing' the interest of the person against whom time has run, improves the position of the possessor: possibly, though not necessarily, by leaving the possessor with an 'indefeasible right to the property'.

This, however, is a different objection—one based, not on how legal changes are brought about, but on what legal changes have actually occurred.

[238] *Nepean v Doe d Knight* (1837) 2 M & W 894, 911; 150 ER 1021, 1028 (Denman CJ); *J A Pye (Oxford) Ltd v Graham* [2003] 1 AC 419 (HL) [33]–[35] (Lord Browne-Wilkinson); Simpson (n 3) 153–54.

[239] *First Report* (n 78) 42.

[240] Sparkes (n 118) 137, 139.

4.3.2 The Objection based on the Doctrine of Tenure

The second objection to the claim that a possessor acquires a legal fee simple estate is that it is inconsistent with the doctrine of tenure. Curwen, for instance, has claimed that 'the doctrine of tenure . . . prevent[s] the creation of more than one fee simple in any plot of land.'[241] This, he argues, is a result of the universality of tenure and the fact that 'the fee simple estate . . . must originate in a Crown grant.'[242]

It is trite law that tenure—the relationship of lord and tenant whereby the tenant holds land of his or her lord—is universal: all land (except the Royal demesne) is held of a lord and, ultimately, of the Crown.[243] 'The grand and fundamental maxim of all feudal tenure', Blackstone averred, is 'that all lands were originally granted out by the sovereign, and are therefore holden, either mediately or immediately, of the Crown.'[244]

The doctrine of tenure was established at a time when '[t]he whole social and political organization of the kingdom rested upon tenure as its foundation.'[245] While many of the incidents of tenure have disappeared and its practical importance has diminished,[246] the doctrine has not been abolished. One consequence of the continued existence of tenure is that some difficult questions arise where a person acquires title to land by possession. Is there a relation of tenure between the possessor and another? If so, who is the possessor's lord? If not, is it really possible for the possessor to have a fee simple estate in the land? Scholars have given different answers to these questions. Christopher Jessel has maintained that, while a squatter has 'a new fee simple estate in the land as from the date of entry', '[t]he squatter's possession does not create a derivative or inferior tenure.'[247] Elizabeth Cooke, on the other hand, has said that a squatter has 'a fee simple held from the Crown.'[248] Both answers give rise to

---

[241] Curwen (n 11) 537.

[242] ibid 538.

[243] Frederick Pollock and Frederic William Maitland, *The History of English Law Before the Time of Edward I* (2nd edn, CUP 1911) vol 1, 232–33; *Attorney-General (Ontario) v Mercer* (1883) 8 App Cas 767 (PC) 771–72 (Earl of Selborne LC); *Mabo v Queensland (No 2)* (1992) 175 CLR 1 (HCA) 46 (Brennan J), 80–81 (Deane and Gaudron JJ); Today, almost all mesne lordships are untraceable, and the courts have been prepared to assume that land is held directly of the Crown: Bridge, Cooke, and Dixon (n 2) para 2-030; *Re Lowe's Will's Trust* [1973] 1 WLR 882 (CA) 886 (Russell LJ).

[244] 2 Bl Comm 53. Compare Co Litt 65a: 'all lands within this realm were originally derived from the Crown'.

[245] Henry W Challis, *The Law of Real Property* (2nd edn, Reeves & Turner 1892) 2.

[246] Bridge, Cooke, and Dixon (n 2) 2-014–2.030.

[247] Christopher Jessel, 'Concurrent Fees Simple and the Land Registration Act 2002' (2014) 130 LQR 587, 600.

[248] Elizabeth Cooke, 'Adverse possession—problems of title in registered land' (1994) 14 LS 1, 6 (hereafter Cooke, 'Adverse possession'). See also H W R Wade, 'Landlord, Tenant and Squatter' (1962) 78 LQR 541, 544–45.

serious difficulties, which spring from the universality of tenure and the survival of escheat.

Escheat 'means the falling-in of the land to the lord'.[249] It is an incident of tenure and, while escheat on the death of the tenant intestate and without heirs was abolished in 1925, escheat still occurs whenever the lord ceases to have a tenant.[250] Upon an escheat, the lord (usually the Crown) is automatically entitled to take possession of the land by virtue of the lordship.[251]

Now, let us suppose that A held an (unregistered) fee simple estate in Blackacre of the Crown, and that B obtained possession without A's consent. B remained in adverse possession for twelve years and, consequently, A's estate was extinguished. Thereafter, B was declared bankrupt and B's trustee in bankruptcy disclaimed the land. There is no evidence that anyone else has an estate in the land. What is the result of this? Under the doctrine of tenure, the land should escheat to the Crown,[252] for there is no tenant.[253] Indeed, to say that no escheat would occur is to deny the universality of tenure. Yet since escheat is an incident of tenure, it must follow, *pace* Jessel, that B is the Crown's tenant.

Cooke's statement, taken at face value, suggests that a squatter *always* holds of the Crown. But it is doubtful that this is correct. Suppose that, in the example above, A had held, not of the Crown, but of a mesne lord, X; and that X, in turn, held of the Crown. In these circumstances, to allow the land, upon the disclaimer by B's trustee in bankruptcy, to escheat to the Crown would be to deny X's rights as the Crown's tenant.

These considerations suggest that the best approach is to accept that, by taking possession, B holds the land of A's lord—a mesne lord if there is one, but otherwise the Crown—by the tenure of common socage for an estate in fee simple. It is true that the claim that A and B hold, severally, the same land of the same lord in fee simple would have been regarded as nonsensical by earlier generations of common lawyers. But this simply reflects the fact that the law of our time is not the same as the law of theirs.

---

[249] T Cyprian Williams, 'The Fundamental Principles of the Present Law of Ownership of Land' (1931) 75 SJ 843, cited with approval in *Scmlla Properties Ltd v Gesso Properties (BVI) Ltd* [1995] BCC 793 (Ch) 800 (Stanley Burnton QC).

[250] *Attorney-General (Ontario)* (n 243) 772 (Earl of Selborne LC): 'when there is no longer any tenant, the land returns, by reason of tenure, to the lord . . . The tenant's estate . . . has come to an end, and the lord is in by his own right'. See also Challis (n 245) 33; Bridge, Cooke, and Dixon (n 2) paras 2-022–2-025.

[251] *Scmlla Properties* (n 249) 802–05 (Stanley Burnton QC).

[252] Depending on the location of the land, the land will escheat to the Crown Estate, the Duchy of Lancaster, or the Duchy of Cornwall.

[253] *Scmlla Properties* (n 249) 802–05 (Stanley Burnton QC).

Is this analysis ruled out by the fact that tenure is said to derive, ultimately, from a Crown grant? Curwen has argued that it is. According to Curwen, the Crown does not, and cannot, grant a new fee simple to a squatter and, therefore, she cannot have a fee simple.[254] The problem with this argument, however, is that it rests on a misunderstanding of Blackstone's 'fundamental maxim'. As Blackstone explained, the proposition that 'all lands were originally granted out by the sovereign' is a 'mere *fiction*'.[255] It is, in other words, a postulate of the theory of tenure.[256] This postulate does not actually prevent, nor provide a good reason for preventing, a squatter from obtaining a fee simple through taking possession.

4.3.3 The Objection based on the Law of Property Act 1925

The third objection is that the claim that a possessor acquires a legal fee simple estate is not consistent with the Law of Property Act 1925. Section 1(1) of the Act provides that the 'only estates in land which are capable of subsisting . . . at law' are 'an estate in fee simple absolute in possession' and a 'term of years absolute'. It has been thought that, where a possessor acquires an inferior fee simple (ie a fee simple that is subject to a superior fee simple), the possessor does not have a fee simple *absolute* and, therefore, the possessor's interest cannot be a legal estate.[257] As others have pointed out,[258] however, the term 'absolute' in section 1(1) of the 1925 Act has a technical meaning: it refers to a fee simple that is not a determinable fee or a fee simple upon a condition. The possessor's interest is not, in the relevant sense of these terms, conditional or determinable.[259] It is, therefore, 'absolute' for the purposes of section 1(1).

4.3.4 The Abandonment Objection

A fourth objection to the claim that a possessor acquires a fee simple estate is that it is not compatible with the law concerning the abandonment of land.

---

[254] Curwen (n 11) 537–39.

[255] 2 Bl Comm 51 (emphasis added).

[256] *Attorney-General v Brown* (1847) 1 Legge 312 (NSWSC) 318 (Sir Alfred Stephen CJ); *Mabo* (n 243) 47.

[257] Rudden (n 232) 68–72; Cooke, 'Adverse possession' (n 248) 4–5.

[258] Law Commission, *Updating the Land Registration Act 2002: A Consultation Paper* (Law Com CP No 227, 2016) para 3.5; Bridge, Cooke, and Dixon (n 2) paras 3-028–3-045.

[259] *Turner* (n 187) [14] (Roth J).

The leading case is *Mount Carmel v Thurlow*.[260] In 1970 an adverse possessor, R, obtained possession of two floors of a mews house in Kensington, which belonged to the claimant. R permitted the defendants to go into exclusive occupation of the premises in 1974 and then left the country. In 1984 R purported to assign his 'estate, rights and title' in the land to the claimant. The claimant sought to recover possession from the defendants, but their claim was rejected. Since the total period of adverse possession exceeded twelve years, the claimant's right was barred by section 15 of the Limitation Act 1980. The claimant argued that, even if this were so, it was entitled to succeed because R had assigned his interest in the land to it in 1984. The Court of Appeal rejected this submission on the ground that, long before the purported assignment, R had 'abandoned any rights to possession which he might have had'.[261]

It is important to keep in mind, when analysing this decision, the distinction between the destructive abandonment of an interest in land ('extinctive abandonment') and the abandonment of possession of land.[262] Extinctive abandonment occurs if an interest is extinguished by virtue of the interest-holder's intention to divest herself of the interest (possibly together with some further element, such as physical separation). According to Stephen Jourdan QC and Oliver Radley-Gardner, the decision in *Thurlow*:

> [can] only be explained on the basis that the title created by R's possession for less than the limitation period was of a different quality to a paper title. Because R in reality had no title, and his rights depended on possession, he lost all his rights when he ceased to have the *animus possidendi*, and so possession.[263]

On this view, *Thurlow* was not a case of extinctive abandonment: since R had a 'possessory title', he automatically lost his title when he lost possession, and he lost possession when he ceased to intend to exercise physical control over the land, irrespective of whether he intended to divest himself of his rights. A major problem with this explanation is that the claims that R 'in reality had no title', and that R's interest 'depended on possession', are not consistent with

---

[260] *Mount Carmel Investments Ltd v Thurlow* [1988] 1 WLR 1078 (CA). See also *Site Developments (Ferndown) Ltd v Cuthbury Ltd* [2010] EWHC 10 (Ch); [2011] Ch 226 [173]–[178], in which Vos J accepted, on the basis of *Thurlow*, that a squatter could abandon her interest.

[261] *Mount Carmel* (n 260) 1088.

[262] See Janine Griffiths-Baker, 'Divesting Abandonment: An Unnecessary Concept?' (2007) 36 CLWR 16, 18. Griffiths-Baker uses the term 'unilateral divesting abandonment' to refer to extinctive abandonment.

[263] Jourdan & Radley-Gardner (n 13) para 20–59. See also para 20–53.

the authorities concerning the nature of the interest acquired by possession; authorities that were not cited or discussed by the Court of Appeal in *Thurlow*.

An alternative explanation is that *Thurlow* is a case of extinctive abandonment: R's title was destroyed, not because he lost possession, but because he manifested an intention to divest himself of his title. There are reasons to think that the Court of Appeal adopted this view. Nicholls LJ, delivering the court's judgment, concluded that the correct inference to be drawn, in the circumstances, was that R 'abandoned any *rights* to possession which he might have had'.[264] The relevant circumstances included the fact that R had 'fled abroad' and thereafter 'never asserted any claim to the property'.[265]

It might be argued that, since fee simple estates cannot be abandoned, *Thurlow* is inconsistent with the claim that a possessor acquires a fee simple estate. There is certainly some authority for the claim that fees simple cannot be abandoned. In *Ironmonger v Bernard International*,[266] for instance, the claimant acquired a fee simple under her husband's will in 1981. The land was vacant from 1991 until 1995, when the defendant entered without the claimant's consent. The claimant obtained an order for possession, and the defendant sought leave to appeal on the ground that the claimant had abandoned the land. The Court of Appeal rejected the defendant's application. Millett LJ (with whom Butler-Sloss LJ agreed) said that, while the land may well have been 'decaying and derelict':

> [i]t was not . . . abandoned; there is no concept in English law of the abandonment of title to land. Land may be left vacant and unoccupied for years; the owner does not thereby lose his title. He cannot lose it unless some other person has been in adverse possession of the property for more than twelve years.[267]

One might think that there is a simple way to reconcile *Ironmonger* and *Thurlow*: fees simple cannot be abandoned, but the limited interest acquired by a possessor can be. It is doubtful, however, that this represents the law. For, in the first place, it is questionable whether the purported reconciliation is consistent with Millett LJ's judgment in *Ironmonger*. Millett LJ asserted that 'title to

---

[264] *Mount Carmel* (n 260) 1088 (emphasis added).
[265] ibid 1087.
[266] *Ironmonger v Bernard International (Estate Division)* (CA, 9 February 1996). Many academics have claimed or assumed that title to land cannot be abandoned: see, eg Swadling, 'Property' (n 2) para 4.511; Griffiths-Baker (n 262) 26.
[267] *Ironmonger* (n 266).

land' cannot be abandoned *without* drawing a distinction between particular categories of title.

Secondly, the Court of Appeal in *Thurlow* simply assumed that it was possible for R to abandon his interest. It seems that this issue was not disputed before the court. Certainly, the court did not examine the point. It focused, instead, on the question of whether, on the facts, it was right to infer that R intended to abandon his interest. Consequently, the court did not engage with the authorities relating to abandonment of title to land, and it did not consider the relevant legal principles or policy considerations. A related point is that, while the Court of Appeal recognised that a squatter may sell or give his interest to another,[268] it did not analyse, in depth, the precise nature of the interest acquired by possession. The court did not consider, for instance, whether R's interest amounted to a freehold estate. Given all this, *Thurlow* is not a strong authority for the proposition that the interest acquired by a possessor may be abandoned.

Accordingly, while a superficial interpretation of the case law might suggest that 'possessory titles', but not fees simple, can be abandoned, it would, in fact, be a mistake to claim that the law has embraced this distinction. The question of whether there is such a distinction has not been considered, let alone authoritatively answered, by the courts. We should, therefore, reject the contention that the law of abandonment is incompatible with the proposition that a possessor acquires a fee simple. The Court of Appeal or the Supreme Court will need to determine, if and when the issue arises, whether the interest acquired by a possessor really can be abandoned. A satisfactory discussion of this question must take into account, among other things,[269] the case law concerning the nature of the interest acquired by possession. If the central argument of this chapter is correct, the salient question will be whether fees simple in general, or inferior fees simple in particular, can be abandoned. The court's answer to this question will determine whether *Thurlow* and/or *Ironmonger* were correctly decided.

---

[268] *Mount Carmel* (n 260) 1086.
[269] Relevant considerations include the impact of abandonment on other persons with an interest in the land, and on the wider community: see Robin Hickey, 'The Problem of Divesting Abandonment' [2016] Conv 28; Malcolm M Combe, 'Abandonment of Land and the *Scottish Coal* Case: was it Unprecedented?' (2018) 22 Edinburgh LR 301.

4.4 The Scope of the Acquisition Rule

We have seen that possession gives rise to a legal fee simple estate. What, pre-cisely, is the scope of this rule? Is it confined to cases in which the possession is adverse? And does it matter whether a registered title exists in respect of the land? It is argued below that the rule applies irrespective of whether the posses-sion is adverse, and irrespective of whether the land is registered.

4.4.1 Adverse and Non-adverse Possession

It is sometimes thought that, so far as the legal consequences of possession are concerned, there is an important distinction between adverse and non-adverse possession: if the possession is adverse,[270] the possessor acquires a legal fee simple estate; if the possession is not adverse, the possessor acquires mere rights of possession, which confer 'trespassory protection' for so long as the rights-holder remains in possession.[271] The better view, however, is that it is *not* a condition of acquiring title by possession that the possession is adverse.

Where a person with a legal fee simple estate grants a contractual licence to another,[272] and the licensee takes possession of the land in accordance with the terms of the licence,[273] the licensee is certainly not in adverse possession as against the licensor. Yet it is undoubtedly the case that the licensee has, by virtue of her possession, a right to exclusive possession that is protected by the law of torts.[274] The licensee can, for instance, recover damages for trespass from a person who lacks a better right and enters onto the land without her

---

[270] A person is in 'adverse possession' if she is in possession of land and the limitation period is run-ning, in her favour, against a person who has a right to possession: *Powell v McFarlane* (1977) 38 P & CR 452, 469 (Slade J); *Pye* (n 238) [32]–[38] (Lord Browne-Wilkinson).

[271] Letitia Crabb, 'The Property Torts?' (2003) 11 Tort L Rev 104, 108–14. See also: Hill (n 29) 31–32; Baker, '*Bruton*' (n 32); Nicholas McBride, *The Humanity of Private Law, Part I: Explanation* (Bloomsbury 2019) 76.

[272] A contract that provides that a party is to have possession of land will, in some circumstances, give rise to, not a lease or a tenancy at will, but a contractual licence: see *Street* (n 19) 826–27 (Lord Templeman); *Mexfield Housing Co-operative Ltd v Berrisford* [2011] UKSC 52; [2012] 1 AC 955 [60]–[64] (Lord Neuberger MR).

[273] It is important to distinguish cases in which a licensee is in possession from cases in which a li-censor is in possession through a licensee. A licensee will be in possession if she has exclusive physical control of the land and an intention to exercise such control on her own behalf and for her own ben-efit: *Pye* (n 238) [40]–[46] (Lord Browne-Wilkinson); *J Alston & Sons Ltd v BOCM Pauls Ltd* [2008] EWHC 3310 (Ch); [2009] 1 EGLR 93. A licensee with such an intention should be distinguished from a licensee who exercises control on behalf of her licensor: *Bannerman Town v Eleuthera Properties Ltd* [2018] UKPC 27 [51]–[54]. cf *Sze To Chun Keung v Kung Kwok Wai David* [1997] 1 WLR 1232 (PC) 1235; Baker, '*Bruton*' (n 32) 497–98.

[274] See section 4.2.1 above. cf Wonnacott (n 11) 69–71; Baker, '*Bruton*' (n 32) 503–04.

consent. Taken by itself, this is consistent with the claim that a licensee, if in possession, has mere rights of possession.[275] But the cases demonstrate that such a licensee has more than this: she has an alienable interest in the land. Consider, for instance, *Rosenberg v Cook*, which was discussed earlier.[276] One question that arose in this case was whether the vendor, who had purported to convey his title to the claimant, was in adverse possession of the land as against a third party. The Court of Appeal maintained that it was not necessary to determine whether the vendor was in adverse possession:[277] as long as he was in possession, which he was, he had a right to exclusive possession that he could convey, and did convey, to the claimant. The decision is, therefore, an authority for the proposition that a possessor acquires an estate in the land—an alienable interest that comprises, inter alia, a right to exclusive possession—irrespective of whether the possession is adverse.

Furthermore, in *Mexfield Housing Co-operative Ltd v Berrisford*, Lord Neuberger MR,[278] giving the leading judgment, maintained that *Bruton v London & Quadrant Housing Trust* 'was about relativity of title', and this can be so only if the title by possession rule is not restricted to adverse possessors. In *Bruton*,[279] a housing trust, which had been granted a licence by a local authority to use a block of flats, agreed that Mr Bruton could occupy one of the flats. The House of Lords held that Mr Bruton was a tenant notwithstanding that his landlord, the trust, had obtained a mere licence from the local authority. One explanation of this decision is that the housing trust, by taking possession of the land, acquired a fee simple estate, and could, therefore, grant a leasehold estate to Mr Bruton.[280] Since the trust's fee simple was inferior to the authority's, Mr Bruton's tenancy did not bind the authority (the licensor),[281] but it was 'binding as such not only on Mr Bruton and the trust, but also on any assignee of . . . the trust'.[282] It might strike one as odd that a person can be, with respect to the same land, a contractual licensee *and* a freeholder. The key is to keep in mind the principle of relativity of title. The authority had a better title

---

[275] cf Amy Goymour, '*Bruton v London & Quadrant Housing Trust* [2000]: Relativity of Title, and the Regulation of the "Proprietary Underworld"' in Simon Douglas, Robin Hickey, and Emma Waring (eds), *Landmark Cases in Property Law* (Hart 2015) 163–64.

[276] *Rosenberg* (n 165).

[277] ibid 165–66 (Brett LJ), 166 (Cotton LJ).

[278] *Mexfield Housing* (n 272) [65].

[279] [2000] 1 AC 406 (HL).

[280] Nicholas Roberts, 'The *Bruton* Tenancy: A Matter of Relativity' [2012] Conv 87; Goymour (n 275). Contrast Baker, '*Bruton*' (n 32). It is true, as Baker explains, that the explanation offered by Roberts, and endorsed by Lord Neuberger MR, is not consistent with the reasons given by the law lords in *Bruton*. The explanation must be regarded, therefore, as a reinterpretation.

[281] *Kay v Lambeth LBC* [2006] UHKL 10; [2006] 2 AC 465.

[282] *Mexfield Housing* (n 272) [65] (Lord Neuberger MR).

than the trust. So, as against the authority, the only rights that the trust had were personal rights under the contractual licence. But, as against the world at large, including Mr Bruton, the trust, by virtue of its possession, had a legal fee simple estate.

The case law supports, therefore, the proposition that the rule that confers fees simple on possessors is not confined to adverse possession. It does not follow, of course, that the act of taking possession *always* generates a legal fee simple estate. If that were so, then every time a freeholder went in and out of possession, she would acquire another fee simple estate, which would be absurd. The law relating to the boundaries of the acquisition rule is unsettled, but the authorities are consistent with the view that a person, by taking possession, will not acquire a legal fee simple if she takes possession under the grant of a new legal estate, or under a pre-existing legal estate that comprises a right to exclusive possession.

4.4.2 Title by Possession and the Land Registration Act 2002

Elizabeth Cooke has written that, in light of the enactment of the Land Registration Act 2002, 'it no longer makes sense, except for those areas of land whose title is not yet registered, to say that title to land in England and Wales is relative. Legal ownership is by registration alone'.[283] This might lead one to think that, if R is the registered proprietor of a fee simple in certain land and S takes possession of the land without R's consent, S will not acquire a title to the land. But, as Cooke recognises,[284] the rule that confers a fee simple on a possessor applies to unregistered *and* registered land. Indeed, certain provisions of the 2002 Act presuppose that, and can operate only if, a person acquires a legal title through taking possession of land.[285] S would, therefore, acquire a fee simple estate that is good as against the world at large, but not as against anyone who has a better title, such as R.

This state of affairs gives rise to some difficult questions concerning the interaction of the common law rules and the registered land system.[286] One

---

[283] Elizabeth Cooke, *Land Law* (2nd edn, OUP 2012) 253.

[284] ibid.

[285] eg Land Registration Act 2002, sch 6(9)(1). See Law Commission, *Land Registration for the Twenty-First Century: A Conveyancing Revolution* (Law Com No 271) para 14.71; Amy Goymour and Robin Hickey, 'The Continuing Relevance of Relativity of Title Under the Land Registration Act 2002' in Amy Goymour, Stephen Watterson, and Martin Dixon (eds), *New Perspectives on Land Registration: Contemporary Problems and Solutions* (Hart 2018) 73–75.

[286] See Goymour and Hickey (n 285); Mark Pawlowski and James Brown, 'Adverse Possession and the Transmissibility of Possessory Rights—the Dark Side of Land Registration?' [2017] Conv 116.

important question is whether the possessor can register her inferior fee simple? This is a contentious issue.[287] Currently, where a person is in possession of land in respect of which another has a registered estate, the Land Registry will reject an application by the possessor to be registered as the proprietor of the estate acquired through possession.[288] The Law Commission has expressed its support for this approach,[289] partly because of its concern that 'entry of a possessory title would enable adverse possessors to circumvent schedule 6 [of the 2002 Act].'[290] Similarly, where a possessor of *unregistered* land seeks to register the estate that she acquired through possession, the Land Registry will reject the application unless the applicant has been in possession for at least twelve years.[291] The thinking is that a person who has acquired a fee simple by taking possession of (unregistered) land should not be registered as the proprietor of such an estate, even with the lowest class of registered title, which is called 'possessory title', unless it is probable that all better titles have been extinguished by section 17 of the Limitation Act 1980. A number of judges in the First-tier Tribunal have maintained, or assumed, that the approach taken by the Land Registry is correct in law.[292] The Law Commission has proposed an amendment to the 2002 Act in order to put the matter beyond doubt.[293]

While the revolution in conveyancing brought about by the Land Registration Act 2002 has, therefore, reduced the importance of title by possession, primarily by amending the rules of adverse possession, the common law rules have not disappeared. Indeed, since estates acquired by possession, and dealings in them, largely operate outside the registered land scheme, English law has, and will continue to have,[294] a dual system of title: a scheme of title by possession exists alongside a scheme of title by registration.

---

[287] Jourdan and Radley-Gardner (n 13) paras 21-30–21-37; Goymour and Hickey (n 285) 75–79, 82–83.

[288] HM Land Registry, *Practice Guide 5: Adverse Possession of (1) Unregistered and (2) Registered land where a right to be registered was acquired before 13 October 2003* (May 2020) para 9 (hereafter *Practice Guide 5: Adverse Possession*).

[289] Law Commission, *Updating the Land Registration Act 2002* (Law Com No 380, 2018) paras 17.89–17.106 (hereafter Law Com 380).

[290] ibid, para 17.98. cf Goymour and Hickey (n 285) 77–79.

[291] *Practice Guide 5: Adverse Possession* (n 288) paras 2, 5.4, 9.

[292] eg *Joslin v Hipgrave* [2015] UKFTT 0497 (PC); *Phillips v Vaughan* [2016] UKFTT 0320 (PC) [208]. See also *Lynn Lewis Ltd v The Environment Agency* [2007] EWL and RA REF/2005/1068; *Heaney v Kirkby* [2015] UKUT 0178 (TCC).

[293] Law Com 380 (n 289) paras 17.103–17.106.

[294] cf Kevin Gray and Susan Francis Gray, *Elements of Land Law* (5th edn, OUP 2009) para 2.2.28: 'It is now widely accepted that the continued existence of two separate systems of conveyancing—the registered and the unregistered—is "absurd" and that the unregistered regime "must be given its quietus"' [citations omitted].

4.5 Conclusion

There has been much debate over the consequences of obtaining possession of land. This chapter has argued that, for the most part, the law is clear and settled: a person acquires, through taking possession, a legal fee simple estate. The traditional view that possession is not a source of freehold title is plausible only if one relies upon historical precedents that were superseded long ago. Holmes and Pollock did not invent the idea that possession is a source of title; they found it in the cases. The rule is, indeed, a judicial creation but, without it, the Real Property Limitation Act 1833 and its successors would not have achieved their aims. The issue that should be debated today is not whether the rule exists, but whether, in the context of the registered land system, the rule should be retained.

5

Possession and Title to Chattels

5.1 Introduction

Serjeant Williams, in his influential notes on Saunders's report of *Wilbraham v Snow*, stated that a possessor was able to 'maintain [trover] against a wrong-doer; for possession is prima facie evidence of property'.[1] This suggests that the protection afforded to possessors of chattels by the law of torts is based on a rule of proof, and that people do not acquire 'property' in respect of chattels simply by taking possession. It is argued in this chapter, however, that while there are some cases that are incompatible with the Strong Proprietary Interest View, so far as chattels are concerned, this view is, in fact, sound. Through taking possession of a chattel, a person generally acquires an interest in the chattel, which is remarkably similar to the interest acquired by taking possession of land. It comprises a right to exclusive possession, as well as certain powers of disposition, including powers to alienate the interest. Moreover, the interest is not possession-dependent: it will survive a loss of possession. The core argument in support of these claims is advanced in section 5.2. Section 5.3 considers, and seeks to rebut, two objections.

5.2 The Incidents of a Possessor's Interest

The aim of this section is to examine the incidents of the interest that is acquired by obtaining possession of a chattel. When considering this issue, it is essential to distinguish the interest acquired simply through taking possession, as where a thief takes another's chattel, from interests acquired as a result of the exercise of a dispositive power. Where, for example, X pledges a painting to Y, Y acquires a new (legal) interest in the painting,[2] which is sometimes

---

[1] *Wilbraham v Snow* (1668) 2 Saund 47; 85 ER 624, 628, cited with approval in *Jeffries v Great Western Railway Co* (1856) 5 El & Bl 802, 805 (Lord Campbell CJ), 806 (Wightman J), 808 (Crompton J).
[2] *Franklin v Neate* (1844) 13 M & W 480; 153 ER 200; *The Odessa* [1916] 1 AC 145 (PC) 157–59 (Lord Mersey). See T Cyprian Williams, 'The True Nature of a Pawnee's Interest in Goods Pawned' (1915) 31 LQR 75; Hugh Beale and others, *The Law of Security and Title-Based Financing* (3rd edn, OUP 2018) paras 5.03–5.12.

Possession, Relative Title, and Ownership in English Law. Luke Rostill, Oxford University Press (2021). © Luke Rostill. DOI: 10.1093/oso/9780198843108.003.0005

called a 'special property'.[3] This interest, which comprises a right to exclude and a power of sale in the event of default,[4] is capable of binding X's successors in title. Such an interest cannot be acquired by simply taking possession of a chattel. If, for instance, Z were to take the painting from Y without Y's (or X's) consent, Z would not acquire the interest of a pledgee. This is demonstrated by the fact that the interest Z would acquire through taking possession would not be capable of binding X, Y, or their successors in title. Y, unlike Z, acquired the interest of a pledgee because X exercised a particular dispositive power in Y's favour. The acquisition of an interest by Y is, therefore, an example of what Ben McFarlane has called 'dependent acquisition', ie the acquisition of an interest that 'derives from, and depends on, the rights of another'.[5] Acquiring an interest through possession, on the other hand, is an example of 'independent acquisition', that is, the acquisition of an interest 'through [one's] own *unilateral* conduct'.[6]

It is argued in this section that the interest acquired independently, through taking possession, has three key features. First, the interest comprises a right to exclusive possession that grounds duties on the rest of the world not to physically interfere with the chattel.[7] Secondly, the interest is not time-limited nor possession-dependent: it will continue to subsist even if the interest-holder loses possession. Thirdly, the interest comprises various dispositive powers, including the power to alienate the entire interest *inter vivos*, or by will. These features will be discussed in turn.

5.2.1 Possession and the Right to Exclusive Possession

The case law supports the proposition that, by taking possession of a chattel, a person acquires a right to exclusive possession, unless the possessor already has such a right. The right grounds duties on others not to physically interfere with the chattel. It is, therefore, a mistake to think that the protection afforded to possessors by the law of torts is achieved solely through rules of evidence or presumption. In this regard, the position with respect to chattels is the same as the position in relation to land.[8]

---

[3] See, eg *Coggs v Bernard* (1703) 2 Ld Raym 909, 916; 92 ER 107, 112 (Holt CJ).

[4] *Donald v Suckling* (1866) LR 1 QB 585 (QB) 594–97 (Shee J), 604 (Mellor J), 612–14 (Blackburn J); *Re Morritt* (1886) 18 QBD 222 (CA).

[5] Ben McFarlane, *The Structure of Property Law* (Hart 2008) 18.

[6] ibid.

[7] In the authorities, this right is often called a right to immediate possession. It may also be called a right to exclude. In this chapter, these terms are generally regarded as interchangeable.

[8] See Chapter 4 (section 4.2.1).

To establish that a possessor actually acquires a right to exclusive possession, it is necessary to examine the law concerning trespass to chattels, the tort of conversion, and liability in negligence for damage to chattels. The tort of trespass to chattels consists of the infringement of a duty not to intentionally interfere,[9] physically,[10] with a chattel. Examples of physical interferences include scratching the panel of a vehicle,[11] picking up jewellery,[12] and shooting an animal.[13] It is beyond doubt that the tort of trespass protects possessors (though this is not to say that it protects *only* possessors).[14] In *Carter v Johnson*,[15] for example, the claimant brought trespass, alleging that the defendant had seized goods that were in his possession. Lord Abinger CB maintained that 'mere possession in the plaintiff is enough against a wrongdoer'.[16] Who, in this context, counts as a 'wrongdoer'? The answer, it seems, is that a defendant (D) is a 'wrongdoer' if: (a) D interferes, without lawful justification, with a chattel that is in the possession of another; and (b) D does not have, as against the possessor, a right to possess it.[17]

The possessor is also protected by the tort of conversion. Conversion involves intentionally interfering with another's chattel,[18] though not every

---

[9] The traditional view is that an unintentional interference may amount to trespass if the interference is a direct result of the defendant's negligence: *National Coal Board v J E Evans & Co* [1951] 2 KB 861 (CA). The law on this point is unsettled. As with trespass to land, the better view is that trespass to chattels is confined to intentional interferences: see *Letang v Cooper* [1965] 1 QB 232 (CA); Simon Douglas, *Liability for Wrongful Interferences with Chattels* (Hart 2011) ch 6 (hereafter Douglas, *Liability*).

[10] *Hartley v Moxham* (1842) 3 Ad & El (NS) 701; 114 ER 675; *Club Cruise Entertainment & Travelling Services Europe BV v Department for Transport (The Van Gogh)* [2008] EWHC 2794 (Comm) [50]–[53]; Simon Douglas, 'Actionable Interferences: A New Perspective on the Chattel Torts' in Simone Degeling, James Edelman, and James Goudkamp (eds), *Torts in Commercial Law* (Thomson Reuters Professional Australia 2011) 88–96. Historically, the interference needed to be 'direct', ie the *immediate* result of the defendant's conduct. It seems, however, that this is no longer a requirement of trespass to chattels: see Douglas, *Liability* (n 9) 97–110.

[11] *Fouldes v Willoughby* (1841) 8 M & W 540, 549; 151 ER 1153, 1157 (Alderson B).

[12] *Kirk v Gregory* (1876) LR 1 Ex D 55.

[13] *Hamps v Darby* [1948] 2 KB 311 (CA).

[14] The orthodox view is that, subject to certain exceptions, a claimant can successfully sue in trespass only if the claimant was in possession at the time of the interference: MA Jones (ed), *Clerk & Lindsell on Torts* (22nd edn, Sweet and Maxwell 2018) para 17-136. But the more principled view is that possession, as defined in Chapter 2, is not necessary and that a right to (immediate) possession suffices: see Douglas, *Liability* (n 9) 31–32. There is support in the case law for this position, eg *Smith v Milles* (1786) 1 Term Reports 475, 480; 99 ER 1205, 1208 (Ashurst J); *White v Morris* (1852) 11 CB 1015; 138 ER 778; *Johnson v Diprose* [1893] 1 QB 512 (CA) 515 (Lord Esher MR) 516 (Bowen LJ); *USA v Dollfus Mieg et Compagnie SA* [1952] AC 582 (HL) 605 (Earl Jowitt); *White v Withers LLP* [2009] EWCA Civ 1122; [2010] 1 FLR 859 [47]–[49] (Ward LJ).

[15] (1839) 2 M & Rob 263; 174 ER 283.

[16] (1839) 2 M & Rob 263, 265; 174 ER 283, 284. See also *Smith* (n 14); *Giles v Glover* (1832) 9 Bing 128, 265–66; 131 ER 563, 615 (Lord Tindal CJ).

[17] *Bourne v Fosbrooke* (1865) 18 CB (NS) 515, 525; 144 ER 545 (CP) 549 (Erle CJ); *Jeffries v Great Western Railway* (1856) 5 El & Bl 802, 805 (Lord Campbell CJ). See also *Russell v Wilson* (1923) 33 CLR 538 (HCA) 548–49 (Isaacs and Rich JJ).

[18] *Walgrave v Ogden* (1589) 1 Leon 224; 74 ER 205; *BMW Financial Services (GB) Ltd v Bhagwanani* [2007] EWCA Civ 1230; [2007] CTLC 280. A bailee will commit a 'statutory conversion', however, if she

intentional interference is a conversion. It is notoriously difficult to provide a comprehensive and concise explanation of the forms of interference that may amount to conversion. What can be said, as Lord Nicholls explained in *Kuwait Airways Corp v Iraqi Airways Co (Nos 4 & 5)*,[19] is that converting a chattel typically involves 'so extensive an encroachment on' the claimant's rights 'as to exclude him from use and possession of the goods'.[20]

It has long been recognised that the law relating to conversion protects possession.[21] An early example is *Basset v Maynard*.[22] The defendant had taken away certain trees that had been cut down by the claimant. The claimant brought an action in trover, maintaining that he was entitled to the trees under a grant from a third party. The defendant argued that this grant was void and that, therefore, the claimant did not have a good title to the trees. The Queen's Bench held that the grant was not void, but according to *Croke's Reports*, Lord Popham CJ and Gawdy and Clench JJ maintained that, even if the grant were void, the claimant would still be entitled to bring trover because 'although the plaintiff had not a good title, yet his having possession of them, being cut down, sufficeth'.[23]

A possessor is also protected by the tort of negligence. In *Rooth v Wilson*,[24] for example, A sent his horse to B, who let it out into his field. The fence that separated B's field from C's field was in a bad state and, as a result, the horse fell into C's field and died. C admitted that he was responsible for the fence, but submitted that B had 'no interest in the horse . . . and therefore cannot sue: the action can only be maintained by the owner of the animal'.[25] B argued that he 'had possession, as a gratuitous bailee, and possession is sufficient, as against a wrongdoer'.[26] The King's Bench held that B was entitled to a monetary remedy. Abbot J said that 'the same possession which would enable the plaintiff to

---

negligently allows goods in her charge to be lost or destroyed: Torts (Interference with Goods) Act 1977, s 2(2).

[19] [2002] UKHL 19; [2002] 2 AC 883.
[20] ibid [39].
[21] *Webb v Fox* (1797) 7 Term Reports 391, 397; 101 ER 1037, 1040 (Lord Kenyon CJ); *Sutton v Buck* (1810) 2 Taunt 302, 309; 127 ER 1094, 1096 (Lawrence J); *Buckley v Gross* (1863) 3 B & S 566, 573; 122 ER 213, 216 (Crompton J); 3 B & S 566, 574; 122 ER 213, 216 (Blackburn J); *Jeffries v Great Western Railway Co* (1856) 5 El & Bl 802, 805; 119 ER 680, 681 (Lord Campbell CJ); *The Winkfield* [1902] P 42 (CA) 54 (Collins MR); *Government of Iran v The Barakat Galleries Ltd* [2007] EWCA Civ 1374; [2009] QB 22 [19] (Lord Phillips CJ).
[22] (1600) Cro Eliz 819; 78 ER 1046.
[23] (1600) Cro Eliz 819, 820.
[24] *Rooth v Wilson* (1817) 1 B & Ald 59; 106 ER 22. See also *Leigh & Sullivan Ltd v Aliakmon Shipping Co Ltd (The Aliakmon)* [1986] AC 785 (HL) 800 (Lord Brandon).
[25] (1817) 1 B & Ald 59, 61
[26] ibid 60.

maintain trespass, would enable him to maintain this action'.[27] Bayley J maintained that '[c]ase is a possessory action; the declaration merely states that it was the horse of the plaintiff', and since B was in possession, the horse could indeed be described as 'the horse of the plaintiff'.[28]

Why is a person who has possession of a chattel able to successfully sue in trespass, conversion, and negligence? It has been thought that a possessor does not actually acquire any rights and that the protection afforded to possessors by the law of torts is based, entirely, on rules of presumption.[29] As we will see,[30] rules of presumption play a role in relation to the measure of recovery. But it is a mistake to think that the protection afforded to possessors is solely based on these rules, for the case law strongly supports the view that possession is a source of rights. In *Bridges v Hawkesworth*, for instance, Patteson J, giving the judgment of the Queen's Bench, maintained that a person who found and took possession of certain bank notes thereby acquired a 'right' in respect of the notes 'as against all the world, except the true owner'.[31] In *R v D'Eyncourt and Ryan*, in which the police had seized money from Ryan, Wills J asserted that Ryan's possession gave her 'the *right* to recover the money from anyone who could not show a better title'.[32] Similarly, in *Parker v British Airways Board*,[33] which concerned a claim by an airline passenger who found a gold bracelet in Heathrow Airport, Eveleigh LJ averred that 'a person in possession has the right to possess'.[34] Donaldson LJ said:

> a finder of a chattel, whilst not acquiring any absolute property or ownership in the chattel, *acquires a right to keep it* against all but the true owner or those in a position to claim through the true owner or one who can assert a prior right to keep the chattel.[35]

In *Waverley BC v Fletcher*,[36] which concerned a dispute between a landowner and a person who found a medieval gold brooch buried in the ground, Auld

---

[27] ibid 62.
[28] ibid. It is true that Lord Ellenborough CJ thought that the action should succeed on the ground that B was liable to A. But it is clear that this is not necessary: *The Winkfield* (n 21).
[29] See section 5.3 below.
[30] See section 5.3.1 below.
[31] *Bridges v Hawkesworth* (1851) 15 Jur 1079, 1082.
[32] *R v D'Eyncourt and Ryan* (1888) 21 QBD 109 (QB) 125 (emphasis added). See also *Costello v Chief Constable of Derbyshire Constabulary* [2001] EWCA Civ 381; [2001] 1 WLR 1437 [14], [31] (Lightman J); *Gough v Chief Constable of the West Midlands Police* [2004] EWCA Civ 206 [15] (Park J).
[33] [1982] QB 1004 (CA).
[34] ibid 1019.
[35] ibid 1017 (emphasis added).
[36] [1996] QB 334 (CA).

LJ, with whom Ward LJ and Sir Thomas Bingham MR agreed, stated that the 'starting point . . . is the firm principle . . . that the finder of an object is *entitled to possess it* against all but the rightful owner'.[37] These statements, and many others, provide support for the proposition that, by taking possession of a chattel, a person acquires a right to exclusive possession, ie a right to exclude that grounds duties of non-interference on other persons. Other persons generally, but not those who have a better right, owe the possessor: (a) a duty not to intentionally interfere, physically, with the chattel; (b) a duty not to intentionally interfere with the chattel in a way that excludes the possessor from the 'use and possession' of the chattel; and (c) a duty not to damage or destroy the chattel by failing to exercise reasonable care.

To show that a possessor acquires a right to exclude, however, does not in itself vindicate the Strong Proprietary Interest View. For one might contend that, while a possessor acquires a right to exclude, this is not a component of an alienable proprietary interest, but a mere right of possession. It is necessary, therefore, to consider whether this contention is correct.

5.2.2 Possession-dependence

Can the interest acquired through possession be regarded as possession-dependent in the sense that, once acquired, it subsists only for so long as the interest-holder remains in possession? A number of eminent legal scholars have given an affirmative answer to this question. Roy Goode and Ewan McKendrick, for example, have said that 'the holder of a purely possessory title loses his real right when he ceases to have possession',[38] and 'only an indefeasible title . . . survives the loss of possession'.[39] Similarly, David Fox has argued that, subject to an important qualification, a 'possessory title' lasts only so long as the possessor has possession.[40] The qualification is that a possessor has a good title as against a defendant whose title derives from the original wrongdoer.[41]

---

[37] ibid 339 (emphasis added).

[38] Ewan McKendrick (ed), *Goode on Commercial Law* (5th edn, Penguin 2016) para 2.07. Possession is defined (at para 2.40) as 'control, directly or through another, either of the asset itself or of some larger object in which it is contained or of land or buildings on or beneath which it is situated, with the intention of asserting such control against others, whether temporarily or permanently'.

[39] ibid para 2.22.

[40] David Fox, 'Relativity of Title at Law and in Equity' (2006) 65 CLJ 330, 344–49.

[41] ibid 345–46. See also James Gordley and Ugo Mattei, 'Protecting Possession' (1996) 44 Am J Comp L 293, 327.

The claim that the interest a person (P) acquires by taking possession is possession-dependent in the way described by Fox can be tested by examining cases in which someone other than P *lawfully* acquired possession, in order to discern whether P's interest survived P's loss of possession. These cases can be usefully divided into two categories. The first are cases in which the former possessor relinquished possession to another. The second are cases in which a person lawfully took the chattel from a possessor and the taker's authority subsequently expired. *Armory v Delamirie*,[42] *Bridges v Hawkesworth*,[43] and *Hannah v Peel*[44] belong to the first category. *Webb v Chief Constable of Merseyside Police*,[45] *Costello v Chief Constable of Derbyshire Constabulary*,[46] and *Gough v Chief Constable of the West Midlands Police*[47] belong to the second. These cases demonstrate that the interest acquired through possession is not possession-dependent.[48]

Hannah v Peel is a good example of a case that belongs to the first category.[49] The defendant, Peel, acquired a freehold estate in a house that he never occupied. The house was requisitioned during the Second World War. While Hannah, the claimant, was stationed at the house, he found a brooch in the crevice of a window frame. He handed it in to the police, who later gave it to the defendant. The claimant demanded the return of the brooch from the defendant, but it was not returned. The claimant commenced proceedings, claiming the return of the brooch or its value, and damages for its detention. The claimant submitted that, since he was the finder of the brooch, he was entitled to its possession as against all persons, except the 'true owner', who was unknown. The defendant submitted that he was entitled to possess the brooch because it was on his land when the claimant found it. Birkett J held that the claimant was entitled to possession and awarded him damages of £66. There was no discussion of whether the claimant was in possession at the time of the defendant's tort, but it is clear that he was not. After the claimant had found the brooch, he handed it to the police, who delivered it to the defendant. The defendant failed to return the brooch when the claimant demanded it. The failure to return the brooch was tortious and, at this time, the claimant was not in

---

[42] (1722) 1 Strange 505; 93 ER 664.

[43] *Bridges* (n 31).

[44] [1945] KB 509 (KB).

[45] [2000] QB 427 (CA).

[46] *Costello* (n 32).

[47] *Gough* (n 32).

[48] For a fuller discussion of the case law, see Luke Rostill, 'Terminology and Title to Chattels: A Case Against "Possessory Title"' (2018) 134 LQR 407, 410–18 (hereafter Rostill, 'Terminology and Title'). See also Patrick Atiyah, 'A Re-Examination of the *Jus Tertii* in Conversion' (1955) 18 MLR 97, 107.

[49] *Hannah* (n 44).

possession. Did the claimant have the 'best title': the supreme right to exclusive possession? Probably not, but the important point is that it did not matter whether he had the best right in the world or an inferior right. The claimant clearly had a right, by virtue of his former possession; and, since the defendant failed to establish that he had a better right than the claimant, the claimant's right bound the defendant. The case illustrates that the interest acquired by taking possession, whether it is supreme or inferior, is not possession-dependent: when the claimant lost possession, his right to exclusive possession continued to bind the rest of the world, except those who had a better right.

The claim that the interest acquired through possession is not possession-dependent is also supported by the second category of cases. Consider, for instance, *Costello v Chief Constable of Derbyshire Constabulary*.[50] The police had seized a car from Costello's possession. They were entitled under section 22 of the Police and Criminal Evidence Act 1984 to seize and retain the car for certain purposes. The question was whether Costello was entitled to possess the car once those statutory purposes were exhausted. The police submitted: (a) that the car was, to the knowledge of the claimant, stolen; and (b) that, on that ground, and though the true owner was not known, they were entitled to refuse to return the car to Costello. At first instance, Judge Styler accepted both submissions. In the Court of Appeal, however, Lightman J, in a judgment with which Robert Walker and Keene LJJ agreed, maintained that, while Judge Styler was fully entitled to reach the conclusion that the car was to the knowledge of the claimant stolen,[51] Costello had a right to possession that bound the police. Lightman J said, '[t]he fact of possession of a chattel of itself gives to the possessor a possessory title and the possessor is entitled to rely on such title without reference to the circumstances in which such possession was obtained'.[52] Accordingly, Costello was entitled to the return of the car when the statutory purposes under which the police retained it were exhausted. Since the police failed to return the car, Costello was entitled to an order for the delivery up, and damages for wrongful detention.[53]

Costello was not in possession when he asked the police to return the chattel. Indeed, his claim was based on the fact that the police had wrongly

---

[50] *Costello* (n 32). See also *Russell v Wilson* (1923) 33 CLR 538 (HCA); *National Crime Authority v Flack* (1998) 86 FCR 16 (FCAFC). For an illuminating discussion of *Costello*, see Joshua Getzler, 'Unclean Hands and the Doctrine of *Jus Tertii*' (2001) 117 LQR 565.

[51] *Costello* (n 32) [8].

[52] ibid [14]. The assertion that a possessor is entitled to rely on her title without reference to the circumstances in which possession was obtained must be reconsidered in light of the decision of the Supreme Court in *Patel v Mirza* [2016] UKSC 42; [2017] AC 467.

[53] *Costello* (n 32) [35].

refused—and were wrongly refusing—to return the car. Nonetheless, Costello was entitled to possession when the police's right to retain the car came to an end. Hence, *Costello* is a case in which the claimant, by virtue of his former possession, had an interest in the car that subsisted notwithstanding that the car was in the possession of another. Moreover, as the car was stolen, an unknown person—the victim of the theft—had a better title to the car than Costello. This shows that there is no distinction, in this regard, between the best title and inferior titles.

According to Fox, a person who has a lesser title can enforce it 'only against third parties who wrongfully dispossess him of the chattel or who derive title through such a person'.[54] However, Costello was not wrongfully dispossessed. The seizure of the car by the police was lawful. The wrong came later: it consisted of the police's refusal to return the car when their right to retain it had expired—at a time, that is, when the police, and not the claimant, had possession of the car. Costello had a right to possession that survived his loss of possession, and this right bound all those who did not have a better right.

The authorities discussed above support the contention that the subsistence of a lesser title is not dependent upon the title-holder retaining possession. Are there any cases that point in the opposite direction? It might be thought that the decision in *Buckley v Gross*[55] provides authority for the view that the subsistence of a lesser title is conditional on the title-holder remaining in possession.[56] Buckley had purchased some tallow from a person who had taken it after it had flowed into the River Thames. The police took the tallow and charged Buckley before a magistrate. The magistrate dismissed the charge, but ordered the tallow to be detained under section 29 of the Metropolitan Police Courts Act 1839. This provision conferred upon the magistrate the power, where 'the owner' could not be ascertained, to 'make such order with respect to such goods or money as to such magistrate shall seem meet'. The police detained the tallow for a time and then sold it to the defendants. Buckley's action in conversion failed. The court held that Buckley had no rights in respect of the tallow at the time of the alleged conversion.

According to Best and Smith's Report,[57] Crompton J maintained that '[t]his action must be founded on possession; here the possession was divested out of the plaintiff'.[58] So, Crompton J's view, it seems, was that the rights acquired by

---

[54] Fox (n 40) 348.

[55] (1863) 3 B & S 566; 122 ER 213; (1863) 32 LJQB 129; (1863) 9 Jur (NS) 986.

[56] cf Fox (n 40) 346–48.

[57] It should be noted that 'the variations in the reports of the judgments in [*Buckley v Gross*] raise questions as to the reliability of various reports': *Costello* (n 32) [22] (Lightman J).

[58] (1863) 3 B & S 566, 573; 122 ER 213, 216.

taking possession are lost if and when the possessor loses possession. It should be recalled, however, that the magistrate had made an order under section 29 of the 1839 Act. Cockburn CJ considered this crucial: Buckley's possession, and the title it gave rise to, were 'taken out of him by virtue of [the magistrate's] enactment'.[59] According to the Chief Justice, then, Buckley's title was extinguished, not when he lost possession, but as a result of the magistrate's order.

Cockburn CJ's analysis is supported by a number of later cases, including *Betts v Metropolitan Police District Receiver*[60] and *Irving v National Provincial Bank Ltd*.[61] In the latter, a magistrate made an order under section 1 of the Police (Property) Act 1897, which is materially the same as section 29 of the 1839 Act, for the delivery of money to the defendant. The police had taken the money from the claimant when he was arrested on suspicion of breaking and entering. He later brought an action against the defendant bank, arguing that his former possession had given him a title to the money that he could assert against it. The claimant's action failed. The Court of Appeal held that the effect of the order under section 1 of the 1897 Act was to divest the claimant of any title he might have had by virtue of his possession. Holroyd Pearce LJ said that the Act 'could have preserved the prior rights of possession in the former possessor. But it has not done so'.[62]

Irving not only supports the view that, in *Buckley v Gross*, the claimant's title was extinguished, not by virtue of the fact that Buckley had lost possession of the tallow, but by virtue of the magistrate's order. It also supports the more general argument advanced in this section, for if the loss of possession itself extinguishes a lesser title, then the reasoning of the Lord Justices in *Irving* would have been superfluous: it would not have been necessary to determine whether the magistrate's order extinguished the claimant's rights. Their Lordships apparently thought that the claimant would not have lost his title had the order not been made, notwithstanding the fact that the claimant had lost possession of the money. It was the magistrate's order, not the claimant's loss of possession, that extinguished the claimant's title.

One might think that the rules that were applied in *Costello* and similar cases regarding the subsistence of titles acquired by possession are confined to cases in which the police have lawfully seized goods from a possessor.[63]

---

[59] (1863) 3 B & S 566, 572; 122 ER 213, 215 (emphasis added).
[60] [1932] 2 KB 595 (KB).
[61] [1962] 2 QB 73 (CA).
[62] ibid 79.
[63] See, eg Norman Palmer (ed), *Palmer on Bailment* (3rd edn, Sweet & Maxwell 2009) para 4-149 (hereafter Palmer, *Bailment*).

When, however, one looks at these cases alongside the first category of cases discussed above, it becomes apparent that they really involved the application of general rules to a particular context. The two categories of cases, taken together, provide clear authority for the view that the subsistence of the interest acquired through possession is not dependent upon the retention of possession. It is a mistake, therefore, to regard possession as giving rise to mere rights of possession.

5.2.3 Alienability

This section considers the third feature of the interest acquired through possession, ie alienability. It is argued that the interest-holder has the power to transfer the interest to others *inter vivos*, or by will. This section focuses on the law of sale because the statutory provisions and case law concerning the sale of goods provide clear support for the contention that the interest acquired by possession can be alienated. If the interest can be alienated by sale, there is no reason to think that it cannot be alienated by deed or delivery during the proprietor's lifetime, or by will.

Section 2 of the Sale of Goods Act 1979 defines three of the law of sale's key terms: 'contract of sale', 'sale', and 'agreement to sell'. A 'contract of sale' is 'a contract by which the seller transfers or agrees to transfer the property in goods to the buyer for a money consideration, called the price'.[64] A 'contract of sale' is either a 'sale' or an 'agreement to sell'. It is a 'sale' if, under the contract of sale, 'the property in the goods is transferred from the seller to the buyer',[65] and it is an 'agreement to sell' if, under the contract of sale, 'the transfer of the property in the goods is to take place at a future time or subject to some condition later to be fulfilled'.[66] Where a contract is an 'agreement to sell', it 'becomes a sale when the time elapses or the conditions are fulfilled subject to which the property in the goods is to be transferred'.[67] Thus, a 'sale' involves a contract and a transfer of 'property' in goods.[68]

---

[64] Sale of Goods Act 1979 (hereafter SGA 1979) s 2(1). cf Consumer Rights Act 2015 (hereafter CRA 2015) s 5. 'Goods' includes 'all personal chattels other than things in action and money': SGA 1979, s 61(1).

[65] SGA 1979, s 2(4).

[66] SGA 1979, s 2(5).

[67] SGA 1979, s 2(6).

[68] Michael Bridge (ed), *Benjamin's Sale of Goods* (10th edn incorporating the Second Supplement, Sweet & Maxwell 2019) para 1-027 (hereafter Bridge, *Benjamin's Sale of Goods*); *Colley v Overseas Exporters* [1921] 3 KB 302 (KB) 310 (McCardie J).

What is the meaning of the term 'property' in these provisions? The Act defines 'property' as 'the general property in goods, and not merely a special property'.[69] One view is that 'general property' means 'true ownership' of goods or, in other words, the best title in respect of goods. It has been thought that Atkin LJ adopted this view in *Rowland v Divall*.[70] His Lordship maintained that 'there can be no sale at all of goods which the seller has no right to sell'.[71]

Graham Battersby and AD Preston have advanced a very convincing argument against the view that only the best title can be transferred by way of sale;[72] and this argument has been endorsed, and lucidly described, by Goode and McKendrick.[73] It will suffice here to make three key points. First, if 'general property' means 'best title' then there could never be a breach of the implied undertaking as to title in section 12(1) of the Act. The implied term, in the case of a 'sale', is that the seller has 'a right to sell the goods'. This has been interpreted as imposing on the seller, inter alia, an obligation to transfer the best title.[74] If every 'sale' necessarily involves a transfer of the best title to the goods, the obligation to transfer the best title 'becomes redundant'.[75] Secondly, the Act explicitly states that section 12(1) does not apply to 'a contract of sale in the case of which there appears from the contract or is to be inferred from its circumstances an intention that the seller should transfer only such title as he or a third person may have'.[76] Thirdly, sections 24 and 25 of the Act enable a person who does not have the best title, by delivering goods 'under any sale', to confer a title that is better than hers; and these provisions would 'make no sense' if there could not be a sale of a lesser title.[77] These considerations lead to the conclusion that the term 'property' in section 2 of the Sale of Goods Act does *not* mean the best title to the goods; inferior titles to goods, acquired through taking possession, can be transferred by way of sale.

These conclusions are also supported by the case law. In *National Employers' Mutual General Insurance Association Ltd v Jones*,[78] for instance, the House of

---

[69] SGA 1979, s 61(1). cf CRA 2015, s 4(1).

[70] [1923] 2 KB 500 (CA). See G Battersby and AD Preston, 'The Concepts of "Property", "Title" and "Owner" Used in the Sale of Goods Act 1893' (1972) 35 MLR 268, 272–74.

[71] [1923] 2 KB 500 (CA) 506. But see D Tiplady, 'When is a Seller not a Seller?' (1988) 51 MLR 240, 243.

[72] Battersby and Preston (n 70).

[73] McKendrick (n 38) paras 7.27–7.28.

[74] McKendrick (n 38) paras 8.23, 11.16; Bridge, *Benjamin's Sale of Goods* (n 68) paras 4-001, 4-002, 4-031.

[75] Battersby and Preston (n 70) 274.

[76] SGA 1979, s 12(1), (3).

[77] McKendrick (n 38) para 7.27.

[78] [1990] 1 AC 24 (HL). See also *Kulkarni v Manor Credit (Davenham) Ltd* [2010] EWCA Civ 69 [43] (Rix LJ).

Lords implicitly accepted that, where a person acquires a title to goods by possession, the title can be transferred by way of sale even if the title is not the best title to the goods. In this case, a thief stole X's car and sold it to another. The car was eventually purchased by A. A sold the car to B, who took possession. B then sold and delivered the car to C, who received it in good faith and without notice of the rights of X. C contended that, by virtue of section 25(1) of the Sale of Goods Act 1979,[79] X did not have a title to the car as against C. By virtue of this provision, if B 'bought or agreed to buy' the car from A, and B obtained, with A's consent, possession of the car, the delivery of the car 'under any sale, pledge or other disposition' to C has the 'same effect' as if B were 'a mercantile agent in possession of the [car] with the consent of the owner'. In *Jones*, the defendant submitted that the term 'owner' in section 25(1) refers to the person with the best title, X. The House of Lords rejected this analysis and held that the effect of the statute was to divest the title of the person who has entrusted the car to the possessor. B acquired possession of the car from A, not X. The result, therefore, was that the sale by B to C had no effect on the rights of X.

The reasoning of the Law Lords presupposes that a possessor acquires a 'general property interest' which can be transferred by way of sale.[80] Lord Goff, giving the leading speech, maintained that the effect of section 25(1) is to 'divest the title of [the] person who has entrusted [the possessor] with the possession of the relevant goods'.[81] His Lordship explained that if (1) B agreed to buy the car from A; (2) B obtained possession with A's consent; and (3) B delivered the car to C under a sale, the effect would be to deprive A, but not X, of his title.[82] This presupposes, of course, that A actually had a title—a general property interest—that he was able to sell to C.[83] Furthermore, Lord Goff thought that the sale by B to C would vest a title in C. Legal scholars disagree over whether, in such circumstances, A's title is destroyed, with the result that C takes B's title without being subject to A's;[84] or whether A's title is transferred to C.[85] Either way, the sale by B to C vests in C a title that is inferior to X's. This is not consistent with the view that only a supreme title can be transferred by way of sale.[86]

---

[79] The defendant also invoked section 9 of the Factors Act 1889, which is not materially different.

[80] See Graham Battersby, 'Acquiring Title by Theft' (2002) 65 MLR 603, 605.

[81] *National Employers'* (n 78) 62.

[82] ibid 61–63.

[83] See Lord Goff's analysis of the situation in which A remains in possession of stolen goods after selling them to B: *National Employers'* (n 78) 62.

[84] William Swadling, 'Property: General Principles' in Andrew Burrows (ed), *English Private Law* (3rd edn, OUP 2013) para 4.492.

[85] Graham Battersby, 'A Reconsideration of "Property" and "Title" in the Sale of Goods Act' [2001] JBL 1, 4–5.

[86] cf *National Employers'* (n 78) 50 (Sir Denys Buckley).

5.2.4 The Incidents of a Possessor's Interest: Conclusions

The analysis above supports the conclusion that, so far as chattels are concerned, the Strong Proprietary Interest View is correct. A person acquires, through taking possession of a chattel, an interest that comprises a right to exclude the rest of the world, but not anyone with a better right, from the chattel. The interest is not possession-dependent; it will survive a loss of possession. And the interest-holder has the power to transfer the interest to others. Accordingly, the view that the law protects possessors of chattels (solely) through the application of rules of evidence and presumption must be rejected: the possessor actually acquires certain rights. The claim that these rights are mere 'possessory rights'—rights of possession that serve solely to protect possession—must also be rejected. The possessor has an alienable proprietary interest, which is similar, in many ways, to the fee simple estate acquired by a possessor of land.

There is a lack of consensus as to what this interest should be called. It is often labelled a 'possessory title' or a 'possessory interest'.[87] There are, however, good reasons to avoid these labels.[88] The interest has also been called an 'absolute interest',[89] an 'ownership interest',[90] and a 'general property interest'.[91] One problem with 'absolute interest' is that the term 'absolute' may reasonably be regarded as signifying that the interest binds everyone without exception. However, the possessor's interest is not necessarily, and will not usually be, absolute in this sense. Alternatively, 'absolute' may be regarded as signifying that the interest is exclusive in the sense that, with respect to a particular chattel, there can be only one such interest. But the thought that the interest is, in this way, exclusive is mistaken. There is, in principle, no limit on the number of 'titles' that may exist in respect of a chattel.

It might be thought that, as 'ownership' also connotes exclusivity, it too is unsuitable. McFarlane has suggested that this problem can be avoided by distinguishing between 'ownership', which refers to the ordinary concept of ownership, and 'an Ownership', which refers to a particular kind of interest that is conferred by English law.[92] Accordingly, one might say that each of A and B is 'an Owner'. It is submitted, however, that the most appropriate term is 'general

---

[87] See, eg *Costello* (n 32) [14] (Lightman J); *The Aliakmon* (n 24) 809 (Lord Brandon); Palmer, *Bailment* (n 63) paras 4-001–4-005; Michael Bridge and others, *The Law of Personal Property* (2nd edn, Sweet & Maxwell 2018) para 10-018 (hereafter Bridge and others, *The Law of Personal Property*).

[88] For an argument in support of this claim, see Rostill, 'Terminology and Title' (n 48).

[89] eg Battersby and Preston (n 70) 268–71.

[90] eg McKendrick (n 38) paras 2.20–2.32.

[91] eg Robin Hickey, *Property and the Law of Finders* (Hart 2010) 167.

[92] McFarlane (n 5) 140–46.

property interest'. This term has a number of advantages. It does not connote exclusivity. And it is used, as we have seen, in the Sale of Goods Act 1979.[93] The term signifies (a) that the interest can be transferred by way of sale (provided that it is an interest in respect of 'goods'); and (b) that the interest is not a limited (or 'special') proprietary interest, such as a pledge. As Robin Hickey has said, the term 'seems adequately to reflect the substance of the law without relying expressly on the terminology of "ownership"', and it can serve 'as a personal property equivalent to "fee simple"'.[94] It is true that 'general property interests' are contrasted with 'special property interests', and some lawyers have thought that possession gives rise merely to a 'special property', not a 'general property'.[95] This thought, however, is premised on a mistaken view of the nature of the interest acquired through possession. If the interest has the features that have been attributed to it in this chapter, it is correct to regard it as a 'general property interest'. One might object to this proposal on the ground that 'general property interest' is a technical term and, unlike ownership, esoteric. But this is not a good objection; in legal discourse, a precise, unambiguous term of art is exactly what is needed.[96] It is suggested, therefore, that the most appropriate label for the interest that a person acquires upon taking possession of a chattel is 'general property interest'.

What is the scope of the rule? The answer is not entirely clear. One relevant consideration is that there is a distinction between obtaining a limited interest, such as a pledge, through taking possession under a grant, and independently acquiring a general property interest through taking possession. Another is that it would be absurd for a person who already has a right to exclusive possession, emanating from a general property interest, to acquire an additional general property interest each time he retakes possession. These factors suggest that a person, P, will acquire a general property interest if P takes possession of a chattel and P does not take under the grant of a limited legal interest (eg a pledge) or under a pre-existing right to exclusive possession.

5.3 Objections to the Strong Proprietary Interest View

The aim of this section is to examine and, ultimately, refute two objections to the Strong Proprietary Interest View so far as it concerns chattels. The first

---

[93] SGA 1979 s 61(1). cf *Sewell v Burdick (The Zoe)* (1884) 10 App Cas 74 (HL) 92–93 (Lord Blackburn).
[94] Hickey (n 91) 167.
[95] See Nicholas Curwen, 'General and Special Property in Goods' (2000) 20 LS 181, 182–83.
[96] cf AD Hargreaves, 'Modern Real Property' (1956) 19 MLR 14, 19–23.

objection, discussed in section 5.3.1, is that the Strong Proprietary Interest View is not compatible with a large set of cases in which the courts presumed that a possessor had 'absolute and complete ownership' of the chattel. The second objection, analysed in section 5.3.2, is that the Strong Proprietary Interest View is not consistent with the law concerning the circumstances in which a defendant can rely on the fact that a third party has a 'better title' than the claimant.

5.3.1 The First Objection: Possession and the Presumption of Ownership

It has been thought that the protection afforded by the law of torts is based, entirely, on a rule of presumption: where a possessor brings an action against a wrongdoer, the court must presume that the possessor is the owner. On this view, the possessor does not actually acquire any rights in respect of the chattel, though, in certain circumstances, possessors will be treated by the law *as though* they had the rights of an owner. One who endorses this view would, therefore, reject the claim, defended in section 5.2.1 above, that a possessor actually acquires a right to exclude.

Are there any cases that provide authority for the claim that a possessor does not truly acquire any rights? There are certainly many cases in which the courts have applied the rule that, where a wrongdoer interferes with a chattel in the possession of another, the possessor must be presumed to be the owner of the chattel.[97] Within this body of case law, however, a distinction should be drawn between cases that are inconsistent with the proposition that a possessor actually acquires a right to exclude, and cases that are compatible with this proposition.

An example of a case that belongs to the first category is *R v Allpress*.[98] In *Allpress*, the Court of Appeal dealt with five appeals arising from confiscation orders made against defendants who had safeguarded or transferred money that represented proceeds of crime. Four of the defendants had acted as couriers or custodians of cash for drug traffickers. It was clear that the applicable confiscation legislation was intended to deprive individuals of benefits they had gained from their criminal conduct.[99] The main issue on the appeals concerned

---

[97] See Luke Rostill, 'Relative Title and Deemed Ownership in English Personal Property Law' (2015) 35 OJLS 31.

[98] [2009] EWCA Crim 8; [2009] 2 Cr App R (S) 58.

[99] *R v May* [2008] UKHL 28; [2008] 1 AC 1028 [48].

the nature and extent of the benefits that the defendants had obtained and, in particular, whether a defendant who receives possession of cash or goods in connection with an offence is liable to a confiscation order in respect of the value of the cash or goods.

One of the arguments advanced by the Crown concerned section 76(4) of the Proceeds of Crime Act 2002. This provides that '[a] person benefits from conduct if he obtains property as a result of or in connection with the conduct'. Section 84(2)(b) states that 'property is obtained by a person if he obtains an interest in it'; and, by virtue of section 84(2)(h), 'an interest' includes 'a right to possession'. The Crown submitted that a carrier or custodian is in possession under a bailment and, consequently, has a 'right to possession' within the meaning of section 84(2)(h).[100] The Crown pointed out that a bailee can sue a wrongdoer in tort and recover the value of the chattel.[101]

The Court of Appeal rejected this argument. Toulson LJ, giving the judgment of the court, accepted that a courier or custodian has 'physical possession',[102] but repudiated the contention that it followed from this that a courier or custodian has a right to possession.[103] His Lordship accepted that 'a bailee can maintain an action for the value of the goods against a third party who wrongly interferes with his possession', but:

> [t]he reason is that . . . as between the possessor and the wrongdoer the law will *presume* 'that the person who has the possession has the property' .... That is far removed from the question whether a mere custodian has a right to possession so as to have an interest in property for the purposes of [s 84(2) of the 2002 Act].[104]

In the Court of Appeal's view, then, a person who is in possession of cash or goods does not have 'a right to possession' for the purposes of the 2002 Act. A possessor can successfully sue, and recover the full value from, a person who tortiously interferes with the goods or cash, but the reason for this is that, as between them, the law will *presume* that the possessor has 'the property'. Toulson LJ's reasoning seems to support, therefore, the view that a possessor is protected by a rule of presumption and does not actually have a right to exclusive

---

[100] *Allpress* (n 98) [64], [65], [76].
[101] ibid [76].
[102] ibid [30].
[103] ibid [69]–[79].
[104] ibid [76] (emphasis added, citation omitted).

possession. But this view is not consistent with the body of case law discussed in section 5.2 above, which Toulson LJ did not consider.

Alongside cases such as *Allpress*, there is a category of cases where a possessor has benefited from the application of a rule of presumption, yet the decision and reasoning of the court is perfectly compatible with the proposition that the possessor has an interest that comprises a right to exclude. The leading case is *The Winkfield*,[105] in which a bailee of letters and parcels sought to recover their full value. Sir FH Jeune P disallowed this claim on the basis that the bailee was not liable to his bailors in respect of the loss of the chattels. The Court of Appeal allowed the bailee's appeal. Sir Richard Collins MR (with whom Stirling and Mathew LJJ agreed) said that the bailee's possession was 'good against a wrongdoer' and that the bailee could 'recover the whole value of the goods'.[106] A possessor's entitlement to recover the full value rests on the fact that, as between possessor and wrongdoer, the 'presumption of law' is that the possessor has 'not a limited interest, but *absolute and complete ownership*'.[107] In contrast, '[a]s between bailor and bailee the real interests of each must be inquired into';[108] and the bailee must account to his bailor for the amount by which the sum received from the defendant surpasses the bailee's true loss.[109]

While the rule applied by Collins MR has been qualified,[110] the authority of *The Winkfield* has never been seriously doubted. Indeed, the case has been cited with approval by numerous law lords in the Privy Council and the House of Lords.[111] Collins MR's explanation as to why a possessor is able to recover the full value from a tortfeasor is, therefore, legally authoritative.[112]

It is important to recognise that Collins MR's reasoning is compatible with the proposition that the person who is treated as the 'true owner' actually has certain rights in respect of the chattel. It is clear, for instance, that the presumption of ownership applies to pledgees.[113] Yet it is beyond doubt that, by virtue of the grant from the pledgor, the pledgee acquires a legal interest that comprises

---

[105] *The Winkfield* (n 21).
[106] ibid 54.
[107] ibid 55, 60 (emphasis added).
[108] ibid 60.
[109] ibid 55. See also *O'Sullivan v Williams* [1992] 3 All ER 385 (CA) 387 (Fox LJ).
[110] See, eg Palmer, *Bailment* (n 63) paras 4-095–4-098. Importantly, the rule is not applicable where the defendant shows, in accordance with section 8(1) of the Torts (Interference with Goods) Act 1977, that a third party has a better right than the claimant: see section 5.3.2 below.
[111] eg *Eastern Construction Co Ltd v National Trust Co Ltd* [1914] AC 197 (PC) 210; *Morrison Steamship Co Ltd v Greystoke Castle* [1947] AC 265 (HL) 278 (Lord Roche), 293 (Lord Porter), 302 (Lord Simonds), 309 (Lord Uthwatt); *Alfred McAlpine Construction Ltd v Panatown Ltd (No 1)* [2001] 1 AC 518 (HL) 581 (Lord Millett).
[112] The *Winkfield* rule has been extended to cases in which the claimant had a right to possession, but was not actually in possession, at the relevant time: *The Jag Shakti* [1986] AC 337 (PC).
[113] *The Jag Shakti* (n 112).

a right to exclusive possession.[114] The position is, therefore, that the pledgee actually has certain rights in respect of the chattel and, in addition, she will be treated as the 'true owner' as against a wrongdoer. It is suggested that a similar analysis applies to those who acquire an interest through possession. Where a person, P, independently takes possession of a chattel without having already acquired an interest that comprises a right to exclusive possession, P acquires, by virtue of her possession, a general property interest. If someone else already has a general property interest in the chattel, P will acquire an *inferior* general property interest. But, by virtue of the rule in *The Winkfield*, P will be treated, as against a wrongdoer, as though P were the 'absolute and complete owner', and P's damages will be assessed on this basis. Understood in this way, there is, in truth, no conflict between *The Winkfield* and the case law discussed in section 5.2 above.

5.3.2 The Strong Proprietary Interest View and the *Jus Tertii*

Is the Strong Proprietary Interest View compatible with the law concerning the circumstances in which a defendant can resist the claimant's action by establishing that a third party has a better title than the claimant? This is not a straightforward matter, for the pertinent body of law is, in some respects, uncertain; partly as a result of this, the legal position has been much debated by scholars.[115] The issue is complicated further by two factors, which have not been sufficiently recognised. The first is that some writers, but not all, treat the *jus tertii* as a defence in the sense described by James Goudkamp:

> the word 'defence' refers only to rules that, when enlivened, result in a verdict for the defendant even though all of the ingredients of the tort in which the claimant sues are present . . . Denials of elements of the tort in which the claimant sues do not qualify as defences when the word 'defence' is used in this way.[116]

Goudkamp notes that defining 'defence' in this way 'brings into focus the fundamental difference between rules that define torts and rules that release

---

[114] *Franklin* (n 2); *The Odessa* (n 2) 157–59 (Lord Mersey).

[115] Atiyah (n 48); CD Baker, 'The *Jus Tertii*: A Restatement' (1990–91) 16 U of Queensland LJ 46; Graham Battersby, 'The Present Status of the *Jus Tertii* Principle' [1992] Conv 100 (hereafter Battersby, 'Present Status'); Douglas, *Liability* (n 9) 26–27; *Clerk & Lindsell* (n 14) para 17-80–17-81.

[116] James Goudkamp, *Tort Law Defences* (Hart 2013) 2.

from liability a defendant whose conduct constitutes a tort'.[117] Scholars have disagreed over how to characterise the *jus tertii*. Anthony Jolly, for instance, thought that, if the defendant establishes that a third party has a better title than the claimant, the defendant thereby shows that the claimant has no right at all:

> the true *jus tertii* is a means of effacing rather than overwhelming the plaintiff's allegation of a right to possession ... The plaintiff alleges a right to possession, and the defendant defeats it not by confession and avoidance but by traverse. The *jus* which the defendant puts forward is not something superior to the plaintiff's right yet compatible with it. It is something which by its very incompatibility disproves the plaintiff's right.[118]

On this view, then, to claim that a third party has a better title than the claimant is to deny that the claimant has been wronged. This presupposes that the Strong Proprietary Interest View is false: that the claimant does not really have any rights in respect of the chattel, but can, by virtue of her possession, invoke the presumption of ownership, which the defendant can rebut, where he is permitted to do so, by showing that a third party has a 'better title'. Patrick Atiyah, on the other hand, treated the *jus tertii* as a defence.[119] He claimed that there is an important distinction between cases in which the defendant shows that she has not wronged the claimant because the claimant 'has no right at all',[120] and cases in which the 'the plaintiff has a better right to possession than the defendant, but ... a third party has a better right than either of them';[121] only the latter involve 'the defence of the *jus tertii*'.

The second complicating factor, which Atiyah and Jolly both seem to have overlooked, is that there is a distinction between: (a) totally defeating the claimant's claim by showing that a third party has a better title; and (b) reducing the claimant's damages by showing that a third party has a better title.[122] Where, for instance, a claimant who has a lesser interest in a chattel (eg an inferior general property interest or a pledge) relies upon the *Winkfield* rule in order to recover the full value of the chattel from a defendant who has

---

[117] ibid 6–7.

[118] Anthony Jolly, 'The Jus Tertii and the Third Man' (1955) 18 MLR 371, 371. Atiyah, in his reply to Jolly, appears to *accept* this point: (1955) 18 MLR 595. Baker has rightly pointed out that this 'seems wholly inconsistent with the views expressed' by Atiyah in his article: Baker (n 115) 61, fn 68.

[119] Atiyah (n 48) 98, 100. See also Battersby, 'Present Status' (n 115); Douglas, *Liability* (n 9) 26–27.

[120] Atiyah (n 48) 100.

[121] ibid.

[122] Law Reform Committee, *Eighteenth Report (Conversion and Detinue)* (Cmnd 4774, 1971) para 58 (hereafter *Eighteenth Report (Conversion and Detinue)*); Palmer, *Bailment* (n 63) paras 4-122–4-124.

tortiously interfered with it, the defendant might seek to show that a third party has a better title than the claimant in order to reduce the damages awarded to the claimant.

If the Strong Proprietary Interest View is correct, the defendant should not be able, generally speaking,[123] to totally avoid liability merely by showing that a third party has a better title than the claimant.[124] If C actually has a general property interest that comprises a right to exclude others, including D, from the chattel, then D, by interfering with the chattel, wrongs C. So far as C's claim that D has wronged C is concerned, the fact that X has a better right is, as Robert Chambers has said, 'irrelevant': D's interference is 'still wrong'.[125] Where, however, C relies upon the presumption of 'absolute and complete ownership' with a view to recovering the full value of the chattel, it is arguable that D should be permitted to rebut the presumption by showing that a third party has an interest that is binding on C. In such circumstances, D is not denying that he has wronged the claimant; he is denying that he has wronged the claimant in the way alleged (ie by infringing the best right). In short, while it is arguable that D should be allowed to invoke the *jus tertii* in support of his denial of the claim that C is the true owner, the *jus tertii* should not provide a defence to C's claim that D has wronged C by infringing C's (actual) right to exclusive possession. The question, then, is whether the authorities are compatible with this analysis? As the law was amended by the Torts (Interference with Goods) Act 1977, it is useful to address the question in two stages. The position before Parliament intervened is examined in section 5.3.2.1. The changes introduced by the 1977 Act are examined in section 5.3.2.2. It is argued that, while the position at common law is, in some respects, uncertain, the case law and the 1977 Act are both compatible with the Strong Proprietary Interest View.

5.3.2.1 The *jus tertii* and the common law

The case law supports,[126] and academics have generally accepted,[127] the proposition that a defendant can wholly avoid liability by establishing that a third party has a better title than the claimant, if the defendant: (a) interfered with

---

[123] The position is different where the defendant interferes with the chattel, or defends the action, by the authority of the third party.

[124] As we saw in the previous chapter, where C has a title to land and seeks to recover from D possession and/or damages for trespass, private nuisance, or property damage resulting from negligence, D cannot defeat C's claim by showing that a third party has a better title: Chapter 4 (section 4.2.2.2).

[125] Robert Chambers, *An Introduction to Property Law in Australia* (3rd edn, Lawbook Co 2013) para 7.65.

[126] *Biddle v Bond* (1865) 6 B & S 225; 122 ER 1179 (QB); *Rogers Sons & Co v Lambert & Co* [1891] 1 QB 318 (CA); *The Jupiter (No 3)* [1927] P 122 (PDA) 137 (Hill J).

[127] eg Baker (n 115) 47–49; *Clerk & Lindsell* (n 14) para 17-80.

the chattel by the authority of the third party; or (b) defends the action on be-half of the third party. Such cases apart, the traditional view is that, at common law, there was a crucial distinction between cases in which the claimant had possession at the time of the alleged tort, and cases where the claimant was not in possession. If the claimant was in possession,[128] the defendant was unable to wholly avoid liability, or reduce the claimant's damages, by showing that a third party had a better title. If, however, the claimant was *not* in possession, the de-fendant was able to totally avoid liability by showing that a third party had a better title (unless the defendant was a bailee who was estopped from denying the title of the claimant/bailor).[129] This view has been endorsed by many dis-tinguished lawyers, including AV Dicey,[130] Frederick Pollock,[131] and William Holdsworth.[132] It is difficult to reconcile the Strong Proprietary Interest View with the contention that, if the claimant was not in possession, the defendant has a full defence. It is no surprise, therefore, that Dicey's statement of the tra-ditional view, which is the earliest, presupposes that the Strong Proprietary Interest View is false. According to Dicey, the defendant, by establishing that a third party has a better title, shows 'that the plaintiff had *no right to possession at all*'.[133]

Is the traditional view correct? There can be no doubt that the position at common law was that, if the claimant was in possession at the time of the defendant's alleged tort, the defendant was not able to avoid liability, or reduce the claimant's damages, by establishing that a third party had a better title.[134] But it is far less clear what the position was where the claimant was *not* in pos-session at the time of the alleged tort.

There are some cases that may appear to support the traditional view. Consider, for instance, *Leake v Loveday*,[135] one of the cases that is usually cited

---

[128] For the meaning of possession, in this context, see Chapter 2 (section 2.3).

[129] At common law, the bailee was generally estopped from denying that her bailor had a good title unless the bailee had been evicted by title paramount or defended the action by the authority of the third party: *Biddle* (n 126); *Rogers* (n 126).

[130] AV Dicey, *A Treatise on the Rules for the Selection of Parties to an Action* (W Maxwell & Son 1870) 356–57.

[131] Frederick Pollock and Robert Samuel Wright, *An Essay on Possession in the Common Law* (Clarendon Press 1888) 91–92. Baker maintained that this view originated with Pollock: Baker (n 115) 46. But the treatise in which Dicey outlines and endorses the view was published in 1870, nearly two decades before Pollock's *Essay on Possession*.

[132] WS Holdsworth, *A History of English Law*, vol VII (Methuen & Co 1925) 421–31. See also: *Eighteenth Report (Conversion and Detinue)* (n 122) paras 51–53.

[133] Dicey (n 130) 357. cf WTS Stallybrass (ed), *Salmond on the Law of Torts* (8th edn, Sweet and Maxwell 1934) 334: 'If ... the plaintiff was not in actual possession ... he must recover on the strength of his title, and proof of the *jus tertii* will destroy the only thing upon which he relies'.

[134] *Nelson v Cherrill* (1832) 8 Bing 316; 131 ER 415; *Carter v Johnson* (1839) 2 Mood & R 263; 174 ER 283; *Jeffries v Great Western Railway* (n 21); *The Winkfield* (n 21).

[135] (1842) 4 M & G 972; 134 ER 399.

by those who endorse the traditional view. The claimant bought some furniture from Cox, who remained in possession. Cox became bankrupt, and the furniture was later seized by the defendant, a sheriff. The defendant sold the furniture and handed over the proceeds to the assignees in bankruptcy. The claimant's action in trover against the defendant failed. According to the headnote, the court held 'that, under the plea of not possessed, the sheriff might set up the title of the assignees'.[136] As Atiyah and others have pointed out,[137] however, the claimant, at the time of the seizure, had no interest in the goods at all: he had never been in possession and the title that had been assigned to him was lost as a result of Cox's bankruptcy. Maule J said, 'Here, the defendants say that the plaintiff has no right to the goods at all. The evidence given by them was offered, not to show the right of third persons, but to prove that the goods were not the property of the plaintiff'.[138]

Now, if the Strong Proprietary Interest View is mistaken, and the Presumed Property View is sound, *Leake v Loveday* might be relied upon by way of analogy. The argument would run thus: just as the defendant in *Leake v Loveday* was able to avoid liability by establishing that the claimant did not really have any rights in the chattel, a defendant should be able to invoke the better title of a third party in order to show that the claimant has no right at all. The analogy can be drawn, however, only if the Strong Proprietary Interest View is false. And the contention that it is false is at odds with the case law discussed in section 5.2 above, which shows that a possessor really acquires a general property interest that comprises a right to exclude. Consequently, there is a crucial distinction between cases such as *Leake v Loveday*, and cases in which the claimant obtained a proprietary interest through possession. In the former, the claimant had no rights in respect of the chattel at the time of the alleged tort and, therefore, the defendant did not wrong the claimant. But in the latter, the claimant acquired, by taking possession, an interest that included a right to exclude others, including the defendant; and the defendant, by interfering with the chattel, infringed the claimant's right. The fact that a third party has a better right than the claimant does not alter the fact that the defendant has wronged the claimant.

Are there any cases that support this analysis? Atiyah relied upon *Bridges v Hawkesworth* and *Hannah v Peel*.[139] But, as CD Baker has observed, 'no reliance on *jus tertii* was placed by the defendants in those cases, nor was it

---

[136] ibid.
[137] Atiyah (n 48) 100–02; Baker (n 115) 59–61; Battersby, 'Present Status' (n 115) 106–10.
[138] (1842) 4 M & G 972, 986; 134 ER 399, 404.
[139] *Bridges* (n 31); *Hannah* (n 44).

considered as a possible defence in the judgments'.[140] Moreover, in both cases the person with the 'better title' was unknown;[141] and it seems that, in those cases where the law permits a defendant to rely upon the better title of a third party, the third party must be identified.[142] Joshua Getzler has suggested that 'with the decision in *Costello*, Atiyah may finally now have the authority he needs . . . to alert the textbook-writers of today to a possible need to rethink the distinction between actual possession and rights to possession in relation to the *jus tertii* defence'.[143] But if the point that Baker advanced against Atiyah with respect to *Bridges v Hawkesworth* and *Hannah v Peel* is sound, it also applies to *Costello*; for in *Costello*, too, the identity of the third party with a better title was unknown.[144]

There is, however, some authority for the contention that, even where the claimant was not in possession at the time of the alleged tort, the general position, at common law, was that it was not a full defence to identify a third party with a better right. In *Barker v Furlong*,[145] for example, S's interest in some furniture was assigned, upon her marriage, to trustees upon certain trusts. S, by her will, left the furniture to C to hold on trust for S's husband and child. C took possession of the furniture and then allowed the husband, D1, to hold and use it. Without C's knowledge or consent, D1, with the assistance of his agent, D2, sent the furniture to a firm of auctioneers, D3, who sold it. C sued D1, D2, and D3 for conversion. D2 and D3 argued that the furniture did not belong to C or S, because 'the property was in the trustees of the [marriage] settlement'.[146] They conceded that if C had 'been in actual possession of the chattels', they would probably have been 'unable to set up the *jus tertii*';[147] but C, they argued, was not in actual possession. Romer J accepted that C was not in actual possession but denied that D1 and D2 were 'at liberty to set up the *jus tertii*'.[148] His Lordship said:

> when there is a right of immediate possession coupled with a title to goods, though the title may be not perfect as against, or may even be liable to be defeated by, the claim of a third person, yet, if that third person has not

---

[140] Baker (n 115) 61.

[141] The same may be said with respect to *Parker* (n 33).

[142] *Rogers* (n 126) 324 (Lord Esher MR); *Costello* (n 32). See also Jolly (n 118) 373; Baker (n 115) 61–62; cf Battersby, 'Present Status' (n 115) 104–05.

[143] Getzler (n 50) 570. For a discussion of *Costello*, see section 5.2.2.

[144] *Costello* (n 32) [15].

[145] [1891] 2 Ch 172 (Ch).

[146] ibid 177.

[147] ibid.

[148] ibid 179.

intervened, a wrongdoer dealing with the chattels cannot set up the title of that third person as an answer to an action against him for his wrongdoing.[149]

Barker v Furlong is sometimes regarded as a case that illustrates that a trustee 'has possession of chattels in the hands of the beneficiary'.[150] But even if it is correct to say that C was in possession at the time of the conversions, the fact remains that Romer J plainly did not think it mattered whether C was in possession or had merely a right to possession: either way, the defendants were not 'at liberty to set up the *jus tertii*'. If this is right, the distinction drawn by Dicey, Pollock, and Holdsworth is erroneous.

The case law suggests, then, that except where the defendant acted or defended under the authority of a third party, the defendant was not able, at common law, to wholly avoid liability by showing that a third party had a better right. Put simply, the *jus tertii* was not a defence. This is perfectly consistent with the Strong Proprietary Interest View.

In some respects, however, the protection provided by the common law to a claimant with an inferior title seems to have gone too far. This concerns the measure of recovery. We have seen that, under the *Winkfield* rule, a claimant with a lesser interest, including an inferior general property interest, is able to recover the full value from a tortfeasor if the claimant was in possession, or had a right to immediate possession, at the time of the tort. The reason is that the law will treat the claimant as though he were the 'absolute and complete owner' (ie the person who has the supreme general property interest in possession) and his damages will be assessed on this basis. The defendant, it seems, was not generally permitted to rebut the presumption that the claimant had 'absolute and complete ownership' by showing that a third party had a better right than the claimant.[151] One question that arises is whether enabling C to recover the full value, where it is known that C is not, in fact, the true owner, is justifiable.[152] Whatever one may think about this general issue, it is difficult to deny that the common law rules sometimes led to very harsh results. To give one example, D could have been subject to a double liability: he could have been required, as a result of one and the same act of interference, to first pay the full value of the chattel to C1, and then to pay the full value to C2 (a person who

---

[149] ibid 180–81.
[150] Edwin Peel and James Goudkamp (eds), *Winfield & Jolowicz on Tort* (19th edn, Sweet & Maxwell 2014) para 18-011. cf *Wilson v Lombank Ltd* [1963] 1 WLR 1294.
[151] *The Winkfield* (n 21).
[152] For a critical analysis of the *Winkfield* rule, see Luke Rostill, 'Possession and Damages for Tortious Interferences with Chattels' (2021) 41 OJLS (forthcoming).

had a better title than C1).[153] The Law Reform Committee rightly thought that this was unjust. It proposed a number of reforms,[154] and many of these were implemented by the Torts (Interference with Goods) Act 1977.

5.3.2.2 The *jus tertii* and the Torts (Interference with Goods) Act 1977

Section 8(1) of the Torts (Interference with Goods) Act 1977 provides that a defendant to an action for 'wrongful interference [with goods] shall be entitled to show, in accordance with rules of court, that a third party has a better right than the plaintiff as respects all or any part of the interest claimed by the plaintiff, or in right of which he sues'. In order for a defendant to rely upon this provision, the third party must be identified.[155] The Civil Procedure Rules require the claimant to identify 'every person who, to his knowledge, has or claims an interest in the goods'.[156] The defendant may apply to the court for a direction that a third party be made a party to the proceedings for the purpose of establishing whether he has a better right than the claimant.[157] Section 7(2) of the 1977 Act states that, where two or more claimants are parties to proceedings, 'the relief shall be such as to avoid double liability of the wrongdoer as between those claimants'. The definition of 'double liability' includes 'the double liability of the wrongdoer which can arise . . . where one of two or more rights of action for wrongful interference is founded on a possessory title'.[158]

Are the rules introduced by and under the 1977 Act compatible with the Strong Proprietary Interest View? It is submitted that they are. Suppose that C takes possession of X's car without X's consent. Thereafter, D takes the car and uses it for her own purposes. C sues D in conversion, claiming the value of the car and damages for consequential loss. D shows, in accordance with section 8(1), that X has a superior general property interest. What is the effect of this? Clearly, C will not be able to recover the value of the car from D. By showing that X has a superior interest, D has rebutted the presumption that C has 'absolute and complete ownership'. But does section 8(1) allow D to avoid liability to C altogether? If C, by taking possession, acquired no rights at all—if the Strong Proprietary Interest View were false—then it would seemingly follow that the effect of rebutting the presumption of ownership is to show that D has

---

[153] *Attenborough v London and St Katharine's Dock Co* (1878) 3 CPD 450 (CA) 454 (Bramwell LJ); *Eighteenth Report (Conversion and Detinue)* (n 122) paras 51–57.

[154] *Eighteenth Report (Conversion and Detinue)* (n 122) paras 58–78.

[155] *Costello* (n 32) [15]. There is some judicial support for the view that the third party must be joined: *de Franco v Commissioner of Police of the Metropolis*, The Times, 8 May 1987 (CA).

[156] CPR 19.5A(1).

[157] CPR 19.5A(2).

[158] Torts (Interference with Goods) Act 1977, s 7(1).

not wronged C at all; and if D has not wronged C, C's claim should fail. But if, as this chapter has argued, C actually acquired an interest in the car by taking possession, then different considerations apply. D wronged C by infringing C's right to exclusive possession, and C should be able to recover appropriate relief from D, such as compensation for the losses that C has suffered as a result of the wrong. The language of section 8(1) is fully consistent with this.[159] It permits D to show that X has a 'better right than [C] as respects *all or any part of the interest claimed by* [C], or in right of which he sues'. C's claim for the full value of the car is based on the proposition that C had 'absolute and complete ownership'; and D has defeated this claim by showing that X has a 'better right'. But insofar as C's claim for damages is based on the rights C actually acquired, and which D actually infringed, X's better title is irrelevant. They are C's rights, not X's; section 8(1) does not concern them. This is in line with the aims of the legislation. To require D to compensate C and X for the losses they have actually suffered is not to subject D to a double liability, but to require D to make amends for infringing distinct rights.[160]

5.4 Conclusion

The main conclusion of this chapter is that the interest acquired through possession is a general property interest. This interest, which is not possession-dependent, comprises a right to exclusive possession, as well as various dispositive powers. These include the power to alienate the interest by deed, delivery, or—provided that the interest is an interest in respect of 'goods'—sale. It is a mistake, therefore, to claim that, by taking possession of a chattel, a possessor acquires mere rights of possession. It is also a mistake to claim that a possessor is protected solely by rules of presumption, though a person who is in possession, or has a right to possession, will generally be presumed to have 'absolute and complete ownership' if a person with a better right cannot be identified. In short, the Strong Proprietary Interest View and (a version of) the Presumed Property View are sound, so far as chattels are concerned.

These conclusions have two important implications. First, the interest acquired through taking possession of chattels is similar to the interest acquired through taking possession of land. In other words, a general property interest

---

[159] The analysis presented here is also consonant with the Law Reform Committee's report: *Eighteenth Report (Conversion and Detinue)* (n 122) paras 66–67, 73–75.
[160] cf *Sevilleja v Marex Financial Ltd* [2020] UKSC 31; [2020] 3 WLR 255 [2] (Lord Reed PSC).

is, in some important respects, similar to a fee simple estate. They both comprise a right to exclude, are capable of lasting forever, are not possession-dependent, and can be alienated *inter vivos* or by will.

Secondly, some influential accounts of the law of personal property ought to be reconsidered. For instance, according to *Goodeve's Modern Law of Personal Property* there are three interests that a person may have in a tangible chattel under English law: (a) 'absolute ownership'; (b) 'mere possession'; and (c) 'bailment'.[161] On this view, if A manufactures a thing and B takes possession of it without A's consent, A has 'absolute ownership' and B has 'possession'. If, however, the main conclusions of this chapter are correct, it is confusing and misleading to regard B as having 'possession'. It is confusing because the same word is being used to refer to two distinct things: first, the conditions that must be met in order to acquire an interest (ie physical control combined with the requisite intention); secondly, the interest that is acquired if those conditions are met. It is misleading because it suggests that the interest is possession-dependent. It is clearer, and more illuminating, to say that B and A each hold a general property interest, and that B's general property interest is inferior to A's. This is not to say, however, that A's and B's positions are in all material respects the same, or that both of them are 'owners'. Indeed, it is argued in Chapter 7 that their positions are, in some important respects, different, and these differences have important ramifications for the applicability of the concept of ownership.

---

[161] RH Kersley (ed), *Goodeve's Modern Law of Personal Property* (9th edn, Sweet & Maxwell 1949) 8–9. See also Norman Palmer and ELG Tyler (eds), *Crossley Vaines' Personal Property* (5th edn, Butterworths 1973) ch 4; Bridge and others, *The Law of Personal Property* (n 87) chs 2, 10.

6

The Grounds of Relative Title

6.1 Introduction

Sir Edward Coke, following Littleton, urged his readers to apprehend the 'arguments and reasons' of the law.[1] Much could be said about how to interpret this instruction. One plausible view is that Coke was, among other things, advancing the sound thesis that, in order to fully understand a rule of law, it is not enough to know what the content of the rule is; it is also necessary to ascertain whether the rule has a legal rationale and, if so, what the rationale is. Consider, for example, the rule against private purpose trusts. One has an impoverished understanding of this rule if one is not aware that the law regards the rule as based (or partly based) on the principle that the administration of trusts should be supervised by the courts.[2] This principle is the legal ground, or one of the grounds, of the rule.[3]

Ascertaining the grounds of a legal rule enhances one's understanding of it in various respects. First, by identifying the legal grounds of a rule, one acquires an understanding of why the law has adopted and/or retained the rule. Secondly, the grounds of legal rules, as Joseph Raz has explained, 'illuminate their point and purpose': they are 'invaluable guides to the interpretation' of the rules and 'help decide what weight to give the [rules] when these conflict with others'.[4] Thirdly, by identifying the grounds of a rule, one identifies some of the legal reasons for the courts to retain or develop the rule.[5] Fourthly, once the legal grounds of the rule have been identified, one can evaluate whether

---

[1] Co Litt 394a, 395b.

[2] *Morice v Bishop of Durham* (1804) 9 Ves Jr 399, 404–05 (Grant MR); (1805) 10 Ves Jr 522, 539–40 (Lord Eldon); *Re Astor's Settlement Trusts* [1952] Ch 534 (Ch) 542 (Roxburgh J). The principle is the basis, or one of the bases, of other rules too: see, eg *McPhail v Doulton* [1971] AC 424 (HL) 450–57 (Lord Wilberforce).

[3] In this chapter, then, the 'legal grounds' of a rule are simply the law's reasons for having the rule. But note that the term is sometimes used in other ways.

[4] Joseph Raz, 'Legal Rights' (1984) 4 OJLS 1, 11.

[5] ibid 9–12.

Possession, Relative Title, and Ownership in English Law. Luke Rostill, Oxford University Press (2021). © Luke Rostill.
DOI: 10.1093/oso/9780198843108.003.0006

they really provide an adequate reason for the retention, or the development, of the rule.[6]

So far, this book has focused primarily on the content of the title by possession rules and their scope of application. We have seen that English law confers extensive proprietary interests on possessors: a fee simple estate in cases involving land, and a general property interest in cases involving chattels. Consequently, it is possible for multiple, competing proprietary interests—interests of the same kind—to exist, concurrently, in respect of the same tangible thing. Since there can be multiple, competing interests (eg multiple fees simple in respect of the same land), it is necessary for the law to rank the interests. The general rule is that an earlier interest has priority over a later interest.[7] If an interest-holder brings an action to recover possession of land, or an action in tort for wrongful interference with land or goods, it generally suffices that the claimant has an interest that is good as against the defendant.[8] The fact that an unconnected third party has a better right is irrelevant (though, as we have seen,[9] the remedy that the claimant is awarded may be affected by proof that an ascertained third party has a better right).

For the reasons outlined above, it is important to consider the grounds of the common law acquisition rules, ie the rules that confer titles—more precisely, fees simple or general property interests—on possessors. There are four important questions about the grounds of the acquisition rules that must not be conflated. First, what are the legal grounds of the rules? In other words, what, according to the law, are the reasons for having the rules? Secondly, are the law's reasons *genuine* reasons for maintaining the rules? If so, are these reasons *adequate*, or are they defeated by other considerations? Fourthly, are there reasons for the maintenance of the rules that have not been recognised by the law?

This chapter seeks to identify what the main legal grounds of the general common law acquisition rules actually are,[10] and whether these grounds provide genuine reasons for the maintenance of the rules. It has already been pointed out in this book,[11] and has long been recognised by

---

[6] An adequate reason is a reason that is undefeated by other considerations: Joseph Raz, *From Normativity to Responsibility* (OUP 2011) 103, 109, 113–14. See also Joseph Raz, *Practical Reason and Norms* (OUP 1999) ch 1.

[7] See William Swadling, 'Property: General Principles' in Andrew Burrows (ed), *English Private Law* (3rd edn, OUP 2013) paras 4.423, 4.424, 4.427.

[8] See Chapter 4 (sections 4.2.1 and 4.2.2.2); Chapter 5 (section 5.3.2).

[9] See Chapter 5 (section 5.3.2).

[10] This chapter does not examine the grounds of the special rules that apply to possessors of land in respect of chattels found in or on the land. For discussion, see Robin Hickey, *Property and the Law of Finders* (Hart 2010) 39–53, 92–95; Michael JR Crawford, *An Expressive Theory of Possession* (Hart 2020) ch 6.

[11] See Chapter 3 (section 3.2.1) and Chapter 4 (section 4.2.2.1).

commentators,[12] that conferring rights to exclude on possessors discourages violence and helps to prevent civil unrest. The law has embraced this reasoning: it regards the need to discourage violence and civil unrest as reasons for protecting possessors. But, as others have explained,[13] these considerations do not justify or provide pro tanto reasons for the maintenance of rules that confer much more than a right to exclude; that is, rules that confer fees simple or general property interests on possessors.[14] This chapter seeks to identify what the legal grounds of the acquisition rules are and whether these provide genuine reasons for the maintenance of the rules.

It has been claimed that, at least so far as chattels are concerned, one of the legal grounds of the acquisition rules concerns the obligations that possessors, or certain categories of possessors, owe to those with a better title. This claim is examined in section 6.2. It is argued that there is a genuine obligation-based reason for conferring a right to exclude, that is not possession-dependent, on possessors who owe a special duty of care for the safety of the chattel. But the scope of the reason is limited. It is not a reason to retain rules that confer general property interests on possessors generally, nor has it been treated as such by the courts.

Section 6.3 advances and defends three claims. First, that the common law acquisition rules are primarily based on the need to provide greater certainty over title to chattels and unregistered land, and to secure the position of possessors and their successors in title. Secondly, that the law's reasons for applying the rule to cases involving registered land are mysterious. Thirdly, that, with regard to chattels and unregistered land, the law has genuine reasons for having the rules; to this extent, they have a valid legal basis, if not necessarily a sufficient one.

The arguments advanced in this chapter do not address the third or fourth questions identified above, that is, the question of whether the law's reasons are adequate or whether they are defeated by other considerations, and the question of whether there may be other reasons for the rules that have not been recognised by the law. These questions go beyond the concern of this book, which aims to provide an account of the legal rules and their grounds, not to assess

---

[12] eg Frederick Pollock and Frederic William Maitland, *The History of English Law Before the Time of Edward I* (2nd edn, CUP 1911) vol 2, 41.

[13] James Gordley and Ugo Mattei, 'Protecting Possession' (1996) 44 Am J Comp L 293; Robin Hickey, 'Possession as a Source of Property at Common Law' in Eric Descheemaeker (ed), *The Consequences of Possession* (Edinburgh UP 2014) 82–83, 92 (hereafter, 'Hickey, 'Possession').

[14] A related point is that these considerations do not justify the *Winkfield* rule, which enables possessors to recover excessive damages: see Luke Rostill, 'Possession and Damages for Tortious Interferences with Chattels' (2021) 41 OJLS (forthcoming) (hereafter, Rostill, 'Possession and Damages').

whether the law is justified. The questions are simply too large to be satisfactorily tackled here. To answer them, one would need to consider, among other things, whether the rules are compatible with sound principles of justice.[15] It is hoped, however, that, by identifying some valid legally recognised reasons for the maintenance of the rules, this chapter will make a modest contribution towards answering those questions.

6.2 Obligation-based Arguments

Some property law scholars have claimed: (a) that the obligations owed by possessors of chattels, or certain categories of possessors, provide genuine reasons for conferring on them an interest that comprises a right to exclude; and (b) that the courts have recognised this. It should be emphasised that these claims concern the conferral of *inferior* titles. Where a person acquires a general property interest by taking possession of a chattel, someone else may, and often will, already hold a general property interest in the chattel. Where this is so, the possessor will acquire an inferior general property interest. The obligation-based arguments are designed to show that the legal basis, or part of the basis, for the acquisition of an inferior general property interest by a possessor has to do with the obligations that the possessor owes to those who have a superior interest. Where a person takes possession of an unowned chattel, the possessor acquires the best general property interest and owes no such obligations.

Robin Hickey has argued that a large set of cases, mostly decided in the 18th and early 19th centuries, adopted and applied the proposition that the acquisition of a proprietary interest by certain categories of possessors, including finders, was premised on their 'obligation to keep the [chattel] safe for its owner'.[16] And, in Hickey's view, the fact that possessors, or certain categories of possessors, are under such a duty '*should* be a fundamental element in justifying' the rules that confer on them a proprietary interest.[17]

How does the (alleged) fact that a possessor is under an obligation to keep the chattel safe provide, or give rise to, a reason to confer a proprietary interest

---

[15] For a recent defence of the view that the rules that confer title on possessors satisfy a 'minimalist standard of fairness', see Crawford (n 10) ch 5.

[16] Hickey, 'Possession' (n 13) 80 (emphasis added). See also Robin Hickey, '*Armory v Delamirie* (1722): Possession, Obligation, and the Evolution of Relative Title to Goods' in Simon Douglas, Robin Hickey, and Emma Waring (eds), *Landmark Cases in Property Law* (Hart 2015) 133–38, 143–44 (hereinafter, Hickey, '*Armory v Delamirie*').

[17] Hickey, 'Possession' (n 13) 80 (emphasis added). See also Hickey, '*Armory v Delamirie* (n 16) 143–49.

on the possessor? One view is that the acquisition of such an interest facilitates the performance of the finder's duty to keep the chattel safe for the person or persons who have a better title to it, and thereby serves the interests of those persons. Hickey explains the point in the following terms:

> the finder's claim is premised upon and exists *to serve and protect* the loser's continuing property. The finder is protected *because* he has made himself responsible to keep the item safely for its loser, and this in turn provides a strong measure of protection for the loser, albeit indirectly.[18]

Similarly, Larissa Katz has claimed that a finder's 'is fundamentally a duty-based position, the possibility of which the law preserves *through* a special right to possess'.[19] The finder's duties, Katz tells us, include a duty to seek out the true owner and to take reasonable care of the goods.[20] So '[t]he finder has a basic responsibility to the owner' and 'it is arguably the discharge of this responsibility that the law protects against interference by third parties'.[21]

The rest of this section examines these views. Section 6.2.1 examines whether the obligations owed by finders, and some other possessors, provide a genuine reason for conferring a general property interest on them. Section 6.2.2 considers whether the law regards the rules that confer a proprietary interest on a finder of chattels (and on other possessors) as justified, or partly justified, by the finder's obligations.

6.2.1 Finders, Wrongful Possessors, and Obligation-based Reasons

To determine whether the obligations owed by certain categories of possessors, such as finders, give rise to a reason to confer a proprietary interest on them, it is necessary to first identify the obligations, or duties,[22] that such possessors

---

[18] Hickey, 'Possession' (n 13) 80 (Hickey's emphases).
[19] Larissa Katz, 'The Relativity of Title and *Causa Possessionis*' in James Penner and Henry E Smith (eds), *Philosophical Foundations of Property Law* (OUP 2013) 206 (emphasis in original). A finder, according to Katz, acquires a 'special right to possess' but 'lacks the full set of beneficial privileges or powers that characterize ownership: she lacks absolute rights to use, sell, consume for her own gain' and she lacks 'the power to create independent property rights in [the] thing, eg liens'. If, however, the arguments advanced in Chapter 5 are correct, the finder's interest comprises the power to create independent property rights and the power to sell.
[20] ibid.
[21] ibid.
[22] These terms are used interchangeably in this chapter.

owe. Once these have been identified, we can consider whether the duties provide, or give rise to, reasons to confer proprietary interests on possessors.

When considering the duties of possessors, it is important not to conflate: (a) the special duties to exercise reasonable care for the safety of goods that are ordinarily owed by bailees and some other persons; and (b) the general duties that, with limited exceptions, every person owes not to physically damage or destroy another's goods through their negligent conduct.[23] These duties are distinct. One important difference relates to interferences by third parties. A bailee is ordinarily under a duty to exercise such care as is reasonable in the circumstances for the safety of the chattel.[24] This duty will be breached if, as a result of the bailee's failure to exercise such care as a reasonable person would take, a third party deliberately damages, destroys, or appropriates the chattel.[25] In contrast, the general duty not to negligently interfere with another's chattel is not breached, and therefore no tort is committed, if, as a result of the duty-bearer's failure to take steps that a reasonable person would take, a third party deliberately damages, destroys, or appropriates the goods.[26] As Lord Goff explained in *Smith v Littlewoods Organisation Ltd*:[27]

> a problem arises when [A] is seeking to hold [B] responsible for having failed to *prevent* a third party from causing damage to [A] or his property by the third party's own deliberate wrongdoing. In such a case, it is not possible to invoke a general duty of care; for it is well recognised that there is no *general* duty of care to prevent third parties from causing such damage.[28]

Lord Goff went on to recognise that there 'are special circumstances in which [B] may be held responsible in law for injuries suffered by [A] through a third

---

[23] See Robert Stevens, *Torts and Rights* (OUP 2007) 10–11; Donal Nolan, 'Assumption of Responsibility: Four Questions' (2019) 72 CLP 123, 136–40 (hereafter Nolan, 'Assumption of Responsibility'). For discussion of what constitutes 'property damage' for the purposes of the general negligence duty see: Simon Douglas, 'Actionable Interferences: A New Perspective on the Chattel Torts' in Simone Degeling, James Edelman, and James Goudkamp (eds), *Torts in Commercial Law* (Lawbook Co 2011); Donal Nolan, 'Damage in the English Law of Negligence' (2013) 4 J Eur Tort L 259.

[24] *Houghland v RR Low (Luxury Coaches) Ltd* [1962] 1 QB 694 (CA); *Morris v CW Martin & Sons Ltd* [1966] 1 QB 716 (CA) 731–32 (Diplock LJ), 738 (Salmon LJ); *Yearworth v North Bristol NHS Trust* [2009] EWCA Civ 37; [2010] QB 1 [46]–[50].

[25] *Coldman v Hill* [1919] 1 KB 443 (CA); *Houghland* (n 24); *Mitchell v Ealing London Borough Council* [1979] QB 1 (QB); *Garlick v W & H Rycroft Ltd* (CA, 30 June 1982).

[26] *Ashby v Tolhurst* [1937] 2 KB 242 (CA); *Mitchell v Glasgow City Council* [2009] 1 AC 874 (HL) [15] (Lord Hope), [39]–[40] (Lord Scott), [55]–[58] (Lord Rodger), [76] (Baroness Hale), [81]–[82] (Lord Brown); *Michael v Chief Constable of South Wales Police* [2015] UKSC 2; [2015] AC 1732, [97]–[102] (Lord Toulson JSC); *Robinson v Chief Constable of West Yorkshire* [2018] UKSC 4; [2018] AC 736, [34]–[37], [50], [70] (Lord Reed JSC), [114]–[115] (Lord Hughes JSC). ;

[27] [1987] AC 241 (HL) (emphases in original).

[28] ibid 270.

party's deliberate wrongdoing', such as where B has assumed responsibility to protect A from such harm, or where B is in a position of control over the third party.[29] But in the absence of such special circumstances, B does not owe a duty of care to A, to protect A from deliberate interferences by third parties.

We have seen that Hickey and Katz regard their obligation-based arguments as applying to finders. Are finders under a special duty to keep the chattel safe? Norman Palmer has claimed that 'finders are bailees only to the limited extent that the custodial rights and obligations of both classes of possessor are . . . in substance the same'.[30] These 'custodial obligations' include the obligation to exercise due care for the safety of the chattel. Is this correct? It seems that it is, at least insofar as it concerns those finders who have *lawfully* taken possession of another's chattel. In England and Wales, the acquisition of possession of another's goods by a finder, without the consent of the proprietor(s), is lawful—that is to say, does not constitute or involve a legal wrong vis-à-vis the proprietor(s)—if B takes possession with the intention of keeping the goods safe for the person(s) who are entitled to them.[31] It appears that such finders are under a duty to take reasonable care to keep the chattel safe, including a duty to exercise such care as is reasonable to protect the chattel from interferences by third parties.[32] Lord Pearson, giving the judgment of the Privy Council in *Gilchrist Watt & Sanderson v York Products*,[33] maintained that such a finder comes under a custodial duty because 'the taking of possession in the circumstances involves an assumption of responsibility for the safe keeping of the goods'.[34] Whether it is correct to say that a finder who has taken possession with the intention of keeping the goods safe has indeed assumed such a responsibility depends on what counts as an 'assumption of responsibility'. In one sense of the term, it appears that such a finder really has assumed responsibility for the safekeeping of the goods. She has assumed responsibility, not in the sense of promising or agreeing to keep the chattel safe, but in the sense that she has taken on the task of keeping the chattel safe for the proprietor(s).[35] Whether it is justified to impose a legal duty to take reasonable care to keep the

---

[29] ibid 272.

[30] Norman Palmer (ed), *Palmer on Bailment* (3rd edn, Sweet & Maxwell 2009) para 26-001.

[31] *Isaack v Clark* (1614) 2 Bulst 306, 312 (Coke CJ); *Hollins v Fowler* (1875) LR 7 HL 757 (HL) 766 (Blackburn J).; See also Hickey, 'Possession' (n 13) 80; Hickey, '*Armory v Delamirie*' (n 16) 135–36.

[32] *Newman v Bourne & Hollingsworth* (1915) 31 TLR 209 (DC); *Thompson v Nixon* [1966] 1 QB 103 (DC); *Gilchrist Watt & Sanderson Pty Ltd v York Products Pty Ltd* [1970] 1 WLR 1262 (PC) 1268–70. Compare: *Kowal v Ellis* (1977) 76 DLR (3d) 546 (Manitoba Court of Appeal); *R v Ngan* [2008] 2 NZLR 48 (Supreme Court of New Zealand) [15]–[20] (Elias CJ, Blanchard and Anderson JJ).

[33] *Gilchrist* (n 32).

[34] ibid 1268.

[35] See Nolan, 'Assumption of Responsibility' (n 23) 128–34, 141.

goods safe on a person who takes on the task is, of course, a further question, which cannot be considered here.[36]

The fact that a person who finds and takes possession of another's chattel in order to keep it safe comes under a legal duty to exercise reasonable care for its safety is significant, because there really are reasons for the law to confer a right to exclude, which is not possession-dependent, on persons who are under such a duty. One is that the conferral by the law of such a right facilitates the performance of the duty, and this, ordinarily, benefits the person or persons with a better title. And—to the extent that it is good for the finder to do her duty—the right, by facilitating the performance of the duty, serves the interests of the finder too.[37] The conferral of a right to exclude facilitates the performance of the duty by generating additional reasons for third parties not to interfere with the thing. The possessor's duty to exercise reasonable care for the safety of another's goods will be breached if, as a result of the possessor's failure to exercise reasonable care, a third party deliberately damages, destroys, or appropriates the chattel.[38] If the law confers on the possessor, B, a right to exclude others, such as C, then C will have an additional duty (or duties) not to interfere with the chattel. This has practical implications for C.[39] If, for instance, C were to wrongfully interfere with the chattel, an action may be brought against her in tort by A or B. Consequently, conferring a right to exclude on the possessor increases the probability that the chattel will remain with the possessor, unspoiled. The right, as Hickey states, 'provides a strong measure of protection for the loser, albeit indirectly'.[40] In this way, the conferral of a right to exclude facilitates the performance of the possessor's duty to keep the chattel safe and serves the interests of the person who has a better title.

Other things being equal, this reason for conferring a right to exclude applies if, and so long as, the possessor has a duty to keep the chattel safe; and, since the duty will not terminate if the right-holder simply ceases to be in possession, the reason applies even if the right-holder ceases to be in possession. Accordingly, where a possessor owes a duty to another to take reasonable care to keep the chattel safe, there truly is a reason for the law to confer on the possessor a right to exclude that is not possession-dependent.

---

[36] For a general discussion of the considerations that support, or might be thought to support, the imposition of a duty on a person who takes on a certain task, see Nolan, 'Assumption of Responsibility' (n 23) 134, 143–46; Sandy Steel, 'Rationalising Omissions Liability in Negligence' (2019) 135 LQR 484, 501–03.

[37] Ordinarily, of course, the conferral of the right will benefit the finder in other ways too.

[38] *Coldman* (n 25); *Houghland* (n 24); *Mitchell* (n 25); *Garlick* (n 25).

[39] See Ben McFarlane, 'The *Numerus Clausus* Principle and Covenants Relating to Land' in Susan Bright (ed), *Modern Studies in Property Law, Volume 6* (Hart 2011) 316–17.

[40] Hickey, 'Possession' (n 13) 80.

It is important to recognise how limited this reason is. First, the argument that we have considered does not show that there is a reason for the law to confer on the possessor an interest that comprises, not just a right to exclude, but also various dispositive powers, including powers to alienate the entire interest, and powers to grant new proprietary interests (eg by pledging the chattel). These broad dispositive powers do not facilitate the performance of the possessor's duty to take reasonable care to keep the chattel safe, or, at least, it is not clear how they do so. It might be pointed out, in response, that the obligation-based argument is one of a number of considerations, which, together, provide a reason, or reasons, for the conferral of an alienable proprietary interest. Hickey has said that:[41]

> the common law's aims in protecting possession . . . appear to be plural, concerning at least: restraint of violence and the preservation of public order; the facilitation of transactions and exchange; and recognition of obligations voluntarily assumed by the possessor.

One might argue that these considerations, perhaps combined with others, provide a rational basis for the rules that confer general property interests on finders.[42]

The obligation-based argument is, however, limited in a second, and more significant, respect. It fails to provide a reason for conferring any rights at all on possessors generally, as opposed to those possessors who are under a duty that would be facilitated by the conferral of a right to exclude. It fails, therefore, to provide a reason for the establishment or maintenance of the acquisition rules that the law has actually adopted. There are two important points to be made here. The first is that a person who is in possession of another's chattels does not necessarily owe a special duty of care. The foundation of the special duty of care that is ordinarily owed by bailees (including lawful finders) is that the bailee, by voluntarily assuming possession of another's chattels, assumes responsibility for their safety.[43] And a possessor will be regarded as voluntarily assuming possession of another's chattels only if the possessor has a sufficient degree of knowledge of the fact that some other person has an interest in them.[44] Where,

---

[41] Hickey, 'Possession' (n 13) 78.

[42] Hickey appears to be of the view that the pertinent factors justify, or provide pro tanto reasons for, conferring alienable proprietary interests on most possessors, including finders: Hickey, 'Armory v Delamirie' (n 16) 144–49.

[43] Gilchrist (n 32); The Pioneer Container [1994] 2 AC 324 (PC); East West Corp v DKBS AF 1912 [2003] EWCA Civ 83; [2003] QB 1509. For a detailed discussion, see Palmer (n 30) paras 1-011–1-046.

[44] The Pioneer Container (n 43); Marcq v Christie Manson & Woods Ltd [2003] EWCA Civ 731; [2004] QB 286. See Palmer (n 30) para 1-018.

for example, A bails goods to B, and B, in turn, bails the goods to C, there can be a relationship of bailment between the head bailee, A, and the sub-bailee, C, only if C has sufficient notice that some other person (apart from B) has an interest in the goods.[45] As Lord Goff explained in *The Pioneer Container*, in the absence of such notice it cannot properly be said that the sub-bailee 'has, by taking the goods into his custody, assumed towards [the head-bailee] the responsibility for the goods which is characteristic of a bailee'.[46] Similar reasoning applies to cases in which a person obtains possession in the mistaken belief that no one has a title better than theirs, and to cases in which a person receives a chattel from another in the mistaken belief that no one has a title that is better than the deliverer's.[47]

In any case—and this is the second point—the obligation-based argument canvassed above does not apply to *wrongful* possessors, irrespective of whether such possessors owe a special duty of care. The conclusion of that argument is that rules conferring a right to exclude on a lawful finder, B, facilitate the performance of B's duty of care and, in so doing, serve the interests of A, who has a better title. The rules promote A's interest in recovering the chattel, unharmed, by discouraging others from appropriating, damaging, or destroying it. This interest is not promoted by conferring rights on wrongful possessors, who are not keeping the chattel safe for A. Hickey acknowledges that his obligation-based argument for conferring a proprietary interest on a finder is not applicable to thieves 'since, by definition, the thief's possession is premised on some high degree of disregard for the property of his victim'.[48] But the point is not limited to thieves: it applies to wrongful possessors generally.

In sum, the obligation-based argument fails, by itself, to provide a genuine basis for the law as it now stands; and, in particular, for the rules that confer general property interests on possessors irrespective of whether they owe a special duty of care, or whether the conferral of such an interest benefits those who hold pre-existing interests. This is not an objection to Katz's view, as Katz recognises that her obligation-based argument for conferring rights on a finder does not apply to wrongful possessors.[49] Interestingly, Hickey suggests that

---

[45] *The Pioneer Container* (n 43)

[46] ibid 342 (cited with approval in *Sandeman Coprimar SA v Transitos y Transportes Integrales SL* [2003] EWCA Civ 113; [2003] QB 1270 [60]; and *Marcq* (n 44) [49] (Tuckey LJ)).

[47] See, eg *Marcq* (n 44).

[48] Hickey, 'Possession' (n 13) 93. See also Hickey, '*Armory v Delamirie*' (n 16) 148–49.

[49] Katz (n 19) 204. Katz argues that it is justifiable, on other grounds, for the law to: (a) confer a 'limited right to possess' on wrongful possessors to protect them against forcible dispossessions; and (b) to protect wrongful possessors as against their bailees: Katz (n 19) 210–14. It was argued in Chapters 4 and 5, however, that, in England and Wales at least, the law does not confer mere limited rights on wrongful possessors; it confers a general property interest.

it may be possible to supplement the obligation-based account, as described above, so as to render it applicable to wrongful possessors.[50] He claims that 'ultimately there is little difference between a wrongdoer in possession of goods' and a lawful finder: just as a lawful finder who refuses to return the goods will be 'strictly liable . . . for the value of the goods', a wrongful possessor will 'find himself strictly liable to some other person for the full value of the goods'.[51] Therefore, Hickey concludes, 'the content of the wrongful possessor's obligation may not in the end differ from the content of the obligation that grounded' the right of a lawful finder.[52] Why will a wrongful possessor usually be under an obligation to pay the full value of the goods to another? Hickey's answer is that 'where no lawful basis for possession can be shown, a possessor will find it very difficult not also to convert the goods' and, as a result of the conversion, the wrongful possessor will be 'strictly liable to some other person for the full value of the goods'.[53]

It is important not to lose sight of the obligation that is thought to provide a basis for the possessor's rights. According to the obligation-based argument expounded above, the relevant obligation is the obligation to keep another's chattels safe. When considering the obligations of wrongful possessors, however, Hickey appears to regard a different obligation as the relevant one, namely, the obligation to pay the full value of the chattels to the proprietor. This arises, in Hickey's view, if the possessor commits the tort of conversion.[54]

An objection to this is that a wrongful possessor will not necessarily be required to pay the value of the chattel to another as a result of committing the tort of conversion. One relevant point here is that a person might commit the tort of trespass by taking possession of a chattel without committing the tort of conversion.[55] Hickey recognises this, but adds that, since it is 'very difficult' for a wrongful possessor to avoid converting the chattel, a wrongful possessor will usually be liable in conversion. There is, however, a second point: where a wrongful possessor has committed the tort of conversion, she will generally be under a duty, or liability,[56] to pay compensation to the right-holder in respect

---

[50] Hickey, 'Armory v Delamirie' (n 16) 144–47. This is not to say that Hickey thinks that the justification applies to all 'wrongful possessors'. He maintains that it may not apply to possessors who have shown 'high degrees of disregard for the continuing property rights of some person better entitled', eg thieves: Hickey, 'Armory v Delamirie' (n 16) 148–49. See also Hickey, 'Possession' (n 13) 93.

[51] Hickey, 'Armory v Delamirie' (n 16)144–45.

[52] ibid 145.

[53] ibid 144–45.

[54] ibid.

[55] Sanderson v Marsden (1922) 10 Ll L Rep 467 (CA).

[56] Private law scholars have debated whether a tortfeasor's legal duty to pay damages arises only if a court orders the tortfeasor to pay damages ('the liability view') or whether an award of damages by a court simply requires the tortfeasor to do what was already her legal duty before the order was made

of the loss caused by the wrong;[57] though, where *The Winkfield* rule applies,[58] the claimant's loss will be assessed on the basis that the claimant is the 'absolute and complete owner' (ie the holder of the supreme general property interest in possession). So, subject to the *Winkfield* rule, where the value of the chattel does not represent what the claimant has lost as a result of the tort, the defendant will not generally be required to pay the value of the chattel to the claimant.

A further objection is that a person might commit the tort of conversion and, as a consequence, be required to pay the value of the chattel, without, at any point, acquiring possession.[59] Suppose that A has a proprietary interest in a chattel that comprises a right to exclusive possession that binds persons generally, including B. In such circumstances, B owes a duty towards A not to convert the chattel. It is possible for B to breach this duty without obtaining possession. If, for example, B deliberately throws a grenade at A's chattel and, as a result, the chattel is destroyed, B will be liable to A in conversion for the value of the chattel.[60]

Hence, it is problematic to claim that the grounds of the rules that confer proprietary interests on wrongful possessors concern the possessor's duty or liability to pay the value of the chattel to another. Not all wrongful possessors are under such a duty or liability, and many wrongdoers who are under such a duty or liability never acquire possession. Since the relevant considerations do not apply only to possessors, nor to all wrongful possessors, they fail to provide a reason for establishing or maintaining a rule that confers proprietary interests on wrongful possessors.

It might be said, by way of response, that the obligation-based argument is simply one component of a suite of arguments that, taken together, provide

('the duty view'): see, eg Stephen Smith, 'Duties, Liabilities, and Damages' (2012) 125 Harv L Rev 1727; John Gardner, 'Damages Without Duty' (2019) 69 UTLJ 412; Sandy Steel and Robert Stevens, 'The Secondary Legal Duty to Pay Damages (2020) 136 LQR 283. The success of Hickey's argument does not ultimately depend on which view is correct. Recasting Hickey's argument as a liability-based argument does not save it from the objections advanced in this section.

[57] If the claimant has suffered a loss and the defendant has obtained a benefit as a result of the conversion, the claimant can elect whether to recover restitutionary or loss-based damages: *United Australia Ltd v Barclays Bank Ltd* [1941] AC 1 (HL). With respect to the latter, '[t]he fundamental object' is to 'award just compensation for loss suffered': *Kuwait Airways Corp v Iraqi Airways Co (Nos 4 and 5)* [2002] UKHL 19; [2002] 2 AC 883 [67] (Lord Nicholls) An exception to the ordinary requirements for causation of loss applies to cases involving successive conversions: see Simon Douglas, *Liability for Wrongful Interferences with Chattels* (Hart 2011) 198–201.

[58] See Chapter 5 (section 5.3.1).

[59] *Douglas Valley Finance Co Ltd v S Hughes (Hirers) Ltd* [1969] 1 QB 738. See Sarah Green and John Randall, *The Tort of Conversion* (Hart 2009) 65–66.

[60] James Goudkamp and Edwin Peel, *Winfield & Jolowicz on Tort* (19th edn, Sweet and Maxwell 2014) para 18-022.

the grounds of the rules that confer proprietary interests on possessors. These other considerations, it may be said, explain why the acquisition rule applies only to possessors and why it extends to possessors generally. But even if that is so, a more fundamental problem with the argument concerning wrongful possessors remains. This is that, even where a wrongful possessor, B, *is* under a duty to pay the full value of the chattel to another, it is unclear how this fact can be, or can give rise to, a reason to confer a right to exclude on B. Hickey provides the following explanation:[61]

> if it is possible to show that trover was allowed on the ground of the possessor's responsibility to some other, this provides a reason that explains not only why possession should be protected, but also why it should be protected by the possessor's acquisition of property. The possessor would be said to have a general claim to the full value of the goods exigible against all the world save those better entitled, *because she in turn must answer for that value to someone better entitled.*

How does the fact that B, as a result of having converted A's goods, 'must answer' to A for their value, count in favour of conferring on B a right to exclude others, such as C? One might claim that, where B's duty to pay the full value of the goods to A results from, or is triggered by, the wrongful interference of a third party, B should acquire a right as against the third party.

In order to defend this, one might adapt an argument that was advanced by JF Clerk in 1891.[62] Clerk was concerned with the circumstances in which a defendant could, and should, be able to defeat a claim for wrongful interference with chattels by setting up the better title of a third party (*jus tertii*). He argued that, where the 'true owner' is known, a bare possessor should be able to recover the value of the goods from a third party who has, without justification, appropriated them *only if*, as a result of the third party's wrongful interference, 'the possessor is liable over to the owner'.[63] Clerk cited, in support of this, *Bacon's Abridgment*: 'A man ought not to be charged with an injury to another without being able to resort to the original cause of that injury, and in amends there to do himself right'.[64] Clerk claimed that three classes of possessors are 'liable over' to the 'true owner' where a third party wrongfully

---

[61] Hickey, '*Armory v Delamirie*' (n 16) 145 (emphasis added).
[62] JF Clerk, 'Title to Chattels by Possession' (1891) 7 LQR 224.
[63] ibid 231.
[64] ibid, citing Matthew Bacon, *A New Abridgement of the Law* (CE Dodd and H Gwillim eds, 7th edn, A Strahan 1832) vol 1, 515.

interferes: (i) possessors who are under a duty to take reasonable care for the safety of the chattel (eg bailees) and whose negligence contributed to the loss of, or damage to, the chattel; (ii) possessors who are 'insurers' of the chattel's safety (eg common carriers and innkeepers); and (iii) possessors who have converted the chattel and against whom an action by the 'owner' is not statute-barred.[65] With respect to this final category, Clerk said:

> [t]he owner is entitled to treat the chattel as having been at the risk of the possessor from the date of the conversion, so as to render him responsible for its loss without further default on his part, whether the loss be caused by fire, theft or otherwise.[66]

By combining aspects of Clerk's views with Hickey's, one can generate the following argument (the 'Original Cause Argument'):

> (P1) If a person (B) is liable to pay the value of goods to another (A) as a result of the conduct of a third party (C), B should be able to recover the value of the goods from C;
> (P2) where B is tortiously in possession of A's goods, B will ordinarily commit conversion as against A and if, following the conversion, the goods are taken or destroyed by C, B will be liable to pay the value of the goods to A as a result of C's conduct;
> (P3) in order to be able to recover the value of the goods from C in conversion, B must have a legal proprietary interest that comprises a right to exclusive possession;
> (P4) therefore, wrongful possessors, such as B, should acquire a legal proprietary interest that comprises a right to exclusive possession.

The Original Cause Argument raises a number of questions. One concerns P2: would B really be liable to pay the value of the goods to A in such circumstances and, if so, is B's liability the result of C's conduct? It is true, as Lord Nicholls explained in *Kuwait Airways Corp v Iraqi Airways Co (Nos 4 & 5)*,[67] that a converter of goods:

---

[65] ibid 231–32.
[66] ibid 232.
[67] *Kuwait Airways* (n 57).

[bears] the risk of being unable to return the goods to their rightful owner. It matters not that he may be prevented from returning the goods due to unforeseen circumstances beyond his control. The reason for his non-return of the goods, or his delay in returning the goods, is neither here nor there so far as his liability to the owner is concerned.[68]

The converter, B, is effectively treated as an insurer of the goods.[69] It is important to recognise, however, that in most cases this will not affect B's liability to A. Suppose that B misappropriated A's goods with a view to eventually selling and delivering them to X.[70] Before B was able to sell the goods to X, they were taken by C. In these circumstances, C's interference does not affect B's liability to A: even if C had not interfered, B would have been required to pay the value of the goods to A. Indeed, where, but for the interference of C, B would have kept the goods for herself, destroyed them, or delivered them to someone other than A, the fact that C has taken or destroyed them will not affect B's liability.

C's interference will make a difference, however, if, but for C's interference, B would have returned the goods to A. If B had returned the goods to A, B would have been liable to pay damages in respect of the loss suffered by A as a result of being temporarily deprived of possession,[71] but B would *not* have been liable to pay the full value of the goods. So, in such circumstances, C's interference affects B's liability to A: the damages that B is liable to pay to A have been enlarged by C's interference. B, it might be said, is liable to pay the full value as a result of C's interference. This is true, provided that it is understood as expressing the proposition that, but for C's interference, B would have been liable to pay a lesser sum. The fact that B has any liability to A is, of course, a result of B's own wrongful conduct.

In certain circumstances, then, P2, if interpreted in a particular way, is true. But there are other problems with the Original Cause Argument. First, the argument is invalid. The conclusion that actually follows from P1 and P2 is: (P3*): B should be able to recover the value of the goods from C. It does not follow that B should be able to recover the value of the goods *in conversion*.[72]

---

[68] ibid [92].

[69] See Lord Hoffmann, 'Causation' in Richard Goldberg (ed), *Perspectives on Causation* (Hart 2011) 7: 'If you convert someone's property, you have to pay for it or give it back. You become insurer of the chattel. It does not matter what would otherwise have happened to it'.

[70] For the sake of simplicity, it is assumed that A has the best general property interest in the goods.

[71] *Moon v Raphael* (1835) 2 Bing NC 310; 132 ER 122; *Chinery v Viall* (1860) 5 H & N 288, 295; 157 ER 1192, 1195 (Bramwell B).

[72] B may have a cause of action against C under s 1(1) of the Civil Liability (Contribution) Act 1978. In *VFS Financial Services (UK) Ltd v Euro Auctions (UK) Ltd*, Judge Richard Seymour QC maintained that, where a chattel is converted by D1 and subsequently converted by D2, and D1 and D2 are each liable to pay the claimant the value of the chattel, a claim for contribution under the 1978 Act would

Empowering B to sue in conversion, by conferring on B a legal interest that comprises a right to exclude, goes far beyond what P1, P2, and P3* support. B's right would bind everyone except those who have a better title. Consequently, B could sue in conversion anyone who appropriates or destroys the goods, irrespective of whether the third party's interference increased B's liability to A. It was pointed out above that, in most cases, the interference of a third party will not affect the converter's liability. If, for example, B, but for C's interference, would have used the goods for her own purposes, disposed of them to someone other than A, or destroyed them, B's liability to A is not affected by C's interference; and, therefore, B's liability is not a result of C's conduct. In such circumstances, the Original Cause Argument provides no reason for allowing B to sue C; yet if B has a right to exclude the rest of the world, B could sue C. Moreover, even in those cases where B *would* have returned the goods to A but for C's interference, B's right to exclude gives her more protection than is justified by the Original Cause Argument. In this situation, B's liability to A is increased due to C's conduct. But if B has a right to exclude, B is empowered to sue others. Suppose that C appropriates the goods. B is then sued by A, and B pays the full value to her. Thereafter, C sells the goods to D. B might sue D in conversion, even though D bears no responsibility for the extent to which B was liable to A.

In sum, the Original Cause Argument uses a sledgehammer to crack a nut. The premises of the argument support, at most, allowing a converter to recover damages from a third party who has enlarged the converter's liability. They provide no reason to confer on converters rights that bind the world. A fortiori, the argument provides no reason for the maintenance of rules that confer general property interests on wrongful possessors.

While, then, there is a sound obligation-based argument for conferring a right to exclude, that is not possession-dependent, on possessors who owe a special duty of care, the reach of this argument is limited. The pertinent considerations do not actually support the general common law acquisition rules; they do not provide pro tanto reasons for their establishment or maintenance.

---

fail because 'each conversion amounts to a separate wrong causing its own separate damage': [2007] EWHC 1492 (QB) [126]. D1 and D2 are not, therefore, 'liable in respect of the same damage' within the meaning of s1(1) of the 1978 Act. But the judge did not consider what the position would be where D1's liability for the value of the chattel is actually a result of D2's interference.

6.2.2 Obligation-based Reasons in the Law

Has the law treated the rules that confer general property interests on possessors as justified, or partly justified, by possessors' obligations or liabilities?
Oliver Wendell Holmes Jr, in his famous lectures on the common law,[73] cited
historical precedents supporting the view that the reason bailees were (generally) able to recover damages from strangers who wrongfully interfered with
chattels in their possession was that bailees were (generally) strictly liable to
their bailors for the loss of chattels.[74] In *Heydon and Smith's Case*, for example,
the court maintained that 'the bailee, or he who hath a special property, shall
have a general action of trespass against a stranger, and shall recover all in
damages, because that he is chargeable over'.[75]

It has been clear for over a century, however, that the bailee's ability to obtain
a remedy from a stranger is not based on the proposition that the bailee is liable to pay damages to the bailor. In *The Winkfield*, the main issue was whether
a bailee of letters and parcels was able to recover their full value, even though
the bailee was not liable to his bailor for the loss of them.[76] The defendant submitted that '[t]he correct view would . . . seem to be that the right of action to
recover the value rested on the liability of the bailee to account to the bailor'.[77]
The Court of Appeal rejected this submission. Collins MR recognised that
'the reason given in *Heydon and Smith's Case*—and itself drawn from the Year
Books—has been repeated in many subsequent cases'.[78] But, after surveying
the case law, Collins MR concluded that 'the statement drawn . . . from the Year
Books . . . has not been treated as law in our Courts'.[79] His Lordship relied primarily on four 19th century cases in which a bailee was 'allowed to recover full

---

[73] OW Holmes Jr, *The Common Law* (Little, Brown and Co 1881) 164–75. See also Hickey, 'Armory v
Delamirie' (n 16) 133–43.

[74] This, it seems, was an inversion of an earlier argument: that the bailee should be strictly liable to the
bailor *because* the bailee had the right to sue wrongdoers: see *Southcot v Bennet* (1600) Cro Eliz 815; 78
ER 1041; Holmes (n 73) 166–67, 170–71; John Baker, *An Introduction to English Legal History* (5th edn,
OUP 2019) 417. Nowadays, the general rule is that bailees must exercise reasonable care for the safety of
the chattels; where the chattels are lost as a result of the interference of a third party, they are not strictly
liable for the loss (unless they have deviated from one of the fundamental terms of the bailment): see
Norman Palmer, 'Bailment' in Andrew Burrows (eds), *English Private Law* (3rd edn, OUP 2013) ch 16.

[75] (1610) 13 Co Rep 67, 69; 77 ER 1476, 1478–79.

[76] [1902] P 42 (CA).

[77] ibid 51.

[78] ibid 58.

[79] ibid 59. This analysis was prefigured by Holmes's, which the Master of the Rolls relied upon.
Holmes thought that 'the reason offered' in the Year Books for the bailee's ability to sue was not 'a true
one' because 'any person in possession, whether intrusted and answerable over or not . . . can sue any
one except the true owner for interference with his possession': Holmes (n 73) 171.

damages against a wrongdoer, where the facts would have afforded a complete answer for him against his bailor'.[80]

It seems that the Court of Appeal accepted, in *The Winkfield*, that the protection afforded to bailees and other possessors by the law of torts is based upon the need to protect possession. Collins MR referred,[81] with approval, to the judgment of Lord Campbell CJ in *Jeffries v Great Western Railway Co.*[82] In *Jeffries*, Lord Campbell said, 'I think it most reasonable law, and essential for the interests of society, that peaceable possession should not be disturbed by wrongdoers'.[83] The acquisition rules help to ensure that those who obtain possession of a chattel will have a right to exclude. They may have such a right by virtue of a pre-existing interest, or because such a right is conferred upon them by another when they take possession (eg under a pledge), or by virtue of the general rule that a person who takes possession, and who would not otherwise have a right to exclude, acquires a general property interest. But, as pointed out in section 6.1, the need to protect possession cannot provide a rational basis for the general acquisition rules.[84] Fortunately, the law has recognised that the general acquisition rules rest on more than the need to protect possession.

6.3 The Security and Certainty of Title

To identify the primary legal grounds of the general acquisition rules, it is necessary to return to, and develop, a point that was made in Chapter 4. The courts, according to the account in Chapter 4, established the rules that confer fee simple estates on possessors of land in order to further purposes that Parliament adopted by enacting the Real Property Limitation Act 1833.[85] One of the lessons of this is that, in order to properly understand the common law acquisition rules, one must appreciate the surrounding legal landscape and the place of the acquisition rules within it. One must, in other words, view the rules as aspects of a system. Within the system of rules that governs proprietary interests in land, there is an important connection between the common law

---

[80] ibid. The four cases are *Sutton v Buck* (1810) 2 Taunt 302; 127 ER 1094; *Burton v Hughes* (1824) 2 Bing 173; 130 ER 272; *Turner v Hardcastle* (1862) 11 CB (NS) 683; 142 ER 964; *Swire v Leach* (1865) 18 CB (NS) 479; 144 ER 531.

[81] *The Winkfield* (n 76) 55.

[82] (1856) 5 El & Bl 802; 119 ER 680.

[83] (1856) 5 El & Bl 802, 805; 119 ER 680, 681.

[84] Nor does it provide an adequate basis for the rule, accepted and applied in *The Winkfield*, that the court should presume that a possessor has 'absolute and complete ownership': see Luke Rostill, 'Possession and Damages' (n 14).

[85] Chapter 4 (section 4.3.1).

acquisition rules and the rules regarding the extinguishment of title to (unregistered) land by lapse of time: these rules, in combination, are regarded by the law as serving certain functions, and were adopted *in order to* serve these functions. Section 6.3.1 explores the grounds of the two sets of rules in greater depth, and defends the claim that the principal grounds of the rules are genuine pro tanto reasons for having the rules. Registered land is considered in section 6.3.2, and the position with respect to chattels in section 6.3.3.

6.3.1 The Security and Certainty of Title to Unregistered Land

It was pointed out in Chapter 4 that the relevant rule of extinguishment, so far as unregistered land is concerned, is the rule established by section 17 of the Limitation Act 1980: 'at the expiration of the period prescribed by this Act for any person to bring an action to recover land . . . the title of that person to the land shall be extinguished'.[86] The rules governing the length of the limitation periods that apply, unless certain cancelling conditions are met,[87] to actions to recover land can be found in section 15 of the Act.[88] The normal limitation period for actions to recover land is twelve years from the date on which the right of action accrued.[89] So far as legal estates in land are concerned, a right of action will accrue in favour of an estate-holder, C, if : (a) another person, D, is in possession of the land without C's consent; and (2) C has (or is regarded as having) a right to exclusive possession as against D.[90] If D is in possession of land and time is running under the Limitation Act in his favour and against C, D is in 'adverse possession' as against C.[91]

The principal legal grounds of the rule of extinguishment in section 17 of the 1980 Act were identified in Chapter 4: the rule is regarded as providing greater certainty as to who has a good title to land, and greater security to possessors and their successors in title. When the Bill that first established the rule was passing through Parliament, Lord Lyndhurst, who had been asked to outline 'the nature and objects' of the bill 'and the principle on which it was founded',[92]

---

[86] The rule is qualified by s 18, which concerns settled land and trusts of land.

[87] For example, the rules established by s 15 do not apply if the person to whom a right of action has accrued is 'under a disability': Limitation Act 1980 (hereafter LA 1980), s 28.

[88] For a detailed discussion, see Stuart Bridge, Elizabeth Cooke, and Martin Dixon (eds), *Megarry & Wade: The Law of Real Property* (9th edn, Sweet & Maxwell 2019) ch 7 (hereafter Bridge, Cooke, and Dixon).

[89] LA 1980, s 15(1).

[90] LA 1980, s 15 and sch 1(1).

[91] LA 1980, Sch 1(8); *J A Pye (Oxford) Ltd v Graham* [2002] UKHL 30; [2003] 1 AC 419 [32]–[38] (Lord Browne-Wilkinson).

[92] HL Deb 14 June 1833, vol 18, col 790.

identified two 'advantages in adopting such a rule': first, 'it would quiet the title to lands'; and, secondly, it would 'give security in possession, and, consequently, ease in letting, and facility in conveying, property'.[93] Lord Lyndhurst rightly believed that these 'advantages' would be secured only if the rules that extinguish title where a person has been in possession of land for a certain period of time were complemented by rules that confer a title on the possessor.[94] Thus, the legally-recognised reasons articulated by Lord Lyndhurst for maintaining the rule in section 17 are also legally-recognised reasons for maintaining the rules that confer fee simple estates on possessors.

This connection between the rules that confer titles on possessors and the rules concerning the extinguishment of title by lapse of time was acknowledged by the Law Commission in its 1998 consultative document on land registration.[95] The Law Commission stated that the 'principal reason for having limitation statutes in relation to real property', and the 'strongest justification', is that:

> title to unregistered land is relative and depends ultimately on possession. The person best entitled to land is the person with the best right to possession of it. The fact that adverse possession can extinguish earlier rights to possess facilitates and cheapens the investigation of title to unregistered land.[96]

Similarly, in *J A Pye (Oxford) Ltd v Graham*,[97] Lord Bingham, having noted that the Grahams, by taking possession of the land, had obtained 'title to [a] considerable area of valuable land' and that, after twelve years, the company's superior title was extinguished, said, '[i]n the case of unregistered land . . . such a result could no doubt be justified as avoiding protracted uncertainty where the title to land lay'.[98] For Lord Bingham, then, the need to avoid uncertainty with

---

[93] HL Deb 14 June 1833, vol 18, col 792. See also *J A Pye (Oxford) Ltd v Graham* [2000] Ch 676 (Ch) 709 (Neuberger J); *J A Pye (Oxford) Ltd v Graham* [2001] EWCA Civ 117; [2001] Ch 804 [43] (Mummery LJ); *J A Pye (Oxford) Ltd v United Kingdom* (2006) 43 EHRR 3 [65]–[67]; (2008) 46 EHRR 45 [74]; *Ofulue v Bossert* [2008] EWCA Civ 7; [2009] Ch 1 [46], [50]–[53] (Arden LJ); Martin Dockray, 'Why do we need Adverse Possession?' [1985] Conv 272, 272–80.

[94] Chapter 4 (section 4.3.1.2).

[95] Law Commission, *Land Registration for the Twenty-First Century: A Consultative Document* (Law Com No 254, 1998) (hereafter LC No 254).

[96] ibid paras 10.9–10.10 (emphases removed). The Law Commission identified two further reasons for having a doctrine of adverse possession: (a) to ensure that 'land remains in commerce and is not rendered sterile'; and (b) to 'prevent hardship' in 'cases of mistake': paras 10.7, 10.8, 10.13. These considerations underpin the scheme of adverse possession introduced by the Land Registration Act 2002: see; *R (Best) v Chief Land Registrar* [2015] EWCA Civ 17; [2016] QB 23 [19]–[22], [44]–[45] (Sales LJ), [106]–[107] (Arden LJ). In relation to unregistered land, on the other hand, the law has treated these considerations as secondary to the considerations identified by Lord Lyndhurst: see Dockray (n 93) 275–77.

[97] [2002] UKHL 30; [2003] 1 AC 419.

[98] ibid [2].

respect to title to unregistered land justifies the destruction of title by lapse of time *and* the acquisition of title by a squatter.

Importantly, the reasons that Lord Lyndhurst identified for the establishment of the rules that confer fee simple estates on possessors, and extinguish the interests of persons against whom time has run, are authentic pro tanto reasons for having such rules, so far as unregistered land is concerned. This is a consequence of the fact that, in connection with such land, English law has: (a) adopted a system of historical entitlement in which the allocation of entitlements at a given time largely depends upon the history of transactions in respect of the land; but (b) lacks a robust and comprehensive record of transactions concerning land. In such circumstances, and in the absence of the rules of adverse possession and title by possession (or rules that play a similar role, such as rules of acquisitive prescription), it will often be impossible to identify, with reasonable confidence, those who actually hold an estate in land.[99]

The undesirable effects of this uncertainty are manifold. First, in many cases, those who have acquired an estate will find it practically impossible, or expensive and time-consuming, to establish their rights, and this may make it difficult for them to enforce their rights. Secondly, as John Stuart Mill noted, there is a real risk that proprietors of land will be 'molested by charges of wrongful acquisition, when by the lapse of time witnesses must have perished or been lost sight of, and the real character of the transaction can no longer be cleared up'.[100] Thirdly, as the Real Property Commissioners explained in 1829, the uncertainty exposes proprietors of land to 'much vexation and expense . . . when they attempt alienation'.[101] Fourthly, those who have been in possession for a long period may be evicted, and the eviction of such a possessor is likely to cause significant harm.[102]

In a system of historical entitlement that lacks a reliable and robust register of title, therefore, there are reasons to take steps to diminish the uncertainty

---

[99] Tackling the difficulty of reliably identifying who has an estate (or, indeed, any other kind of proprietary interest) in land, and the related problem of insecurity of title, were the principal objectives of successive campaigns for general and compulsory land registration: see AH Manchester, *A Modern Legal History of England and Wales 1750–1950* (Butterworths 1980) 306–10; AWB Simpson, *A History of the Land Law* (2nd edn, OUP 1986) 280–83; Bridge, Cooke, and Dixon (n 88) paras 4-067–4-075.

[100] John Stuart Mill, *Principles of Political Economy* (JW Palmer 1848) vol 1, 257. See also *Cholmondeley v Clinton* (1820) 2 Jac & W 1, 139–40; 37 ER 527, 577 (Sir Thomas Plumer MR); *Trustees of Dundee Harbour v Dougall* (1852) 1 Macq 317 (HL) 321 (Lord St Leonards LC); Richard Epstein, 'Past and Future: The Temporal Dimension in the Law of Property' (1986) 64 Washington ULQ 667, 676–80.

[101] *First Report made to His Majesty by the Commissioners appointed to inquire into the Law of England respecting Real Property* (1829) House of Commons Papers (Paper No 263) Volume X, 41 (hereafter *First Report*). See also Dockray (n 93) 277–84; Alain Pottage, 'The Originality of Registration' (1995) 15 OJLS 371, 383–85.

[102] *First Report* (n 101) 39; Mill (n 100) 257; Epstein (n 100) 676.

of title and the insecurity of possession. The general acquisition rules, when combined with the rule in section 17 of the Limitation Act 1980, make it easier to ascertain who has a title, and who has a good title, to land. If a person, P, is in possession of land and claims to hold a fee simple, one can be reasonably confident—on account of the general acquisition rules—that P *has* a fee simple. If P was dispossessed by P2, and P2 was dispossessed by P3, P can establish that she has a better title—specifically, a right to exclusive possession emanating from a superior fee simple—by proving her prior possession; consequently, the dispute over possession is easily resolved. Thus, as Richard Epstein has written, the principle of relativity of title 'gives a clear and expeditious temporal rule to resolve conflicting claims'.[103] Moreover, if the land is unregistered and P, or P and her predecessors in title, were in possession for at least twelve years, it is reasonably safe to assume that no one has a superior right. Thus, the rules 'facilitate conveyancing by making it safe in practice to investigate an unregistered title only for a comparatively short period'.[104] Finally, by securing the position of those who, by themselves or in conjunction with their predecessors in title, have been in possession for twelve years, the rules 'avoid the real risk of injustice in the adjudication of stale claims',[105] and prevent the harm that would result from the eviction of those who have been in possession for a substantial period of time.[106]

We saw in Chapter 4 that the common law acquisition rules are not confined to adverse possession: a person who takes possession, not under a lease or a pre-existing fee simple, but nonetheless lawfully (under a licence, for example) thereby acquires a fee simple estate.[107] It has been argued in this section that the principal grounds of the rules concerning the destruction of title by lapse of time are also the main grounds of the general acquisition rules, and this might lead one to wonder whether the acquisition rules should apply only to adverse possessors.

While, as we have seen, the core objectives of the doctrine of adverse possession, in relation to unregistered land, can be achieved only by conjoining the acquisition rules with the rule in section 17 of the Limitation Act 1980, it does

---

[103] Epstein (n 100) 675. See also JE Penner, *The Idea of Property in Law* (OUP 1997) 148–49; Thomas W Merrill, 'Ownership and Possession' in Yun-Chien Chang (ed), *Law and Economics of Possession* (CUP 2015) 23–24. Of course, these are not the only pertinent considerations and relativity of title is not unqualified: see Chapter 5 (section 5.3).

[104] Dockray (n 93) 278.

[105] *J A Pye (Oxford) Ltd v Graham* [2001] EWCA Civ 117; [2001] Ch 804 [43] (Mummery LJ). See also David Fox, 'Relativity of Title at Law and in Equity' [2006] CLJ 330, 338.

[106] Dockray (n 93) 274–76 rightly emphasised that a countervailing consideration is that the rules may cause great harm to those against whom time has run.

[107] Chapter 4 (section 4.4.1).

not follow that the legal grounds of the rules provide reason to confer titles only on adverse possessors. The rule in section 17, when combined with the common law acquisition rules, facilitates the establishment of a *good* title (ie a title that will be forced on an unwilling purchaser under an open contract).[108] The common law acquisition rules, by themselves, make it easier to reliably identify who has *a* title and, in conjunction with the basic temporal priority rule, who among two or more ascertained persons has a *better* title. One advantage of having a rule that confers titles on possessors generally, and not merely on adverse possessors, is that, in many cases, it will be easier to ascertain who has a title and who, among two or more parties, has a better title. To return to the example discussed above, if the common law acquisition rules applied only to adverse possessors, then, in an action to recover possession from P3, it would not be enough, other things being equal, for P to prove her prior possession. P would also need to show that the possession was adverse and, thus, that time was running in her favour under the Limitation Act. To do this, P would need to establish that a right of action had accrued to another, and it may well be difficult for P to establish this. Accordingly, in many cases, the rules would fail to provide a 'clear and expeditious' means for the resolution of disputes over possession.[109]

6.3.2 Registered Land and Title by Possession

One question that has not been satisfactorily addressed is the question of why the common law acquisition rules continue to apply to land in respect of which there is a registered (freehold or leasehold) estate. The Law Commission, in the report upon which the Land Registration Act 2002 is based, claimed that the principal reasons for maintaining the rules that confer a fee simple on a possessor and extinguish the estate of the person against whom time has run, do not 'apply where title is registered'.[110] The fundamental basis of this claim is the proposition that 'the registration of a person as proprietor of land of itself vests in him or her the relevant legal estate (whether freehold or leasehold)'

---

[108] *Emmet & Farrand on Title*, vol 1, paras 5.002–5.006, 5.018, 5.080–5.082, 5.090 (Release 121 30 April 2020); Bridge, Cooke, and Dixon (n 88) paras 7-014, 14–075–14.076.

[109] Epstein (n 100) 675. See also Pollock and Maitland (n 12) 42; Merrill (n 103) 23–24.

[110] Law Commission, *Land Registration for the Twenty-First Century: A Conveyancing Revolution* (Law Com No 271) para 14.3 (hereafter LC No 271). See also *J A Pye (Oxford) Ltd v Graham* [2000] Ch 676 (Ch) 709–10 (Neuberger J); [2002] UKHL 30; [2003] 1 AC 419 [2] (Lord Bingham); Lynden Griggs, 'Possessory Titles in a System of Title by Registration' (1999) 21 Adelaide L Rev 157. cf Alison Clarke, 'Use, Time, and Entitlement' (2004) 57 CLP 239, 246–63.

and '[t]he ownership of the land is therefore apparent from the register'.[111] Consequently, the Law Commission proposed, and the Land Registration Act established,[112] 'a wholly new system of adverse possession' in respect of registered land.[113] One important change was the disapplication of the rules concerning the extinguishment of title by lapse of time: sections 15 and 17 of the Limitation Act 1980 do not apply to registered estates in land.[114] Yet, as we saw in Chapter 4,[115] the common law acquisition rules were not amended: if, for instance, R has a registered fee simple in Blackacre and S dispossesses R, S will acquire an unregistered fee simple estate.

This state of affairs gives rise to the following issue. Parliament, by enacting the Land Registration Act 2002, disapplied the rule of extinguishment in section 17 of the Limitation Act 1980 on the ground that the principal considerations that underpin the rule do not apply to registered estates in land. But those grounds are also the primary grounds of the common law acquisition rules. Why, then, do the common law acquisition rules continue to apply to registered land? It cannot be that that they are necessary in order for the new scheme of adverse possession to fulfil its objectives because, where a person who is in adverse possession of registered land meets the conditions established by that scheme, a form of statutory transfer occurs: the registered estate is transferred to the adverse possessor.[116] It might be said that the common law acquisition rules protect, and are regarded by the law as protecting, possession, and that this applies to registered land just as it applies to unregistered land.[117] This is true, but, as we have seen,[118] possession can be protected by conferring a right to exclusive possession on the current possessor; the need to protect possession is not a reason to confer a fee simple estate. Possibly, there are reasons for the common law acquisition rules to apply to land in respect of which there is a registered leasehold or freehold estate,[119] but it appears that no such reasons have been endorsed by the law. In other words, the acquisition rules, so far as they apply to such land, appear to lack a valid legal basis.

---

[111] LC No 271 (n 110) para 14.3.

[112] Land Registration Act 2002 (hereafter LRA 2002), ss 96–98, sch 6.

[113] LC No 271 (n 110) para 14.2.

[114] LRA 2002, s 96(1), (3).

[115] Chapter 4 (section 4.4.2).

[116] LRA 2002, sch 6(9).

[117] See Amy Goymour and Robin Hickey, 'The Continuing Relevance of Relativity of Title Under the Land Registration Act 2002' in Amy Goymour, Stephen Watterson, and Martin Dixon (eds), *New Perspectives on Land Registration: Contemporary Problems and Solutions* (Hart 2018) 76–77. See also LC No 254 (n 95) para 10.43; LC No 271 (n 110) para 14.10.

[118] See section 6.1 above. See also Christopher Jessel, 'Concurrent Fees Simple and the Land Registration Act 2002' (2014) 130 LQR 587, 606. cf Clarke (n 110) 262.

[119] For discussion, see Crawford (n 10) 138–41.

6.3.3 The Security and Certainty of Title to Chattels

English law has not adopted a general scheme of registration for proprietary interests in chattels.[120] This is not surprising for, as Henry Smith has said, '[i]t would be too expensive and not worthwhile to have registries for objects like paper cups, shoes, and watches'.[121] For similar reasons, interests in chattels can generally be conveyed and granted *inter vivos* without documentation. A person who has a general property interest in a piano, for instance, may transfer the interest to another by delivering the piano to the transferee with the intention of transferring the interest;[122] there is no need to use a deed. As a result of all this, entitlements to chattels will, very often, depend upon acts and transactions that cannot be easily ascertained, or which cannot be discovered at all. There are, of course, various ways in which the law might tackle this problem.[123] One approach is to adopt a doctrine of relative title, including the rules that enable general property interests to be acquired through possession.[124] Where such a doctrine has been adopted, it is usually safe to assume that a person who is in possession of a chattel, and who does not claim to have a limited legal interest (such as a pledge),[125] has a general property interest. Consequently, where a claimant claims to have a right to exclusive possession emanating from a general property interest, she can ordinarily establish this by proving that she was in possession. This facilitates the resolution of disputes over chattels.[126] In other words, with respect to chattels as with respect to land,

[120] While there is no general scheme of registration of interests in chattels, certain registration requirements apply in particular contexts. For example, the general rule is that 'charges' created by a company must be registered: Companies Act 2006, s 859A. See Ewan McKendrick (ed), *Goode on Commercial Law* (5th edn, Penguin 2016) paras 24.30–24.56.

[121] Henry E Smith, 'The Elements of Possession' in Yun-Chien Chang, *Law and Economics of Possession* (CUP 2015) 85. See also Ben McFarlane, *The Structure of Property Law* (Hart 2008) 80–87, 104–11.

[122] *Cochrane v Moore* (1890) 25 QBD 57 (CA).

[123] Many legal systems have responded to the problem by, among other things, adopting certain rules of presumption. In Scotland, for example, there is a rebuttable presumption that the possessor of a corporeal moveable is the owner: *Prangnell-O'Neill v Lady Skiffington* [1984] SLT 282 (IH); Kenneth Reid and others, *The Law of Property in Scotland* (Law Society of Scotland/Butterworths 1996) para 130. Similar rules exist in the French and German legal systems: see Sjef van Erp and Bram Akkermans (eds), *Cases, Materials and Text on Property Law* (Hart 2012) 99, 145.

[124] For a defence of the claim that there are reasons to supplement the acquisition rule with a rule that requires the court to presume, in the absence of evidence to the contrary, that a person who has been shown to have a general property interest has the best such interest: see Rostill, 'Possession and Damages' (n 14).

[125] Where a claimant who brings a claim for wrongful interference with goods has a limited legal interest (eg the interest of a pledgee), the claimant must disclose this in the particulars of claim: CPR 19.5A(1). There is a small risk that a possessor with a limited interest will dishonestly claim to hold a general property interest.

[126] See, eg *Hannah v Peel* [1945] KB 509 (KB); *Costello v Chief Constable of Derbyshire* [2001] EWCA Civ 381; [2001] 1 WLR 1437. See also Simon Roberts, 'More Lost Than Found' (1982) 45 MLR 683, 686–87; Graham Battersby, 'Acquiring Title by Theft' (2002) 65 MLR 603, 609–10.

the rules provide a 'clear and expeditious' means for the resolution of competing claims.[127] And, in a society in which most people generally abide by the law, the rules will primarily benefit, in the aggregate, those who are in possession lawfully.[128]

We have seen that, with respect to land, the common law acquisition rules are complemented by a statutory rule of extinguishment and that, together, these rules are regarded by the law as promoting certainty of title and proving greater security to possessors and their successors in title. The same can be said with regard to chattels. Section 3(2) of the Limitation Act 1980 establishes that a 'title' to a chattel will be 'extinguished' if: (a) a cause of action in conversion has accrued to the title-holder; (b) the period for bringing the action has expired; and (c) the title-holder has failed to recover possession of the chattel during that period. The normal limitation period for actions in tort, including actions in conversion, is six years from the date on which the cause of action accrued.[129] The rule that is now found in section 3(2) of the 1980 Act was originally established by the Limitation Act 1939. The Law Revision Committee, in the report upon which the 1939 Act was founded,[130] explained that, where a chattel is converted, there is a 'clear argument in favour of the extinction of' the claimant's title because the action is 'analogous to an action to recover land'; and, as in the case of land, there is a need to clear the title, though 'the necessity for clearing the title is of far less importance in the case of chattels'.[131] Thus, the Law Revision Committee and, later, Parliament, recognised that the considerations underpinning the rule that extinguishes title to land are also reasons for extinguishing title to chattels in certain circumstances. When the Law Reform Committee reconsidered the law of limitation in the 1970s, it concluded, in the report upon which the 1980 Act is based,[132] that the basic rule should be retained. The committee recognised that the rule serves 'to protect defendants from stale claims',[133] and that it is also in line with 'the policy of not disturbing long possession'.[134] The objective of protecting long possession clearly could

---

[127] Epstein (n 100) 675.

[128] Pollock thought that, 'for the very reason that possession in fact is the visible exercise of ownership, the fact of possession, so long as it is not otherwise explained, tends to show that the possessor is owner': Frederick Pollock and Robert Samuel Wright, *An Essay on Possession in the Common Law* (Clarendon Press 1888) 25.

[129] Limitation Act 1980 (hereafter LA 1980), s 2. Special rules apply to cases involving successive conversions or theft: see LA 1980, ss 3(1), 4.

[130] Law Revision Committee, *Fifth Interim Report (Statutes of Limitation)* (Cmd 5334, 1936).

[131] ibid para 24. Ultimately, the Law Revision Committee decided to make no recommendation on whether title should be extinguished.

[132] Law Reform Committee, *Twenty-first Report (Final Report on Limitations of Actions)* (Cmnd 6923, 1977).

[133] ibid para 1.7.

[134] ibid para 3.14.

not be achieved if the rules concerning the extinguishment of title by lapse of time were not complemented by rules that confer titles on possessors.

The law has, then, adopted the rules that extinguish titles to chattels and unregistered land by lapse of time, *and* the rules that *confer* titles to chattels and unregistered land on possessors, in order to provide greater certainty over title—over who has a title, who has a better title, and whether a given title is likely to be defeated by another—and to enhance the security of possessors and their successors in title. The law's reasons are, it has been argued, genuine reasons for having these rules. These conclusions are significant: they illuminate the internal logic of the law and they are relevant to, though by no means exhaustive of, the project of determining whether, all things considered, the rules are justified.

7

Ownership and Relativity of Title

What is the relationship between relativity of title and ownership? If X acquired a fee simple estate in respect of Whiteacre by obtaining possession of the land, and a general property interest in respect of a car through taking possession of it, does X *own* Whiteacre and the car? Many eminent land lawyers have maintained that, in English law, land cannot be owned.[1] And some writers have asserted that chattels cannot be owned either.[2] If these claims are correct, then X does not own the land or the car. It is argued in section 7.2, however, that both claims are mistaken, and that, in truth, land and chattels can be owned in English law.

The conclusion that land and chattels can be owned gives rise to another question: where there are competing titles (ie fees simple or general property interests), is each title-holder an owner? Do they have competing, or relative, ownerships? It is argued in section 7.3 that, while the holder of the supreme title may have ownership, there are good reasons to think that the holder of an inferior fee simple in land does not own the land and the holder of an inferior general property interest in a chattel does not own the chattel.

The questions addressed in sections 7.2 and 7.3 cannot be properly answered unless one knows what ownership is. Consequently, the first section of this chapter considers the nature of ownership.

7.1 Ownership in General

What is it to be the *owner* of a thing? It is important to emphasise that this is a philosophical, not legal, question; it is a question about the nature of ownership in general. Are there any propositions about the nature of ownership

---

[1] eg AD Hargreaves, *An Introduction to the Principles of Land Law* (2nd edn, Sweet & Maxwell 1944) 43 45; EH Burn and J Cartwright, *Cheshire and Burn's Modern Law of Real Property* (18th edn, OUP 2011) 48; Kevin Gray and Susan Francis Gray, *Elements of Land Law* (5th edn, OUP 2009) para 1.3.3; Mark Wonnacott, *Possession of Land* (CUP 2006) 38–39.

[2] eg William Swadling, 'Trusts and Ownership: A Common Law Perspective' (2016) 24 Eur Rev Private L 951, 958–61 (hereafter, Swadling, 'Trusts and Ownership').

Possession, Relative Title, and Ownership in English Law. Luke Rostill, Oxford University Press (2021). © Luke Rostill. DOI: 10.1093/oso/9780198843108.003.0007

in general that are true and illuminating? Two points are relatively uncontroversial. First, ownership necessarily involves relations among: (a) a person or group of persons (the owner); (b) an ownership object (a thing); and (c) other persons (non-owners).[3] Accordingly, whenever and wherever there is ownership, there is an owner, there is a thing that is owned, and there are non-owners.

Secondly, ownership must be distinguished from other relations among persons with respect to things. The yearly tenant of certain residential premises may regard the land as her home, but she is not the owner. If you were to ask her whether she wishes to be a homeowner, she might tell you that she is quite happy renting. Or perhaps she would say that she hopes, one day, to own her own home. But if she were to tell you that the house is hers, you may wonder whether she misunderstood the question or whether you have misunderstood the facts. Of course, in particular contexts it might be useful to deploy the term 'ownership' broadly, to refer to a very wide range of relations among persons with respect to things. But to make this a universal practice and to deny that 'ownership' picks out a particular category of relations—albeit one with fuzzy edges—is to lose sight of distinctions that are of importance to legal, political, and social theory,[4] and which are utilised by non-specialists to conceptualise and structure interpersonal relationships in respect of things.[5]

What, then, is it to be the owner of land or chattels? One issue that has been much discussed by property theorists is whether having a right to exclude others from a thing is a necessary and sufficient condition of having a property right.[6] Whatever the answer to this question,[7] it is clear that having a right to exclude others from certain land or a particular chattel is not a sufficient

---

[3] JW Harris, *Property and Justice* (OUP 1996) 5, 119–30 (hereafter Harris, *Property and Justice*); Tony Honoré, 'Property and Ownership: Marginal Comments' in Timothy Endicott, Joshua Getzler, and Edwin Peel (eds), *Properties of Law: Essays in Honour of Jim Harris* (OUP 2006) 131 (hereafter Honoré, 'Property and Ownership'); Stephen R Munzer, 'Property and Disagreement' in James Penner and Henry E Smith (eds), *Philosophical Foundations of Property Law* (OUP 2013) 303–04 (hereafter, Munzer, 'Property and Disagreement'). cf Thomas C Grey, 'The Disintegration of Property' (1980) 22 Nomos 69, 69–71.

[4] See Jeremy Waldron, *The Right to Private Property* (Clarendon Press 1988) 37–61.

[5] For discussion of the influence on property theory 'of the *pre*-theoretical understanding of what private ownership is', see Avihay Dorfman, 'Private Ownership and the Standing to Say So' (2014) 64 UTLJ 402.

[6] See, eg Thomas W Merrill, 'Property and the Right to Exclude' (1998) 77 Neb L Rev 730; Hanoch Dagan, *Property: Values and Institutions* (OUP 2011) ch 2; Simon Douglas and Ben McFarlane, 'Defining Property Rights' in James Penner and Henry E Smith (eds), *Philosophical Foundations of Property Law* (OUP 2013).

[7] Unfortunately, the debate over the significance of the right to exclude has, on some occasions, been marred by a failure to clearly specify whether the subject matter of the analysis is the concept of ownership, the concept of a proprietary interest, or the concept of an institutional system of property. There are undoubtedly important relations between these, but if we fail to separate them, there is danger of talking past one another.

condition of being the owner of the land or chattel.[8] The yearly tenant of a house has a right to exclude others from the house, and the pledgee of a pawned car has a right to exclude others from the car; but the tenant does not own the house and the pledgee does not own the car.

In recent years, many political and legal theorists have emphasised that proprietors, including owners, have, with respect to their things, a special sphere of practical authority over others.[9] Owners have authority over others in the sense that, within certain limits, their say-so can determine what others may do, or must not do, with respect to their things.[10] As Arthur Ripstein has said, 'what the owner . . . says goes. If it is your house, you can ask me to leave; if it is your umbrella, you get to decide whether I can use it when it rains'.[11] Even within the private domain, however, there are many forms of authority over others with respect to things, and many of those who have such authority are not owners. The yearly tenant of a house, for example, has authority over others with respect to the house, but she is not the owner.

What differentiates the owner from the yearly tenant? It might be said that the owner's position is special because her authority is supreme. One who wishes to defend this position might draw on the work of Larissa Katz. For, according to Katz, '[w]hat it is for a thing to be mine, in the sense that I own it, is that my decision-making authority is supreme among private actors'.[12] A major problem with defining the owner's position hierarchically, however, is that, in a given system, an individual's authority over others with respect to a thing might be supreme among private actors, and yet its scope might be so greatly restricted, or its exercise so generally directed, that the individual does not occupy what we would recognise as the position of an owner.[13]

---

[8] See Dorfman (n 5) 403–04; Larissa Katz, 'Property Law' in John Tasioulas (ed), *The Cambridge Companion to the Philosophy of Law* (CUP 2020) 377 (hereafter Katz, 'Property Law').

[9] eg Waldron (n 4) 38–40; Larissa Katz, 'Exclusion and Exclusivity in Property Law' (2008) 58 UTLJ 275 (hereafter, Katz, 'Exclusion and Exclusivity'); Dorfman (n 5); Arthur Ripstein, *Private Wrongs* (HUP 2016) ch 2; David Owens, 'Private Authority' (2019) 19 Jerusalem Rev LS 1; David Owens, 'Property and Authority' (2019) 27 J Political Philosophy 271. See also Robert Nozick, *Anarchy, State and Utopia* (Blackwell 1974) 171.

[10] Where a person has ownership in law, the owner's authority over others, qua legal owner, is conferred or recognised by law; and the owner is both an authority and a subject: see John Gardner, 'Private Authority in Ripstein's *Private Wrongs*' (2016) 14 Jerusalem Rev LS 52, 58.

[11] Arthur Ripstein, 'Property and Sovereignty: How to Tell the Difference' (2017) 18 TIL 243, 244. To say that owners *have* authority over others is not to say that the owner's authority is justified. For discussion of the distinction between de facto (ie recognised) authority and legitimate authority see Joseph Raz, 'Authority and Justification' (1985) 14 Philosophy and Public Affairs 3, 5, 13–14; Leslie Green, *The Authority of the State* (OUP 1988) 60.

[12] Katz, 'Property Law' (n 8) 378. See also Katz, 'Exclusion and Exclusivity' (n 9) 289–95.

[13] For similar reasons, Waldron has criticised attempts to define ownership as the 'greatest interest in a thing': see Waldron (n 4) 48. Interestingly, Katz, in recent work, has identified three 'dimensions' to what she sees as the perpetual, exclusive, and supreme office of ownership: (a) the ability to make binding decisions about what can be done with a thing (ie to 'set the agenda' with respect to it);

What we need is an account of ownership that will enable us to understand how the position of an owner differs from that of non-owners who have authority over others with respect to things. Tony Honoré's account, which is the most influential contemporary analysis of ownership in the English language, enables us to do just that.[14] The main aim of the remainder of this section is to defend this claim. Honoré's account, it will be argued, is largely correct, and has great explanatory power, although some key aspects of his thinking have been misunderstood, and the account is incomplete in at least one significant respect.

The aim of Honoré's account is to provide 'an accurate analysis of ownership', ie 'the liberal concept of full individual ownership'.[15] His method is to begin by describing the features of ownership in 'simple cases' in which one would not hesitate to say 'X owns that thing'.[16] These are cases in which a single person owns—in the full, liberal sense— a single material thing. By giving an explication of such cases, Honoré is able to give an account of the 'standard case' (or 'basic model') of ownership. The existence of peripheral cases of ownership does not mean that it is futile to delineate the basic model, '[o]n the contrary, such a delineation is essential in order that it may be possible to assess the strength of the analogies in the peripheral cases'.[17] Indeed, a major reason for adopting the methodology is that 'once the standard case of full ownership has been depicted, the variants and possible alternatives stand out more clearly in contrast, and are easier to understand and assess'.[18]

(b) entitlements to certain benefits (such as fruits and profits) and the responsibility for certain burdens; and (c) the ability to sell the thing, gift it, abandon it, or destroy it: Larissa Katz, 'Property's Sovereignty' (2017) 18 TIL 299, 300–07. One thing that is striking about this is how close it comes to Honoré's account of ownership (discussed below), which is not to say that there are no important differences.

[14] AM Honoré, 'Ownership' in AG Guest (ed), *Oxford Essays in Jurisprudence* (OUP 1961) 107(hereafter Honoré, 'Ownership'). The essay was reprinted, with some minor alterations, in Honoré's *Making Law Bind* (OUP 1987) ch 8 (hereafter Honoré, *Making Law Bind*). Honoré's analysis has been discussed on numerous occasions and many theorists have accepted that the analysis correctly identifies, for the most part, the features of ownership, though theorists have disagreed over how to interpret the features and how they are connected: see, eg Lawrence C Becker, *Property Rights: Philosophic Foundations* (Routledge & Kegan Paul 1977) ch 2; Waldron (n 4) ch 2; Stephen R Munzer, *A Theory of Property* (CUP 1990) ch 2 (hereafter Munzer, *A Theory of Property*); Harris, *Property and Justice* (n 3) ch 8; JE Penner, 'The "Bundle of Rights" Picture of Property' (1996) 43 UCLA L Rev 711, 739–64 (hereafter Penner, 'Bundle of Rights').

[15] Honoré, *Making Law Bind* (n 14) 161.

[16] Honoré, 'Ownership' (n 14) 110. A similar approach has been taken by others, eg Frank Snare, 'The Concept of Property' (1972) 9 APQ 200, 202.

[17] Honoré, 'Ownership' (n 14) 111. cf Bruce A Ackerman, *Private Property and the Constitution* (Yale University Press 1977) 26–27; Grey (n 3) 70; Shane Nicholas Glackin, 'Back to Bundles: Deflating Property Rights, Again' (2014) 20 LEG 1, 4.

[18] Honoré, 'Ownership' (n 14) 107–08. See also Waldron (n 4) 30–31, 49–50. It is, of course, a separate question whether a legal system *should* institute or recognise the basic model: whether, in law, any individual should have ownership in the full liberal sense. This is not a question about the nature of ownership, but about the reasons for and against having ownership. It can be properly answered only if one knows what the basic model of ownership is.

Some of the complicated cases that Honoré refers to are borderline cases of ownership in which it is intrinsically unclear whether any person is the owner. Therefore, alongside the standard case of ownership, there are: (a) non-standard, or peripheral, cases of ownership in which some of the incidents are missing;[19] (b) borderline cases in which whether a person does or does not have ownership is indeterminate;[20] and (c) cases in which a person clearly does not have ownership of a thing even though some of the features of ownership are present. For some thinkers, it is a defect of Honoré's analysis that it recognises that there are borderline cases of ownership, and that the boundaries of ownership are in this way imprecise.[21] But, if this is a defect, it is the concept of ownership itself that it defective,[22] not Honoré's account. As Aristotle said, a 'discussion will be adequate if it has as much clearness as the subject-matter admits of'.[23] To describe the boundaries as being sharper than they are is not to provide a better account of ownership, but to misdescribe it.

What, in the standard case, is ownership? Honoré's answer is that it is made up of eleven 'incidents'—or, more appropriately, *features*—though he acknowledges that there are 'alternative ways of classifying' them.[24] The eleven features are:

(1) the right to exclude the rest of the world, though not necessarily everyone, from the thing;[25]

(2) the liberty 'to use [the thing] at one's discretion', subject to certain limited restrictions;[26]

(3) the right to manage, which is constituted, or partly constituted, by powers to determine who may use the thing and how it may be used;[27]

(4) the right to the income that can be derived from the thing (eg fruits and rents);[28]

---

[19] Honoré, 'Ownership' (n 14) 111.

[20] ibid. Honoré does not actually use the term 'borderline case' but he does refer to cases in which 'no obvious linguistic convention governs the answer' to whether a person is the owner.

[21] eg Kenneth Campbell, 'On the General Nature of Property Rights' (1992) 3 KCLJ 79, 91. It is significant that Campbell's preferred account of ownership is hierarchical and, consequently, inherits the weaknesses of such accounts.

[22] There is, however, no good reason to think that the concept is so indeterminate as to be entirely useless for practical and theoretical purposes: see Munzer, *A Theory of Property* (n 14) 31–36; Waldron (n 4) 26–31, 49–50.

[23] Aristotle, *Nicomachean Ethics* (WD Ross tr, OUP 1954) 1094b 13–14.

[24] Honoré, 'Ownership' (n 14) 113.

[25] ibid, 113–14. Honoré also calls this a 'right to possess' or to have 'exclusive physical control'. He appears to regard these terms as interchangeable (and they often are used synonymously in legal contexts). Whatever it is called, it seems that the right is fundamentally a right that others keep off—exclude themselves from—the thing. cf JE Penner, *Property Rights: A Re-Examination* (OUP 2020) 8 (hereafter Penner, *Property Rights*).

[26] Honoré, 'Ownership' (n 14) 116.

[27] ibid 116–17. Honoré uses the term 'rights' broadly: it encompasses: (a) rights that ground duties; (b) liberties; (c) normative powers; and (d) immunities.

[28] ibid 117–18.

(5) the right to the capital, which consists of 'a power to alienate the thing and the liberty to consume, waste or destroy the whole or part of it';[29]

(6) the right to security, which is, or includes, a general immunity against expropriation;[30]

(7) unlimited transmissibility, which means that the owner's interest 'can be transmitted to [her] successors and so on ad infinitum';[31]

(8) absence of term, which means that, unlike a lease, the interest is not certain to determine on a particular date or on the occurrence of an event that is certain to occur;[32]

(9) the duty not to use the thing to harm individuals;[33]

(10) liability to execution, which is the liability of the interest 'to be taken away for debt';[34] and

(11) residuary character, which means that, where ownership is encumbered by other interests (eg a lease), the owner has a residuary right in the thing owned and, as a result, the extinguishment of the other interests will generally enure, mediately or immediately, for the benefit of the owner.[35]

Some of the features of ownership, as described by Honoré, are complex and consist of *various kinds* of normative entities (rights, liberties, powers, and so forth).[36] The 'right to the capital', for example, comprises powers of alienation as well as liberties to consume, waste, and destroy. Furthermore, some of the features (eg absence of term) are not constituted by rights or other kinds of normative entities; rather, they are features predicated of other features that are constituted by normative entities.[37]

A number of theorists have doubted whether the ninth feature is really a standard feature of ownership.[38] The basis of the doubt is that at least some of the duties that Honoré has in mind typically apply to persons irrespective of whether

---

[29] ibid 118.
[30] ibid 119–20.
[31] ibid 120.
[32] ibid 121–22.
[33] ibid 122.
[34] ibid 123.
[35] ibid 126–28. See also Waldron (n 4) 56–57. For an argument in support of the claim that having the ultimate (or 'greatest') residuary right is a necessary condition of ownership, see Campbell (n 21) 91–97.
[36] To say that some of the incidents consist of normative entities, including rights and powers, is *not* to say that any of the incidents should be regarded as constituted by Hohfeldian jural relations. Honoré's analysis of ownership is not Hohfeldian. Indeed, Honoré explicitly rejected Hohfeld's scheme: see AM Honoré, 'Rights of Exclusion and Immunities Against Divesting' (1959–60) 34 Tulane L Rev 453, 456–58. For discussion of whether it is possible to provide a Hohfeldian interpretation of Honoré's eleven features, see Penner, *Property Rights* (n 25) 3–12.
[37] A similar point has recently been made by Penner in his *Property Rights* (n 25) 10, fn 34.
[38] Waldron (n 4) 32–33, 49; Harris, *Property and Justice* (n 3) 32–33; Penner, 'Bundle of Rights' (n 14) 761–62.

they are owners. The owner's duty not to use his car to intentionally run down his neighbours, for example, is not a duty that, in terms of its content or basis, is connected to his status as owner; *everyone* is under such a duty. Accordingly, Jeremy Waldron has proposed that 'a better approach is to treat prohibitions on harmful behaviour as general constraints on action, setting limits to what may be done in a given society'.[39] The revised version of Honoré's essay recognises that the duty not to use a car to run people over is 'not confined to owners' and adds,'[t]he owner's position is special in that he must not allow others to use his car in these harmful or potentially harmful ways'.[40] This response gives rise to the question of whether owners are, typically, under a duty to prevent harmful use, or any similar duty, qua owners.[41] It is not necessary, however, to answer this question here. The aim of this chapter is to defend the claim that land and chattels can be owned in English law and the success of this argument, as we will see, does not depend upon whether the duty to prevent harm is a feature of the standard case of ownership.[42]

In connection with the third feature, the 'right to manage', Honoré discusses the sphere of management of the owner of a deckchair: she may 'validly license others to sit in it, lend it, impose conditions on the borrower, direct how it is to be painted or cleaned, contract for it to be mended in a particular way'.[43] This example brings to light an important point: the owner's management powers— and, indeed, the owner's other powers—are largely *undirected*.[44] That is to say, they are not governed by duties regulating their exercise.[45] This, in turn, illustrates a feature of ownership that is implicit in Honoré's account of the eleven incidents, and which he has drawn attention to in other writings.[46] It is what Jim Harris has called 'self-seekingness':[47] in the standard case, the owner may generally use the thing, and exercise her powers, to pursue her self-interest. In this respect, the owner of a car can be contrasted with a person who holds a title

---

[39] Waldron (n 4) 32.

[40] Honoré, *Making Law Bind* (n 14) 174.

[41] For discussion, see Penner, 'Bundle of Rights' (n 14) 761–62; Chris Essert, 'The Office of Ownership' (2013) 63 UTLJ 418, 446–47.

[42] Penner has also questioned whether the tenth incident, liability to execution, is part of the nature of ownership: Penner, 'Bundle of Rights' (n 14) 762–64. For similar reasons, it is not necessary here to determine whether this is correct, and the analysis proceeds on the assumption that liability to execution is a feature of ownership.

[43] Honoré, 'Ownership' (n 14) 116.

[44] For discussion of the distinction between directed and undirected powers, see Joseph Raz, 'The Inner Logic of the Law' in his *Ethics in the Public Domain* (OUP 1994) 238, 242.

[45] Duties directing the exercise of powers should not be conflated with conditions of validity.

[46] Honoré, 'Property and Ownership' (n 3) 136–37.

[47] Harris, *Property and Justice* (n 3) 5, 31. This is not to say that there are no limits on the owner's freedom to use the thing to pursue her own interest.

to a car on trust for another: the trustee, unlike the owner, is under a duty to deal with the car in the best interests of another person, the beneficiary.[48]

Are the standard features necessary conditions for a person to be the owner of a thing? Honoré states that the 'incidents are not individually necessary, though they may be together sufficient, conditions' of ownership.[49] The claim that the eleven features are jointly sufficient conditions of ownership is correct. It is also true that not every feature is individually necessary: there are non-standard cases of ownership in which some of the features are missing. Significantly, while Honoré recognised that there are non-standard cases in which some of the eleven features are absent, he never claimed that the presence, with respect to a particular person or a particular thing, of *any* of the eleven incidents, or *any* combination thereof, is sufficient for the person to have ownership of the thing.[50] That claim is clearly false. It entails that a person who holds a fee simple on trust for another has ownership of the land; that a weekly tenant of a house has ownership of the house; and that a pledgee of a watch has ownership of the watch.

Honoré's account correctly identifies, at least for the most part,[51] the standard features of ownership. It is true that, in the simple case, the features that Honoré identifies (or most of them) are present. Moreover, the account, properly interpreted, possesses a significant degree of explanatory power. For instance, it illuminates the differences between basic and peripheral cases of ownership and, in so doing, it enables us to see why, in some cases, we might be unsure as to whether a person is the owner of a thing. Suppose that L, who holds Blackacre for an estate in fee simple, grants the land to T for a term of 1,000 years. Is T the owner of Blackacre? It is not easy to answer this question. A weekly or yearly tenant of land would ordinarily not be said to own the land, but those who hold very long leases are more frequently described as owners. Honoré's account provides an explanation of this. Armed with his analysis, we can compare T's long lease with the standard case of ownership and identify the similarities and differences. This enables us to see that T's interest in Blackacre comprises many of the standard features of ownership, including a

---

[48] *Buttle v Saunders* [1950] 2 All ER 193 (Ch); *Cowan v Scargill* [1985] Ch 270 (Ch).

[49] Honoré, 'Ownership' (n 14) 112–13.

[50] Honoré never endorsed what Merrill and Smith have described as 'a commonplace of academic discourse', namely, the thesis that 'any distribution of rights and privileges among persons with respect to things can be dignified with the (almost meaningless) label "property"': Thomas W Merrill and Henry E Smith, 'What Happened to Property in Law and Economics?' (2001) 111 Yale LJ 357, 357. This thesis is entirely at odds with Honoré's views and it is regrettable that he has been associated with it: see, eg Glackin (n 17) 3.

[51] This qualification leaves open the possibility that the ninth and/or tenth incidents should not be regarded as features of the standard case of ownership.

right to exclude the world from Blackacre, powers to determine who may use Blackacre and on what terms, and a general immunity against expropriation. On the other hand, the liberty to waste is missing. Absence of term, which is an important feature, is also missing, but the distinction between an interest that can last forever and an interest that can last for 1,000 years is of limited practical importance. This is why T's interest bears a greater resemblance to the standard case of ownership than the interest held by a weekly tenant.

Honoré's account is, however, incomplete in one significant respect: it does not provide an adequate explanation of the relations among the various incidents.[52] That there are certain connections between the features is obvious and not denied by Honoré. For instance, an owner might restrict her personal liberty to use the thing by granting a lease to another, or she might remove or modify a person's duty not to interfere with the thing by granting a licence. Moreover, some of the features are dependent on others in the sense that they cannot exist without them.[53] The incident of transmissibility, for instance, cannot be present unless there is at least one right or other normative entity that can be transmitted. Similarly, the eighth incident, absence of term, presupposes that there is at least one right or other normative entity that can last forever.

Other claims concerning the relations among the features are, however, more contentious. One significant set of questions concerns justificatory relations. Is there a single justificatory foundation for the various features? Are certain features grounded or partly grounded by others? Are we to locate the incidents, or some of them, in a nested justificatory structure? These questions cannot be satisfactorily answered unless one considers the grounds of ownership. Honoré does not examine these matters in his essay, which seeks to identify the standard features of ownership, not to provide a justificatory argument. They have, however, been discussed by others, including James Penner.[54] In the 1990s, Penner defended the thesis that the 'right of property' is grounded by a single human interest, namely, 'the interest in exclusively determining the use of things'.[55] He claimed that the various features of the 'right of property'—including the right

---

[52] See Dorfman (n 5) 405.

[53] cf Glackin (n 17) 4, who claims that the incidents have 'no substantive, essential connection to each other'. According to Glackin, this claim is an aspect of the 'bundle theory' of ownership and '[o]pinions differ as to whether Honoré ... can be grouped with the bundle theorists': Glackin (n 17) 3, fn 7. There is no reason to think, however, that Honoré endorsed this theory. Indeed, his analysis is not compatible with it.

[54] For other views, see Arthur Ripstein, 'Possession and Use' in James Penner and Henry E Smith (eds), *Philosophical Foundations of Property Law* (OUP 2013); Dorfman (n 5); Ernst J Weinrib, 'Ownership, Use, and Exclusivity: The Kantian Approach' (2018) 31 Ratio Juris 123; David Owens, 'Property and Authority' (2019) 27 J Political Philosophy 271; Hanoch Dagan, *A Liberal Theory of Property* (CUP 2020).

[55] JE Penner, *The Idea of Property in Law* (OUP 1997) 49 (hereafter Penner, *The Idea of Property*).

to exclude, the power to abandon, the power to confer licences to use, and the power to give the right to others—serve and protect this interest.[56] Therefore, Penner argued, we should reject the 'substantive bundle of rights' thesis, ie the thesis that 'property is a naturally complex relation that should be regarded as an historically contingent association of various rights'.[57]

One cannot identify the justificatory relationships among the features of ownership without considering the justification of ownership; but, armed with Honoré's account, one can, it seems, identify ownership without identifying its grounds or the justificatory relations among its incidents. Accordingly, this chapter proceeds on the basis that it is possible to determine whether land and chattels can be owned in English law without discussing the grounds of owner-ship. If this approach is defensible, enough has been said to enable us to return to English law.

7.2 Ownership of Land and Chattels in English Law

Applying Honoré's account to English law reveals that land and chattels can be—and, in some cases, are—owned. Suppose that, under English law, X has an unregistered fee simple absolute in possession in Blackacre and that X is in possession of the land. Suppose, also, that X is the only person with such an es-tate in Blackacre, that there are no lesser estates in it, and that X holds directly of the Crown. The view that X is indeed the owner is supported by the fact that this accords with our ordinary usage of the term 'ownership' and, more impor-tantly, by the fact that all of the standard features of ownership are present.

First, X has a right to exclude the world at large from the land.[58] Secondly, X may, subject to some fairly narrow restrictions,[59] use the land as she wishes.[60]

---

[56] ibid ch 4. See also Penner, 'Bundle of Rights' (n 14) 739–67. For a recent statement of Penner's views, see Penner, *Property Rights* (n 25) ch 1.

[57] Penner, 'Bundle of Rights' (n 14) 722. On the other hand, '[t]he bundle of rights perspective on pro-perty is entirely innocuous if regarded merely as an elaboration of the scope of action that ownership provides. In that vein, the right to property does comprise a bundle of rights—the right to use, consume, destroy, and transfer what one owns, and so forth . . . . There is nothing wrong with this': Penner, Bundle of Rights' (n 14) 741.

[58] See, eg *Anchor Brewhouse Developments Ltd v Berkley House (Docklands Development) Ltd* [1987] 2 EGLR 173 (Ch); *Bocardo SA v Star Energy UK Onshore Ltd* [2010] UKSC 35; [2011] 1 AC 380.

[59] These include planning and environmental restrictions. While some of these restrictions are sig-nificant, it remains the case that X is generally free to use the land as he wishes: see Simon Douglas, 'The Content of a Freehold: A "Right to Use" Land?' in Nicholas Hopkins (ed), *Modern Studies in Property Law, Volume 7* (Hart 2013) 363–64.

[60] *Tapling v Jones* (1865) 11 HLC 290, 311–12; 11 ER 1344, 1353 (Lord Cranworth); *Rhone v Stephens* [1994] 2 AC 310 (HL) 317 (Lord Templeman); Susan Bright, 'Of Estates and Interests: A Tale

She is under no general duty not to interfere with the land. Thirdly, X has powers of management, ie powers to determine who may use the land and how it may be used.[61] She may, for instance, permit Y to reside on the land as a lodger, or to display an advertisement on the land. X also has what Honoré called a 'right to the income'. For example, crops that are growing on the land are regarded as part of the land and, upon severance, X will acquire a title (ie a general property interest) in respect of them.[62] Moreover, X can allow others to use the land for reward: she may, for example, grant a lease to another at a rent.[63] Fifthly, X has the power to convey her entire interest to someone else;[64] and, within certain limits, she is permitted to destroy components of the land (eg buildings and trees),[65] or to waste or consume them.[66] Sixthly, X has a general immunity against expropriation, which is protected by the Human Rights Act 1998 and the European Convention on Human Rights.[67] Her interest possesses the incidents of transmissibility and absence of term: it can be transmitted to successors indefinitely and is capable of lasting forever.[68] Ninthly, X is under certain duties not to allow others to use the land to harm others. For example, X must not authorise another to unreasonably interfere with X's neighbour's use and enjoyment of land.[69] And X must not allow a state of affairs that unreasonably interferes with his neighbour's use and enjoyment of land to continue.[70] Tenthly, X's estate may be taken away for debt. Where, for example, X becomes bankrupt, the fee simple will vest in the trustee in bankruptcy immediately on her appointment.[71] Finally, X's estate has a residuary character: if the estate becomes encumbered by another interest (eg a lease), X will continue to hold a fee simple estate in the land and, accordingly, the extinction of the

---

of Ownership and Property Rights' in Susan Bright and John Dewar (eds), *Land Law: Themes and Perspectives* (OUP 1998) 534–36; Douglas (n 59) 362–64.

[61] See, eg *Winter Garden Theatre (London) Ltd v Millennium Productions Ltd* [1948] AC 173 (HL). See also Bright (n 60) 537–38.

[62] *Mills v Brooker* [1919] 1 KB 555 (DC). This assumes, of course, that X has not granted a right to the crops to another person: see *Back v Daniels* [1925] 1 KB 526 (CA) 542 (Scrutton LJ).

[63] See, eg *Street v Mountford* [1985] AC 809 (HL).

[64] See *Re Brown* [1954] Ch 39 (Ch); Stuart Bridge, Elizabeth Cooke, and Martin Dixon (eds), *Megarry & Wade: The Law of Real Property* (9th edn, Sweet & Maxwell 2019) para 3-012. There are, of course, rules governing how these powers can be validly exercised: see, eg Law of Property Act 1925, s 52; Land Registration Act 2002, ss 4, 27.

[65] *Phipps v Pears* [1965] 1 QB 76 (CA) 83 (Lord Denning MR).

[66] Henry W Challis, *The Law of Real Property* (2nd edn, Reeves & Turner 1892) 191.

[67] Human Rights Act 1998, ss 1(1)(b), 4, 6; Article 1 of Protocol 1 to the European Convention on Human Rights.

[68] Bridge, Cooke, and Dixon (n 64) paras 3-005, 3-008, 3-029.

[69] *Lawrence v Fen Tigers Ltd* [2014] UKSC 46; [2015] AC 106.

[70] *Sedleigh-Denfield v O'Callaghan* [1940] AC 880 (HL).

[71] Insolvency Act 1986, ss 283, 283A, 306, 436(1).

encumbrance will, mediately or immediately enure to the benefit of X (or X's successor).

The position with respect to chattels is similar. Suppose that Y has the supreme general property interest in a car and that, accordingly, there is no general property interest in the car that is better than Y's. In such circumstances, the eleven standard features of ownership are present.[72]

What reasons are there, then, for thinking that land or chattels cannot be owned in England and Wales? There appear to be five considerations that have led commentators to this conclusion: (a) the doctrine of tenure; (b) the doctrines of estates; (c) the fact that there may be multiple, independent titles (fees simple) in respect of the same land; (d) the difficulty of ascertaining who has the best title; and (e) the lack of an action that exclusively protects ownership. It has been thought by some that (c), (d), and (e) apply, *mutatis mutandis*, to chattels and that, therefore, chattels cannot be owned either. The remainder of this section seeks to show that none of these considerations actually support the proposition that land or chattels cannot be owned.

7.2.1 Landownership and Tenure

It was pointed out in Chapter 4 that, in England and Wales, tenure is universal: all land (except the Royal demesne) is held, immediately or ultimately, of the Crown.[73] According to AD Hargreaves, 'if tenure exists, then the tenant cannot be the 'owner' of the land'.[74] This is not an uncommon view.[75] The question that must be addressed, therefore, is whether tenure really is incompatible with landownership. And to answer this question, it is necessary to consider how tenure affects the position of a person who holds a fee simple estate.

The doctrine of tenure governs the relationship between lord and tenant.[76] More specifically, it governs the rights and other advantages, and the obligations, of the lord and the tenant. The rights, obligations, and so forth that attach to tenure are called the incidents of tenure.[77] The incidents of a particular

---

[72] Michael Bridge and others, *The Law of Personal Property* (2nd edn, Sweet & Maxwell 2018) para 2-006.

[73] Chapter 4 (section 4.3.2).

[74] AD Hargreaves, 'Terminology and Title in Ejectment' (1940) 56 LQR 376, 376. See also Hargreaves (n 1) 43–45.

[75] See, eg Gray and Gray (n 1) para 1.3.3; Wonnacott (n 1) 38–39.

[76] See AWB Simpson, *A History of the Land Law* (2nd edn, OUP 1986) ch 1; Bridge, Cooke, and Dixon (n 64) ch 2.

[77] Simpson (n 76) 15–20.

tenure depend upon what kind of tenure it is. While, historically, there were many kinds of feudal tenure,[78] nowadays there is just one kind that is of any importance, namely socage tenure.[79] All the other kinds were (with one possible, minor exception) abolished by the Tenures Abolition Act 1660 and the 1925 legislation.[80] In most cases,[81] the only incident of tenure that has not disappeared is escheat: when the tenant's fee simple determines, her lord becomes entitled to possession (eg where the tenant files for bankruptcy and her trustee in bankruptcy disclaims the land).[82]

Returning to X and her fee simple in Blackacre, does the fact that the land will escheat to the Crown if X's fee simple determines entail that X is not the owner of the land? It does not. Even if, by virtue of the rules on escheat, the Crown does have a residuary right in Blackacre,[83] which is one of the incidents of ownership, it would be a mistake to regard the Crown as the owner, for central features of ownership are missing. The Crown has, for example, no right to exclude the world from the land: it acquires a right to possession only if and when the land escheats.[84] It has no powers of management. And it is not legally permitted to use, consume, waste, or destroy the land. In contrast, so far as X and Blackacre are concerned, every feature of ownership is present. This shows that X owns Blackacre and the Crown does not. We should, therefore, reject Hargreaves's claim that tenure and ownership are incompatible. X is a tenant in fee simple, but she is also the owner of Blackacre. As Waldron has said, 'the forms of a feudal system . . . have been adapted by the English law to express the modern reality of private property in pieces of land'.[85]

It is important to recognise the distinction between X's position vis-à-vis the Crown, on the one hand, and the position of the holder of a fee simple encumbered by a lease, on the other. Suppose that A, who has the best fee simple estate in Blueacre, leases the land to B for five years. Until the lease expires, B is

[78] Simpson (n 76) 6–15; Bridge, Cooke, and Dixon (n 64) paras 2-007–2-013.

[79] Bridge, Cooke, and Dixon (n 64) paras 2-019–2-030. There is one kind of *non-feudal* tenure that is of importance in the modern law, ie leasehold tenure. But, for present purposes, this is irrelevant.

[80] Lawyers have disagreed over whether frankalmoin has been abolished. One view is that it was abolished by the Administration of Estates Act 1925, sch 2, pt 1: Bridge, Cooke, and Dixon (n 64) para 2-019, fn 43.

[81] Some cases are more complicated. For example, where, prior to the coming into force of the Law of Property Act 1922, land was held by copyhold tenure, the 1922 Act preserved a number of rights and obligations, including any rights of the lord or tenant to mines and minerals: Law of Property Act 1922, ss 128(2), 138, sch 12(4)–(6).

[82] *Scmlla Properties Ltd v Gesso Properties (BVI) Ltd* [1995] BCC 793 (Ch).

[83] For arguments to the effect that the Crown, or mesne lord, has no existing rights in the land, but a mere expectancy, see Campbell (n 21) 91–95; Penner, *The Idea of Property* (n 55) 149–52.

[84] Co Litt 18b; *Scmlla Properties* (n 82) 803–04 (Stanley Burnton QC). See also Challis (n 66) 33; Simpson (n 76) 47–48.

[85] Waldron (n 4) 36.

generally permitted to use the land as she sees fit: she has a right to exclude the world from the land, powers of management, and so forth. Yet the landlord, A, will be regarded as the owner of the land, not B. It might be thought that, if A is the owner, this in tension with the argument that, so far as X and Blackacre are concerned, X is the owner, not the Crown. There are, however, important differences between A's position vis-à-vis B, and the Crown's position vis-à-vis X. First, B's interest, unlike X's, lacks certain features of ownership, including absence of term and the liberty to waste. Secondly, even if it is correct to regard the Crown as having a residuary interest in Blackacre, the interest is of limited practical importance, because the possibility of the land escheating to the Crown is remote. In contrast, A's reversionary fee simple in Blueacre is a significant interest, for it is certain that B's lease will come to an end.

7.2.2 The Doctrine of Estates and Relativity of Title

It has been thought that, since there can be several estates in land, each held by a different person, *estates* in land can be owned, but not *land*.[86] Suppose P holds a fee simple in Greenacre; P's tenant, Q, has a ninety-nine-year lease; R, a sub-lessee, has a weekly tenancy; and S, an adverse possessor, has an inferior fee simple. Who is the owner of the land—P, Q, R, or S? This is an interesting question. We will consider, in section 7.3, whether a person who has an inferior fee simple has ownership. But we are concerned here with whether, in English law, land *can* be owned. The fact that there may be multiple estates in land, including multiple fees simple, is not at all inconsistent with the view that persons can, and do, own land in English law. Even if, in the example above, no one owns the land, this is perfectly consistent with the claim that X is the owner of Blackacre in the simple case where she has the only estate in the land. As Honoré pointed out, the argument that, in view of complicated cases, it would be better not to speak of ownership of land at all, 'ignores the many straightforward cases in which there is a single tenant in fee simple and no competing title'.[87] A similar point applies to chattels.

---

[86] See Gray and Gray (n 1) para 1.3.3; FH Lawson, *Introduction to the Law of Property* (Clarendon Press 1958) 9.
[87] Honoré, 'Ownership' (n 14) 140.

7.2.3 The Difficulty of Identifying the Best Title

It might be thought that the example involving X and Blackacre is wholly unrealistic. X, it was said, has the best fee simple estate in Blackacre. Yet, in the real world, there is often uncertainty as to whether a given fee simple is truly the best. According to the authors of *Megarry & Wade*:

> O may be 'owner' of Blackacre, but it is always theoretically possible for someone to come forward and prove a better title, as by proving that he or she owns the reversion on a long term of years which has now expired.[88]

This does not show, however, that land cannot be owned. If correct, it shows that the person who has the best fee simple cannot be identified with absolute certainty. But why should this matter? It will often suffice, for practical purposes, that the best fee simple can be identified with reasonable certainty; and, even with respect to unregistered fees simple,[89] one can, in certain circumstances, be reasonably confident that a given person has the best fee simple.[90] Similarly, one can, in certain circumstances, be reasonably confident that a particular person has the best title to a chattel.[91]

7.2.4 The Protection of Proprietary Interests

It has been thought that chattels and land are not objects of ownership in English law because there are no actions in English law that exclusively protect ownership, or in which it is necessary to prove ownership. William Swadling has forcefully defended this view. He argues that 'there is no concept of ownership in English law'.[92] The reason is that, in order to successfully bring an action for the recovery of possession of land, or to obtain a remedy in the property torts, it is necessary to prove, not that one has ownership, but that one

---

[88] Bridge, Cooke, and Dixon (n 64) para 7-012.

[89] For discussion of the position with respect to registered fees simple, see Bridge, Cooke, and Dixon (n 64) paras 6-023–6-038.

[90] Lawson (n 86) 39–41; Martin Dockray, 'Why do we Need Adverse Possession?' [1985] Conv 272; Alain Pottage, 'Evidencing Ownership' in Susan Bright and John Dewar (eds), *Land Law: Themes and Perspectives* (OUP 1998).

[91] See Lawson (n 86) 38.

[92] William Swadling, 'Unjust Delivery' in Andrew Burrows and Lord Rodger of Earlsferry (eds), *Mapping the Law: Essays in Memory of Peter Birks* (OUP 2006) 281.

has a right to exclusive possession: '[t]he common law has no equivalent of the Roman *vindicatio*', ie an action in which it is necessary to prove ownership.[93]

If this is meant to be an argument for the claim that land and chattels cannot be owned in English law, it is invalid.[94] It does not follow from the fact that the claimant does not need to prove that she is the owner of the thing, that she is not the owner. Swadling might not disagree with this. The point, as he has expressed it elsewhere, is that 'it is *never important* to identify the person with the best fee simple, for no benefits attach to having such status'.[95] Since one does not need to prove that one has the best title, the best title is legally irrelevant, or so Swadling argues.

It is true that there is no action that exclusively protects the best title. But, as we saw in Chapter 5,[96] in some circumstances it is legally relevant whether one has the best title to a chattel or an inferior title.[97] Where, for example, C brings an action in conversion against D, and C was in possession of the chattel, or had a right to immediate possession, at the time of the alleged tort, the law will presume that C has 'absolute and complete ownership', ie the best title; or, more precisely, the supreme general property interest in possession.[98] It is open to D to defeat this presumption, and to thereby prevent C from recovering the 'full value' of the chattel, by showing that a third party has a superior general property interest.[99] This shows that, at least with respect to chattels, it matters, in some cases, whether one has the best title. We will see in the next section that the distinction between best titles and inferior titles is important in land law too.

7.3 Ownership and Relative Title

If land and chattels can be owned in English law, the question arises whether, by virtue of the rules concerning the acquisition of property through possession, there can be *competing* ownerships. Suppose that O used some leather to manufacture a bag and, thereafter, P took possession of the bag without O's

---

[93] ibid 283.

[94] A similar point is advanced in Bridge (n 72) para 2-009.

[95] Swadling, 'Trusts and Ownership' (n 2) 959.

[96] Chapter 5 (section 5.3).

[97] For a wide-ranging discussion of the role that ownership has played in judicial reasoning, see JW Harris, 'Ownership of Land in English Law' in Neil MacCormick and Peter Birks (eds), *The Legal Mind* (Clarendon Press 1986); Harris, *Property and Justice* (n 3) ch 6.

[98] Chapter 5 (section 5.3.1).

[99] Chapter 5 (section 5.3.2).

consent. When P took possession, she acquired an inferior general property interest. The best general property interest is held by O. Is it correct to regard each of them as (independent) owners of the bag? According to Pollock, '[t]he possessor'—in this case, P—'is in a relative sense an owner':[100] P has 'a right which, though subject to whatever better rights may exist, is invested as against the world at large with all the incidents of ownership'.[101] It might be thought that this is a compelling argument. If O has ownership, and if P's interest has the same content as O's, then P must have ownership too.

It is argued in this section, however, that Pollock's view is mistaken. There is an important distinction between, on the one hand, those who hold the *supreme* fee simple in respect of certain land or the *supreme* general property interest in respect of a particular chattel and, on the other hand, those who hold an inferior fee simple or an inferior general property interest. The holder of the best title, at least where it is unencumbered by other interests, is the owner, but the holder of an inferior fee simple or an inferior general property interest does not have ownership.

Many scholars have claimed that, where a possessor acquires an inferior title, the content of the possessor's interest is the same as the content of the interest held by the person or persons with a better title.[102] When assessing this claim, it is important to identify what the relevant 'interest' is thought to be. Ben McFarlane, for example, would say that, in the example above, O and P each have a particular kind of interest, which he calls 'Ownership'.[103] This is 'a right to immediate exclusive control of a thing forever'.[104] Now, to claim that O and P each have a right to immediate exclusive control forever is, of course, not to claim that their legal positions, with respect to the bag, are entirely the same. Nor is it to claim what Pollock claimed, ie that P's interest has all the incidents of ownership.[105]

Does P's interest have all the incidents of ownership? According to Honoré, P's interest 'has every incident of ownership except security against divesting' and, therefore, '[t]here is much to be said' for treating O and P as 'independent owners rather than as persons sharing a single, split ownership'.[106] But the proposition that P's interest possesses 'every incident of ownership except security

[100] Frederick Pollock, *A First Book of Jurisprudence* (5th edn, Macmillan 1923) 189.
[101] ibid 188.
[102] eg Pollock (n 100) 188–89;Ben McFarlane, *The Structure of Property Law* (Hart 2008) 140–46; Simon Douglas, *Liability for Wrongful Interferences with Chattels* (Hart 2011) 26; Swadling, 'Trusts and Ownership' (n 2) 959.
[103] McFarlane (n 102) 146.
[104] ibid 140
[105] McFarlane makes clear that he is concerned, not with the general concept of ownership, but with a specific type of proprietary interest recognised by English law, which he calls 'Ownership', and which has been called herein a 'general property interest'.
[106] Honoré, 'Ownership' (n 14) 140.

against divesting' is false. The second incident, the liberty to use the thing as one sees fit, is missing. Since O's interest binds P, P owes certain duties of non-interference to O.[107] P was under a duty not to take the bag in the first place: by intentionally taking it, P committed the tort of trespass to chattels. And if P took it with the intention of keeping it, P committed conversion.[108] Moreover, P is under a continuing duty not to treat the bag as her own.[109] And while P has various powers of management and alienation, P is under a duty not to exercise many of these powers. For example, she must not exercise her power to transfer her interest by delivering the bag to another,[110] and she must not pledge it.[111] She is also under a duty not to destroy the bag.[112] O, on the other hand, is in a very different position. O is generally permitted to use the bag as she sees fit. She may destroy it. And she may exercise her powers of alienation and management as she wishes.

The adoption of a Hohfeldian approach might conceal, or appear to minimise the importance of, the differences between the positions of O and P.[113] This is a consequence of the logic of the Hohfeldian scheme of jural relations. For, according to Hohfeld, a jural relation (right–duty; liberty–no right; power–liability; immunity–disability) is always a tripartite relation between exactly one person, one other person, and an act-description.[114] A liberty, for example, is always a liberty to act in a certain way *relative to* one other person.

On a Hohfeldian analysis of the example above, O has various rights against P. For example, O has a right against P that P does not destroy the bag. Since the correlative of a right is a duty, P owes O a duty not to destroy the bag. The opposite of a duty is a liberty. So, since P owes O a duty not to destroy the bag, P does *not* have a liberty *as against* O to destroy the bag. P's position vis-à-vis O can be contrasted with P's position as against a third party, Q, who does not have an interest in the bag. P does not owe Q a duty not to destroy the bag. Therefore, P has, *as against* Q, a liberty to destroy the bag. Indeed, P has such a liberty as

---

[107] For an account of these duties, see Chapter 5 (section 5.2.1).

[108] *Lancashire & Yorkshire Railway Co v MacNicoll* (1918) 88 LJKB 601 (KB).

[109] *Kuwait Airways Corp v Iraqi Airways Co (Nos 4 & 5)* [2002] UKHL 19; [2002] 2 AC 883 [39]–[44] (Lord Nicholls).

[110] *Hollins v Fowler* (1875) LR 7 HL 757 (HL).

[111] *Parker v Godin* (1728) 2 Strange 813; 93 ER 866.

[112] *Fouldes v Willoughby* (1841) 8 M & W 540, 547; 151 ER 1153, 1156 (Lord Abinger CB).

[113] WN Hohfeld, 'Some Fundamental Legal Conceptions as Applied in Judicial Reasoning' (1913) 23 Yale LJ 16.

[114] John Finnis, 'Rights: Their Logic Restated' in his *Collected Essays: Volume IV, Philosophy of Law* (OUP 2011) 378.

against everyone except O. So, applying the Hohfeldian scheme, it is a mistake to say that P does not have a liberty to destroy the bag. P has liberties to destroy the bag *as against everyone but* O.[115]

On a Hohfeldian approach, therefore, it is not possible to say simply that one has a general liberty to act in a certain way. This is significant because it was said above that one difference between O's legal position and P's is that O, but not P, is generally permitted to use the thing as she sees fit. To capture the difference between the positions of O and P on a Hohfeldian approach, one would need to say that O has certain liberties as against everyone, but P has certain liberties against everyone but O. While P will wrong O if she destroys the bag, O will wrong no one if she destroys it herself. The key is to recognise that, on any view, this distinction is important. We can see this by considering how O and P should behave, according to the law. Since, in law, P is under a duty not to destroy the bag, P *should not* destroy the bag. On the other hand, as O does not owe a duty not to destroy the bag to anyone, O may destroy it.

There are, therefore, important legal differences between the respective positions of the holder of the supreme title and the holder of an inferior title. Other things being equal, the holder of the supreme title is permitted, in law, to use the thing, within certain limits, as she sees fit. The holder of an inferior title, in contrast, is not. Furthermore, the holder of the supreme title is usually permitted to destroy the thing, but the holder of an inferior title is not. And whereas the holder of a supreme title may exercise powers of management and alienation, the holder of an inferior title is, so far as many of these powers are concerned, under a duty *not* to exercise them. It is, therefore, a mistake to claim that a person who has an inferior fee simple or an inferior general property interest has every incident of ownership. Indeed, given the extent of the restrictions, and the significance that freely using and determining the use of things has to the idea of ownership,[116] there is a strong case for concluding that the holder of an inferior fee simple does not own the land, and the holder of an inferior general property interest does not own the chattel. If this is right, the holder of an inferior title is not, in fact, a 'relative owner'.

---

[115] See Douglas and McFarlane (n 6) 220–21. For a critique of Hohfeld's conception of liberties, see Penner, *Property Rights* (n 25) ch 3.

[116] Honoré rightly described the liberty to use the thing as one wishes as a 'cardinal feature of ownership': 'Ownership' (n 14) 116. And, as section 7.1 explains, it is implicit in Honoré's whole analysis that the owner is generally permitted to exercise her powers as she sees fit.

7.4 Conclusion

Some scholars have thought that, since English law is a multititular system in which multiple fees simple may exist in respect of the same land, and multiple general property interests may exist in respect of the same chattel, ownership is of no importance. Others have drawn a different conclusion: that a person who takes possession of a thing that belongs to another becomes a relative owner and, consequently, there may be multiple, independent ownerships. A third group has argued that these two views rest on a false premise—ie that there can be multiple fees simple or multiple general property interests—and that the correct view is that a person who takes possession of another's land or chattels acquires a more limited interest (eg a mere right of possession).

The truth, it has been argued, is that there may be two or more fees simple in respect of certain land, and two or more general property interests in respect of a particular chattel. But it does not follow that each estate-holder or interest-holder is a relative owner. Nor does it follow that ownership is irrelevant. The person who has the supreme fee simple or the supreme general property interest will usually have ownership. But a person who has an inferior fee simple does not own the land and a person who has an inferior general property interest does not own the chattel. The distinction between supreme interests and inferior interests is important. The holder of the best interest is, in general, legally permitted to deal with the thing as she wishes. The holder of an inferior interest is not. Furthermore, where a claimant has an inferior title, the defendant may, at least in cases involving chattels, reduce the size of the claimant's damages by identifying a person with a superior interest. While, then, English law is a system that recognises relativity of title, it is also a system that recognises and protects ownership.

Index

For the benefit of digital users, indexed terms that span two pages (e.g., 52–53) may, on occasion, appear on only one of those pages.

abandonment
  destructive abandonment v
    abandonment of possession, 91, 92
  grounds of power of, 163–64
  of titles to land, 91, 92–93
absence of term, incident of, 159, 160,
  162–63, 164–66, 167–68
absolute and complete ownership *see*
  presumption of absolute and
  complete ownership
absolute interest, 112
  see also general property interest; legal
    ownership interest
acquisition of property
  dependent v independent, 99–100
  see also causative events; modes of
    acquisition or loss
acquisition, rules of
  v rules of presumption, 26, 27, 35, 36
action for the recovery of land
  nature of, 63, 169–70
  protection of prior possession, 79–80
  see also ejectment
adverse possession
  accrual of right of action, 82, 87, 145
  justifications of, 84, 145–49
  nature of, 83, 94, 145
  protection of, 3–4, 32–33, 84–87
  and registered land, 83–84, 96–97,
    146n.96, 149–50
  transfer of title by virtue of, 82–84, 85
  see also disseisin; extinguishment of title
    by lapse of time; limitation periods;
    possession
alienability *see* alienable v non-alienable
  rights; dispositive powers
animus possidendi see intention to possess

Aristotle, 159
assumption of responsibility, 132–34, 135–36
  see also duties of care; tort of negligence
Atiyah, Patrick, 118–19, 120–22
authority, practical
  conferred or recognised by law, 157n.10
  de facto v legitimate, 157n.11
  with respect to things, 157–58

Bacon, Matthew, 139–40
bailment
  duties of bailees, 132–34,
    135–36, 139–40
  protection of bailees, 115–17, 143–44
  sub-bailments, 135–36
  see also assumption of responsibility;
    finders; pledges
Baker, CD, 121–22
Baker, John, 64
Blackstone, William, 62–63, 88, 90
Bridge, Michael, 9–10
bundle of rights thesis, the substantive,
  162n.50, 163–64

causative events, 25–26
certainty of title, 5–6, 129, 144–49, 151–53
Chambers, Robert, 119
chattels, meaning of *see* tangible chattels
choses in possession *see* tangible chattels
claims to proprietary interests, 25–26, 35–
  36, 39, 85n.224
Clerk JF, 139–40
Coke, Edward, 127
confiscation orders, 114–16
constructive possession, 10
contractual licences, 94–96
  see also licensees

control *see* exclusive physical control
conversion, tort of, 101–2, 103–4, 106–7,
    136–42, 152, 169–70, 171–72
Cooke, Elizabeth, 88–89, 96
Curwen, Nicholas, 81–82, 85–87, 88, 90

damages
    and conversion, 137–42, 170
    contribution, claim for, 141–42n.72
    and the Winkfield rule, 116–17, 118–19,
        123–25, 137–38, 143–44
    see also jus tertii; secondary duty to pay
        damages
defences, nature of, 117–18
Dennis, Ian, 47–48
Dias, RWM, 13
Dicey, AV, 119–20, 123
dispossession
    reasons to protect possessors from,
        28–30, 128–29
disseisin, 53, 64, 75, 78, 85
    v adverse possession, 53–54, 85–87
Dixon, Martin, 4–5
duties of care
    general v special, 132–34, 135–37
        with respect to chattels, 102–3,
            132–34, 135–36, 139–40
        with respect to land, 58–59
duties not to use things to harm others, 159,
    160–61, 164–66

ejectment
    nature of, 62–64
    protection of prior possession, 68–71,
        72–77, 79–80
Epstein, Richard, 147–48
escheat, 89, 166–67
Essert, Christopher, 60–61
evidence, rules of, 3, 37
exclusive physical control
    nature of, 16–19
    see also possession
extinguishment of title by lapse of time, 82–
    83, 84–85, 87, 144–50, 152–53
    see also adverse possession; limitation
        periods

fee simple
    absolute, 55n.17, 90

acquisition through possession, 4–5, 32–
    33, 54–62, 67–68, 72–93, 94–97, 98
    core incidents of, 55–56
    destruction by abandonment, 92–93
    inferior v superior, 90, 93, 170–73, 174
    presumption of, 3, 23, 34–35, 38–39, 49,
        50–51, 53–54, 64–67
        conceptual objections to, 42–51
    see also ownership; tenure
finders
    and agents, 21–22
    duties of, 130, 131, 133–34, 135–37
    and employees, 21–22
    and the intention to possess, 20–21
    lawful finders v wrongdoers, 20–21,
        133–34, 136–37, 138
    reasons for protecting, 130–31, 134–37
Fox, David, 30, 35, 38–40, 104–5, 107

general property interest
    acquisition by manufacture, 170–71
    acquisition by possession, 5, 33, 99–113,
        114–17, 119, 123, 124–26, 176
    inferior v superior, 116–17,
        170–73, 174
    nature of, 100, 110, 112–13
    transfer by delivery, 151–52
    utility of label, 112–13, 126
    v limited legal interests, 5,
        99–100, 112–13
    see also sale of goods

Getzler, Joshua, 121–22
Glover, Richard, 45–46
Goode, Roy, 30, 104, 110
goods
    for purposes of law of sale, 109n.64
    see also sale of goods
Gordley, James, 32, 67–68, 75–77
Goudkamp, James, 117–18
grounds of legal rules
    nature and significance of, 5–6, 127–28

Hargreaves, AD, 32, 37, 53–54, 69–70,
    76–77, 81–82, 166, 167
Harris, Jim, 161–62
Hart, HLA, 40–41
Hickey, Robin, 25–26, 42–43, 50, 112–13,
    130–31, 133–34, 135, 136–39, 140

Hohfeldian jural relations, 160n.36, 172–73
Holdsworth, William, 119–20, 123
Holmes, Oliver Wendell Jr, 1, 32, 67–68, 98, 143, 143n.79
Honoré, AM (Tony), 1, 25–26, 158–64, 168, 171–72

illegality, defence of, 106
immunities, 31–32
    against expropriation, 159, 162–63, 164–66
intention to possess
    nature of, 19–21
    proof of, 21
    requirement of, 16, 19
issues of fact v issues of law, 47–48

Jessel, Christopher, 88–89
joint possession see possession
Jolly, Anthony, 117–19
Jourdan, Stephen, 91–92
judicial decisions
    importance of identifying grounds of, 41
jus tertii
    avoiding liability v reducing extent of liability, 70–71n.135, 118–19, 124–25
    defence v denial of wrongdoing, 117–18, 119
    and ejectment/actions to recover land, 70–71, 79
    possession v right to possession, 119–23
    and private nuisance, 71n.135, 119n.125
    and tortious interferences with chattels, 117–25, 139–40, 170, 174
    and trespass to land, 58, 71n.135, 119n.125

Katz, Larissa, 131, 133–34, 136–37, 157
Kersley, RH, 9–10

land, nature of, 1–2n.5
land law v personal property, 6, 125–26
legal interests, nature of, 9–10, 31–32
legal ownership interest, 1, 2, 33, 112
    see also absolute interest; general property interest
legal rights see rights
liability to execution, incident of, 159, 161n.42, 164–66

liberties, 31–32, 172
    to consume things, 159, 160, 164–66, 167
    to destroy things, 159, 160, 164–66, 167–68, 171–73
    to use things, 159, 163–64, 165–66, 167–68, 171–72, 173
    to waste things, 159, 160, 162–63, 164–66, 167–68
licensees
    acquisition of possession by, 94–95
    nature and grounds of interest acquired through possession, 94–96, 148–49
Lightwood, JM, 67–68, 71–72
limitation periods
    and conversion, 152–53
    and ejectment/actions for the recovery of land, 64, 82–84, 145
    and registered land, 83–84, 149–50
    see also adverse possession; extinguishment of title by lapse of time
Lyndhurst, Lord, 84, 87, 145–46, 147

McFarlane, Ben, 33, 99–100, 112–13, 171
McKendrick, Ewan, 30, 104, 110
Maitland, Frederic William, 28–29, 64
Mattei, Ugo, 32, 67–68, 75–77
Mill, John Stuart, 147
modes of acquisition or loss, 25–26
multititular system
    and English law, 33–34, 174
    meaning of, 1

negligence, tort of
    and chattels, 102–4, 132–34, 143–44, 169–70
    and land, 58–59, 169–70
    property damage, nature of, 132n.23
    see also assumption of responsibility; damages; duties of care; jus tertii
Nolan, Donal, 60–61

obligation-based reasons see reasons
ownerless things see res nullius
ownership
    and estates in land, 164–69, 170–73, 174
    and general property interests, 166, 170–73, 174

ownership (*cont.*)
  incidents of, 159–63, 165–66
  justification of, 158–59n.18, 163–64
  legal significance of, 6, 170–74
  nature of, 155–64
  protection of, 169–70
  and relativity of title, 3, 6, 32, 155, 164–
      66, 168–69, 171–73, 174
  and self-seekingness, 161–62
  standard v non-standard cases, 158–63
  and tenure, 164, 166–68
  v trusteeship, 161–62
  v yearly tenancy, 156–57, 162–63
  see also presumption of absolute and
      complete ownership

Palmer, Norman, 133–34
parliamentary conveyance theory, 85
Penner, James, 163–64
physical control *see* exclusive physical
      control
pledges, 99–100, 116–17, 151–52
Pollock, Frederick, 3, 7–9, 17, 28–29, 32, 53,
      67–68, 98, 119–20, 123, 170–71
Posner, Richard, 1
possession
  acquisition of, 15
  and the acquisition of property, 4–5,
      55–81, 99–113
  and agents, 21–22
  borderline v clear cases, 10–11, 13–14
  of chattels on, under, or attached to
      land, 12–13, 16, 22, 103–4, 105–6,
      128n.10
  and employees, 21–22
  evidence of property in chattels, 99
  evidence of seisin, 32, 37, 53–54, 64–67,
      73, 76–77
  exclusivity of, 22
  held jointly, 22
  lawful v wrongful, 94–96
  and licensees, 19, 21, 94–95
  loss of, 15
  meanings of, 4, 8–10, 11–13, 15, 126
  nature of, 4, 14–22
  subject matter of, 23–24
  through another, 21–22
  see also constructive possession exclusive
      physical control; intention to
      possess; right of possession

possession-dependent right, 26, 27–28
  see also possessory right view; right of
      possession
possessory rights/interests
  meanings of, 2, 32–33, 112
  see also rights of possession
possessory right view, the, 27–31, 36
  and chattels, 104–9
  and land, 61–62, 66–67, 71, 91–92
powers, 31–32
  directed v undirected, 161–62
  dispositive, 55–56, 72, 73, 74–75, 77–79,
      80–81, 99–100, 109, 135, 159, 160,
      163–66, 171–72
  permissive, 159, 161–64, 165–66, 172
predictive theories of legal rights *see* rights
presumed property view, the, 34–36
  and chattels, 99, 103–4, 113–17, 121, 125
  conceptual objections to, 42–51
  and land, 64–67, 76–77
presumption
  bases of, 45–46
  evidential v persuasive, 45
  nature of, 38, 43–46, 49–51
  rebuttable v irrebuttable, 45, 50–51
  rules of, 3, 34–35, 38, 43–46, 48–51,
      151n.123
  see also fee simple; presumption of
      absolute and complete ownership;
      rules of acquisition v rules of
      presumption
  presumption of absolute and complete
      ownership, 5, 34–35, 116–17,
      118–19, 123–25, 129n.14, 137–38,
      143–44, 170
  conceptual objections to, 42–51
priority rules, 33–34, 39, 128
private nuisance, tort of, 59–61, 169–70
private purposes trusts, 127
proceeds of crime *see* confiscation orders
proof
  of facts, 46, 48–50
  law of, 48–49
property rights *see* proprietary interests
propositions
  factual v legal, 46–48, 49
  legal v non-legal, 47–48
proprietary interests
  general features of, 31–32, 156–57
  types of, 1, 2–3, 9–10, 126

Radley-Gardner, Oliver, 91–92
Raz, Joseph, 47–48, 127–28
real actions, 62–63, 64, 87
Real Property Commissioners, 63, 82–83, 147
reasons
    adequate v pro tanto, 127–30
    obligation-based, 129, 130, 131–32, 134–
        37, 138–40, 141–42, 143–44
registered land
    campaigns for establishment of, 147n.99
    and title by possession, 4–6, 96–97,
        129, 149–50
    see also adverse possession
registration of company charges, 151n.120
relativity of title
    general principle, 2, 34, 39, 70–71, 79–80,
        119, 121–23, 128
    limits of, 4, 71n.135, 119–25, 128
    see also jus tertii; ownership
res nullius, 2n.13, 130
residuary character, incident of, 159,
    164–66, 167–68
reversionary injury, 55n.17
reversionary interest v possessory interest,
    2n.16, 55n.17
right of entry
    acquisition of, 53, 64, 85
    features of, 53, 64–65, 85–86
    loss of, 64, 85
right of possession
    and chattels, 104–9
    and land, 53–54, 66–67, 71, 79–80,
        91–92, 94
    grounds of, 28–30, 67, 128–29, 150
    nature of, 27–28
right to exclude
    meaning of, 55n.15, 100n.7, 159n.25
    see also right to exclusive possession
right to exclusive possession
    grounds of, 28–30, 67, 128–29, 130–31,
        134–37, 138–39, 140, 141–42, 144,
        145–49, 150, 151–53, 159, 162–64
    over chattels, 100–4
    over land, 55, 59, 60–61, 164–66, 167–68
right to manage things, 159, 161–66,
    167–68, 171–72, 173
right to security, 159, 164–66
right to the capital, 159, 160, 164–66, 171–72
right to the income, 159, 164–66
right to use and enjoy land, 55, 59–61

rights
    alienable v non-alienable, 26, 28, 73, 74–75
    legal rights, predictive theories of, 40–41
    over chattels or land, 28
    v other normative relations, 31–32,
        159n.27, 160
    in respect of wild animals, 28n.16
    see also alienable v non-alienable rights;
        Hohfeldian jural relations
Ripstein, Arthur, 157
Rudden, Bernard, 85–86

sale of goods
    agreement to sell, 109
    by buyer in possession, 110–11
    contract of sale, 109
    implied undertaking as to title, 110
    sale, nature of, 109, 110
    and the transfer of general property
        interests, 110–11
Salmond, John, 7
Savigny, Friedrich Karl von, 1, 29–30n.23
secondary duty to pay damages
    duty view v liability view, 137–38n.56
security of possession, 5–6, 129,
    144–49, 151–53
seisin
    acquisition/loss of, 53, 85
    establishment of, 64–66
    legal consequences of, 53–54, 75, 78
    status in modern law, 85–87
Shartel, Burke, 8–9
Simpson, AWB, 53, 85
Smith, Henry, 151–52
Sparkes, Peter, 69–71, 87
special property, 33, 99–100, 112–13, 143
squatters see adverse possession
strict liability in property torts, 56n.24, 101–2
strong proprietary interest view, the,
    31–34, 36
    and chattels, 99–125
    and land, 54–62, 67–68, 72–93, 94–97
Swadling, William, 3, 33, 42–43, 46–49,
    50–51, 169–70
Sweet, Charles, 53–54

tangible chattels, nature of 1n.4
tenure
    and the acquisition of title by
        possession, 88–90

tenure (*cont.*)
  Crown grant, 90
  incidents of, 88–89, 166–67
  nature, 88, 166–67
  scope of, 88, 166
types of, 167
Thayer, JB, 43–44, 45–46, 50
title
  good title, 148–49
  meanings of, 25–26, 35–36, 85n.224
transmissibility, incident of, 159,
      163, 164–66
trespass to chattels, 101, 103–4, 137–38,
      143, 169–70, 171–72
  see also damages; jus tertii

trespass to land, 56–59, 66–67, 169–70
  see also damages; jus tertii

Ullmann-Margalit, Edna, 44, 45–46
unregistered land, importance of, 4–5, 97

vagueness, nature of, 10–11
vindicatio, 169–70

Waldron, Jeremy, 160–61, 167
Winkfield rule, the *see* damages;
      presumption of absolute and
      complete ownership
Wiren, SA, 54–55, 76–77
Wonnacott, Mark, 23